David Laing, William Carew Hazlitt

Early popular poetry of Scotland and the northern border

David Laing, William Carew Hazlitt

Early popular poetry of Scotland and the northern border

ISBN/EAN: 9783743341876

Manufactured in Europe, USA, Canada, Australia, Japa

Cover: Foto ©Thomas Meinert / pixelio.de

Manufactured and distributed by brebook publishing software (www.brebook.com)

David Laing, William Carew Hazlitt

Early popular poetry of Scotland and the northern border

Early Popular Poetry of Scotland and the Northern Border

Edited by David Laing LL.D. in 1822 and 1826

Re-arranged and Revised with Additions and a Glossary

By W. Carew Hazlitt

IN TWO VOLUMES

VOL. I

LONDON
REEVES AND TURNER
WELLINGTON STREET, STRAND
1895

[All Rights reserved]

PREFACE

PARTLY as a companion to the similar work on "Early English Popular Poetry," in four volumes, in the "Library of Old Authors," the present undertaking has been carried out, agreeably to a plan which the late Dr. Laing had long entertained, but never accomplished, of amalgamating two works published by him in 1822 and 1826, namely, "Select Remains of the Ancient Popular Poetry of Scotland" and "Early Metrical Tales." In the performance of this task, I have felt it to be my duty to introduce such corrections and alterations as Dr. Laing himself would have probably thought fit and requisite, had he executed it in his lifetime. The Appendices and Errata have been superseded; and one piece, "Roswal and Lillian," which was common to both compilations, has of course not been repeated; nor was it deemed expedient to retain the "Bludy Serk," by Robert

Henryson, since it is to be found in that writer's Collected Works, 1865. But the striking tale of "John the Reeve," which Dr. Laing was unable to recover, or at all events to print, has been inserted, as it belongs, if not to Scotish ground, to the Durham or Northumberland border, and may be regarded as one of the most remarkable compositions of its rather numerous class. For a similar reason, the Cumberland legend of "Adam Bel" has been re-edited from the earliest extant copies, and I have made room for the interesting, if somewhat late, *fabliau* of the "Lovers' Quarrel."

The opportunity of reimpression almost necessitated such changes in the preliminary remarks as the lapse of sixty or seventy years has effected in the state of literary discovery and knowledge. But the verbal or textual revision has been advisedly limited, as a rule, to words and passages where an apparent *lacuna* in the narrative or defect in the sense made a resort elsewhere indispensable; and this observation affects almost exclusively the earlier pieces in the series. At the same time, the adoption of an eclectic text is more permissible perhaps where all the extant MSS. or printed editions are more or less illiterate copies, presenting a medley of English and Scotish diction, and having no high claim as philological monuments; and it has further to be borne in mind that a leading aim in these volumes is to portray the manners and sentiments of the Scots rather than to illustrate the language of the country, for which our immediate material is only casually available. In making emendations in works of this class, there is not the same sacrilegious violence as in altering the language of an autograph, or even an ancient MS. The corruptions and mistakes in many cases can only be regarded as the fruit of repeated reproduction by uneducated copyists or careless typographers. It is to a certain extent curious, however, to trace in the mixed or hybrid orthography the operation by which transcribers stealthily adapted the older forms to the speech of the locality where they resided: like an ancient building in part restored with some of the rooms left in their original state.

The dark religious bigotry which distinguished early Scotish life and character promoted in more than one way the destruction of the popular literature of all kinds immediately connected with that long poor and unhappy country; and the circumstances naturally tend to surround it with an interest and a charm, which scarcely manifest themselves in so powerful a degree toward the more copious and important survival of ballads and romances illustrating the history and manners of Southern Britain, even when, as it not unfrequently happens, the latter can be shown to have been the actual place of parentage, and the Scotish version to be more or less a copy. On the other hand, we have instances where a Northern production no longer exists in its pristine garb, and has to be accepted with what must be treated as corruptions at the hands of a Southern or perhaps Midland scribe. Such has been the fate of the singularly fascinating and instructive fable of "John the Reeve;" and where the dialectic, or at least textual changes are less pronounced or less general, the difficulty of ascertaining with any precision the original source is so frequent, that Sir Walter Scott acted quite discreetly in declining to draw the line with too much confidence, and in assigning certain pieces to the borderland between the two kingdoms.

For interesting historical and critical notices of many of the relics here assembled together, the reader may be referred to Dr. Irving's "History of Scotish Poetry," edited by Dr. Carlyle, 1861. In that work, however, we do not meet with so full an account of the "Tales of the Priests of Peebles" as the special excellence and value of that remarkable relic merited. I have pointed out the curious association of the first Tale with a real personage resident at Newcastle-on-Tyne in the fifteenth century.

I hope that it will be considered that the distribution of the Prefaces, which formerly made a distinct section, most inconvenient for reference, and the addition of a Glossary, are two improvements. Where I could not meet with a satisfactory explanation of a word or expression, I have admitted it with a note of the place where it occurs.

It may be predicated without undue presumption of the Collection thus reconstructed and augmented, that it embraces a fairly representative gathering of the popular romances and minstrelsy of North Britain and the Border, and a notable body of rare, if not unique, remains, however regrettable in our eyes may be the loss of many others unquestionably once in existence, and even in print, as well as the necessity of employing in some instances comparatively modern impressions or defective MSS., owing to the unfortunate disappearance of older or completer copies.

W. C. H.

BARNES COMMON, SURREY,
October 1894.

ADVERTISEMENTS

PREFIXED TO THE

FORMER EDITIONS[1]

LITTLE or no apology, it is conceived, will be now looked for, on submitting to the public a Collection, such as this is, of our ANCIENT POPULAR POETRY: neither is it necessary to detain the reader with any general reflections which the nature of its contents might be supposed to suggest. The remains of the Early Poetical literature of our country, and, indeed, of most nations, are allowed to possess a value, sanc-

---

[1] The present writer, who had the honour of being personally acquainted with the late David Laing, desired to preserve such portions of the prefatory notices attached to the two books now consolidated as seemed to be of permanent interest and application, and has therefore woven them into one text. The titles of the volumes are as follow:—(i.) Select Remains of the Ancient Popular Poetry of Scotland. Printed at Edinburgh, MDCCCXXII. 4to. (ii.) Early Metrical Tales; including the History of Sir Egeir, Sir Gryme, and Sir Gray-Steil. Edinburgh, MDCCCXXVI. Small 8vo.

tioned by time, of which neither prejudice nor fashion can deprive them, and this may be thought sufficient to justify any attempt that is made for their preservation. They are valuable, no less in enabling us to trace the history and progress of our language, than in assisting us to illustrate ancient manners and amusements, of which they often contain the liveliest representations.

The history of Scotish Romance-Poetry, owing to the peculiar circumstances attending its transmission to modern times, is unfortunately involved in great obscurity. Although the more ancient of these remains occasionally bear internal evidence of having proceeded from the celebrated Makars of the Northe Countreye, we remain in ignorance respecting the individuals who contributed so much to the amusement of our ancestors in these remote times, and even possess little or no positive evidence that might help us to distinguish the productions of Scotish writers from those of the English minstrels. This may indeed be esteemed a matter of extreme unimportance, since the most valuable specimens of romantic fiction that are extant, have in one shape or other been made public. The "Sir Tristrem," for instance, has received every possible advantage in the illustrations of its distinguished editor, Sir Walter Scott. The "Geste of King Horn," perhaps the next in point of antiquity, has been faithfully printed by Ritson; and the "Lyf of Alexander" (erroneously assigned to an English poet in the age of Edward II.), is given with no less accuracy by Weber in his excellent Collection of Metrical Romances.

These Tales and Romance-Poems are very inconsiderable in number when compared with those which belong to the sister-kingdom. But from various allusions to be found to the number and popularity of such compositions in Scotland at an early period, it is evident that this portion of our ancient literature, in its transmission to modern times, must have suffered in a more than common degree; in the words of Bishop Percy, "it has been handed down to us with less care than any other writings in the world." Nor indeed was it to be conceived, at the time "Quhen gude Makars rang weill into Scotland," that our native minstrels should have been behind their neighbours, either for invention or facility of composition, in thus contributing to the amusement of their countrymen. In proof of the general esteem in which these works of fiction were held, it may here be sufficient to mention what has been incidentally recorded of two of the most renowned of the Scotish monarchs.

When the followers of Robert the Bruce, in his retreat to the Isle of Rachrin, at the close of the year 1306, had to be ferried over Loch Lomond in a boat which held but three persons at a time; that "gude king" is said by his venerable biographer to have amused them for "a night and a day," by reading portions of the Romance of Ferumbrace.[1] After giving a brief detail of that part of the narrative which relates how Roland and his companions, the *dousiperes* of France, with only one attendant, manfully held out the Tower of Egrymor, when besieged by the Soudan of Babylon and a whole host of Saracens, the Archdeacon of Aberdeen declares—

> "The gud king upon this máner
> Comfort thaim that war him ner;
> And maid thaim gamyn and solace,
> Till that his folk all passyt was."[2]

From the same authority we learn, that on other occasions Robert the Bruce was wont to "comfort" his adherents in their difficulties by relating to them

> "Auld storyis of men that wer
> Set in tyll hard assayis ser."

The other instance alluded to is of James the First of Scotland, who, according to the contemporaneous narrative of the very tragical fate

---

[1] This is evidently the Romance of Fierabras, but it must have been a different and earlier translation from the French than that quoted by Mr. Ellis in his abstract of the story. (Metrical Romances, vol. ii. p. 369, &c.)

[2] Barbour's Bruce, book ii. line 858-862. Dr. Jamieson's 4to edit. 1820.

of that accomplished Prince, spent the night previous to his assassination "*yn* REDYNG OF ROMANS, *yn syngyng and pypynge, yn harpyng, and yn other honest solaces of grete pleasance and disport.*"

Were direct evidence, therefore, wanting, we might be warranted to infer that compositions, which afforded delight and were familiar to our kings, would neither be unknown nor disregarded by their subjects. But deeply as we cannot but regret the loss which the early literature of Scotland has sustained in the almost total destruction of these tales of romantic and legendary fiction,—it is a subject of inquiry which might lead to a discussion disproportionate to the size and contents of these volumes. One circumstance, however, may be mentioned, to show that these compositions were not uncommon *in a written state* at a remote period; although, with the exception of charters, hardly any MSS. (and not one in verse), written in Scotland, are known to be extant of an older date than the middle of the fifteenth century: —Sir James Douglas of Dalkeith, the ancestor of the Earls of Morton, in his last will and testament, dated in the year 1390, bequeaths to his son and heir, "OMNES LIBROS MEOS TAM STATUTORUM REGNI SCOCIE QUAM ROMANCIE."[1]

---

[1] Original deed, in the possession of the Earl of Morton.

In the present volumes, a few Metrical Tales, from copies of a comparatively recent date, are collected, together with some Scotish poems which appear to have enjoyed more than a common degree of popularity. That most of these existed in copies of a much earlier time will be seen from the respective notices which are subjoined. The chief object in submitting this little Collection to the public is the hope that it may be the means of bringing some of these productions to light in a more antique garb. But whether or not the appearance of the volumes shall contribute in any way to a more careful and extended research after such remains, the Editor flatters himself that he performs an acceptable service in rendering attainable some few of these "delectable" compositions, which even in their present state (modernised and corrupted as most of them confessedly are), will nevertheless be allowed to possess no ordinary charms for those who are gratified with the simple and unaffected strains which gave delight to our ancestors. To such as feel any interest in the revival of the literary productions of remoter ages, the Editor may use the words of an old English writer, and say,

> "Accept my paynes, allow me thankes,
>   If I deserue the same,
> If not, yet lette not meaning well
>   Be payde with checke and blame.

> For I am he that buylde the bowre,
>   I hewe the hardened stone;
> And thou art owner of the house,
>   The paine is mine alone.
> I burne the bee, I hold the hyue,
>   The Sommer toyle is myne;
> And all bicause when Winter commes
>   The honie may be thine."[1]

The professed object of this work was to bring together some of the rarer pieces of the ancient vernacular Poetry of Scotland. Accordingly, an endeavour has been made to collect such as either still remained unpublished, or had appeared only in a corrupted or imperfect state: and if, in the prosecution of this design, the Editor has been unsuccessful, it has, at least, arisen from no want on his part of diligence and assiduity. For it has been well observed by the ingenious Headley, that "to constitute a relish for the Black-Letter (a term by which we may understand whatever relates to antiquarian knowledge), a certain degree of literary Quixotism is highly requisite: he who is unwilling to penetrate the barren heath and solitary desert; he who cannot encounter weariness, perplexity, and disgust; he who is not actuated by an enthusiasm for his employment, is no true knight, and unfit for such service."[2] More especially is this the case when, in order

---

[1] Tragical Tales, &c., by George Turbervile, 1587. 8vo, bl. l. sign. Biii.

[2] Select Beauties of Ancient English Poetry, 8vo, p. vii.

to publish the early remains of our National Poetry with the correctness and fidelity which is requisite, recourse must be had to ancient and discordant manuscripts, where the obscurity of the language, or the labour of decyphering them, is the least perplexing or difficult part of the undertaking.

The reader will observe that the various pieces contained in it have, at least, in their favour, the claim of antiquity, since all of them are given from sources anterior to the close of the sixteenth century. These are carefully pointed out in the short notices which it was thought necessary to prefix to the poems for their better illustration. At the same time, many other curious reliques might have been found worthy of being brought to light; and it will be gratifying to the Editor if this publication prove in any way conducive to a more extensive research after the scanty and too long neglected remains of this portion of our Ancient Literature.

In the following stanzas of "The Palice of Honour," by Bishop Douglas, written in 1503, several curious tales are alluded to, most of which probably are no longer in existence:—

"I saw Ralf Coilȝear with his thrawin brow
Craibit Johne the Reif, and auld Cowkewpis Sow
And how the Wran came out of Ailssay
And Piers Plewman that maid his workmen few
Greit Gowmakmorne and Fyn Makcoull and how

They suld be Goddis in Ireland as thay say
Thair saw I Maitland upon auld Beird Gray
Robene Hude, and Gilbert with the quhite hand
How Hay of Nauchtoun flew in Madin land.

The Nigromansie thair saw I eik anone,
Of Bentyas, Bongo, and Freir Bacone,
With many subtill point of Juglary
Of Flanders peis maid mony precious stone.
Ane greit laid sadill of a siching bone,
Of ane Nutemug thay maid a Monk in hy
Ane Paroche Kirk of ane penny py.
Ane Benytas of ane Mussill maid and Aip
With mony uteir subtill mow and jaip."
—Edit. 1579, p. 56.

Of some of the pieces which have hitherto eluded discovery, a short list may here be subjoined, as the best mode of exciting attention; and the Editor should feel happy to receive information respecting any of them, or of similar compositions, either in a printed or manuscript state, which may have escaped his researches. This list might have been easily enlarged:—

THE TALE HOW THE KING OF ESTMORELAND MAREIT THE KINGIS DOCHTER OF WESTMORELAND. A supposed modernised copy of this romantic tale is printed *infrâ*.

THE TALE OF THE THREE FUTTIT DOG OF NORROWAY. Mentioned in the "Complaynt of Scotland," 1549: or, indeed, any of the *taylis, fabillis*, or *pleysand storeis* enumerated in that curious work.

THE EARL OF ERROL'S TESTAMENT, in Scotish metre, by Robert Alexander, Advocate, printed at Edinburgh some time after the year 1541.

CHRIST'S KIRK ON THE GREENE. Any edition prior to that printed in the year 1663.

ADVERTISEMENTS

THE BATTLE OF HARLAW. Anno 1411. Printed in the "Evergreen," by Allan Ramsay, from (as supposed) a modernised copy. Any edition prior to that of 1668.

SIR EGEIR, SIR GRYME, AND SIR GRAY STEILL. A good text of this story occurs in Bishop Percy's Folio MS., as edited by Furnivall and Hales. Any edition prior to that of 1687. Comp. introductory notice to the text, *infra*.

The present work must necessarily have a very limited circulation, yet trusting that such a Collection is neither unworthy of public attention, nor of the care that has been bestowed in forming it, the Editor, with all due feeling of grateful esteem, would inscribe it as a slight but sincere tribute of respect to the Distinguished Author, to whom, of all others, the literature of his native country is most deeply beholden :—Whose zeal in its cause has been shown, no less in a friendly and generous encouragement of those engaged in its cultivation, than in his own successful exertions in behalf of the unregarded and traditionary productions of former ages;—and who has, at the same time, so eminently sustained and extended the reputation of our national literary character, by those original compositions which have shed so much lustre over the Minstrelsy and Romance of Scotland, and have happily displayed the extent and fertility of his own surpassing genius.

[DAVID LAING.]

[EDINBURGH, 1822-6.]

CONTENTS

OF VOL. I

	PAGE
PREFACE	vii
ADVERTISEMENTS PREFIXED TO THE FORMER EDITIONS	xiii
THE AWNTYRS OFF ARTHURE AT THE TERNE WATHELYN	1
THE PYSTYL OF SWETE SUSAN	43
ORFEO AND HEURODIS; OR KING ORFEO	59
THOMAS OF ERSYLDOUNE AND THE QUENE OF ELF-LAND	81
THE FERMORAR AND HIS DOCHTER	112
THE BATTLE OF HARLAW	116
THE THRIE TAILES OF THE THRIE PRIESTS OF PEBLIS	127
TAYIS BANK	169
THE EPISTILL OF THE HERMEIT OF ALAREIT TO THE GRAY FREIRS	175
THE TALE OF COLKELBIE SOW	179
THE TALE OF RAUF COILƷEAR	212
JOHN THE REEVE	250
THE LAYING OF LORD FERGUS'S GAIST	284

CONTENTS

	PAGE
SIR JOHN ROWLL'S CURSING	289
ANE BALLET OF THE NINE NOBLES	300
THE DUIK OF ORLYANCE IN DEFENCE OF THE SCOTS	304
A POEM BY GLASSINBERRY	307
THE RING OF THE ROY ROBERT	313

The awntyrs off Arthure at the Terne Wathelyn.

THE Romance which follows bears such a close resemblance in subject, style, and manner to "the Knightly tale of Golagrus and Gawane,"[1] that both have generally been attributed to one and the same author. It was a style of composition for which, for a length of time, the Northern Poets were particularly renowned; for although the use of alliteration was not entirely peculiar to them, it was, at least, one distinguishing feature of their compositions. Thus Chaucer makes "his Persone" to say

——"I am a Sotherne man
I can not geste, Rom, Ram, Ruf, by my letter,
And, God wote, rime hold I but litel better."

George Gascoigne, in his *Certayne Notes of Instruction*,[2] has the following reference to this curious passage:—"In making a delectable poem," he says, "it is not enough to roll in pleasant woordes, nor yet to thunder in Rym, Ram, Ruff by letter, (quoth my maister Chaucer,) nor yet to abounde in apte vocables, or epithets, unlesse the invention have in it also *aliquid salis*."

The antiquity of these tales is unquestionably considerable; and but for our knowledge of other similar alliterative poems, of which the dates are ascertained, and go far to rival these in point of obscurity, we might be justified in

---

[1] Reprinted, with other similar pieces, from the original copies, under the editorship of David Laing, 4to, 1827.

[2] Works by Hazlitt, 1869, i. 500.

carrying them back to a very remote period. The only conjecture that can be offered respecting their author is founded on the slight allusion in Dunbar's "Lament for the Death of the Makaris," where he says—

> Clerk of Tranent eik he hes tane
> That made the aventers of Sir Gawane.[1]

As different poems of the Adventures of Sir Gawane are known, we are prevented from ascribing one or other of them to Clerk with any degree of certainty; besides, we have the authority of Andrew of Wyntoun for assigning them to Hucheon, another of our early Poets (by whom the reader will find a specimen, in the same alliterative style, in the present volume). Wyntoun says—

> "He made the gret Gest of Arthure,
> And the Awntyre of Gawane."

The Editor has been favoured by his friend, Dr. Robert Anderson, whose attachment and valuable contributions to our national literature are well known, with a sight of some remarks on this ancient romance, by the late Alexander Thomson, Esq. They occur among the Collections which he had made for a History of Scotish Poetry. The following extract will evince the discrimination which he was capable of showing, and the value that might have been attached to his labours had he proceeded farther in completing such an important undertaking:—

"The most glaring imperfections of this Romance [Gawan and Galoran of Galloway] is undoubtedly its deficiency in unity of action, the two parts being entirely unconnected. In this respect it is inferior to the former, although the appearance and behaviour of the ghost displays more of fancy and of poetry than anything to be found in the Gawan and Gologras. It is, however, to be wished that this marvellous incident had constituted the latter half of the poem, as the entrance of Galoran, at the banquet of Arthur, would have opened the piece in a striking manner; and the whole of that story must have been more interesting had it pre-

---

[1] See them collected and edited by Sir F. Madden, 4to, 1839; and some have been re-edited for the E. E. Text Society.

ceded and not followed the supernatural adventures. The same error, in point of arrangement, I have often regretted in the 'Romance of the Forest,' where the woes and wanderings of the two lovers, although sufficiently interesting in themselves, are read almost with a perfect indifference after the terrific scenes at the castle.

"Although the characters are not marked with that strength of pencil which distinguished those of Gawan and Gologras, that defect is perhaps compensated by the introduction of two female personages; and the circumstance of a wedding making part of the catastrophe, gives it more the air of a modern performance."

The author of these Romances, whoever he may have been, has certainly added something new to the poetry of his country. In them there is both originality of incident and manner:—for although they doubtless were founded on popular tradition, the author surely would not have chosen such an intricate and cumbrous mode of versification had they been mere translations, or had he profited by the example of the numerous productions of English Romance-poetry during its best period, namely, from the middle of the fourteenth to the early part of the fifteenth century.

Three copies of this Romance are known to be extant. The one now adopted is preserved in the Cathedral Library, Lincoln. The others are the Douce MS., formerly belonging to Mr. Baynes, of Gray's Inn, and printed by Pinkerton; and the Ireland MS., first published by Mr. Robson,[1] and unknown to the earlier editors. The Douce MS. consists of eleven leaves, in folio, written in a very fair and legible hand, in the reign of Henry VI. It was thought unnecessary to swell out the pages by noticing all the minute variations and discrepancies between the three manuscripts, since in every line some difference in orthography, in omission, or transposition is found.[2]

---

[1] Three Early English Metrical Romances, edited by John Robson, Camden Society, 1842. The reader may be usefully referred to Mr. Robson's able and elaborate Introduction. See Ritson's Letter on this subject in *Gentleman's Magazine*, Jan. 1793.

[2] The Ireland MS. equally varies from that here employed, and some of its readings are clearly superior,

Whatever seems material, is, however, carefully pointed out, and the words or lines in the text, printed within inverted commas, are those which the Douce copy has furnished, unless it be otherwise stated.

To the Reverend Mr. Gray of Lincoln the Editor owes his best thanks for the kind and friendly manner in which he facilitated his object during the time required for making some transcripts from the Thornton MS.

Here byggnnes the awntyrs off Arthure at the Terne Wathelyn.

I.

IN Kyng Arthurs tym ane awntir by tyde,[1]
By the Terne Wathelyn,[2] als the buke tellis;
Als he to Carelele was commen, that conqueroure kyde,[3]
With Dukes, and with ducheperes, that with that dere[4] duellys,
For to hunte at the herdys, that lang hase bene hyde; 5
And one a day thay tham dighte to the depe dellis,
To felle of the ffemmales in the fforeste, 'and frydde,'[5]
Faire in the ffernysone tyme, by ffrythis,[6] and fellis:

---

and have been adopted. Dr. Laing entered into particulars as to the contents of the Lincoln MS., a volume now so well known to all interested in these matters, that it seemed superfluous to reproduce the information.

[1] 'In the tyme of Arthur an aunter by tydde.'

[2] 'Turnewathelan,' Tearn Wadling, or Tarn Watling, in Cumberland.

[3] 'And conquerour kydde.' [4] 'The dere.'

[5] 'In forest and frydde.' MS. L. reads, 'in the fforeste wele frythede.'

[6] 'Fayre by the Firmysthamis, in frithes.'

Thus to the wode are thay wente, the wlonkaste
    in wedys,
  Bothe the Kynge, and the Qwene,
  And all the doghety by dene,
  Schir Gawane gayeste one grene,
Dame Gayenour he ledis.

II.

And thus Schir Gawane the gay, dame Gayenour
    he ledis,
In a gletterande gyse, that glemet full gaye;
With rich rebanes reuerssede,[1] who that righte
    redys,
Arayit with rubes[2] one royalle arraye:
Hir hude was of hawe hewe[3] that hir hede
    hydys,
Wroghte with pelours, and palle, and perrye to
    paye;
Schruedede in a schorte cloke, that the rayne
    schrydes[4]
Sett ouer with safyrs,[5] full sothely to saye;
  And thus wondirfully was all the wyghtis
    wedys,
  Hir sadill semyde of that ilke,
  Semlely sewede with sylke:
  One a muyle als the milke,
Gayely scho glydis.

---

[1] 'With riche ribaynes reuersset.'
[2] 'Rubes of rial.'
[3] 'Of herde hawe.'
[4] 'Schurde in a schort cloke that the rayne shedes.'
[5] 'With saffres and seladynes, set by the sides.'

III.

Thus alle gleterande golde gayely scho glydis
The gates, with Schir Gawane, by a grene welle;
Nane bot hym selfe one a blonke, by that birde bydis,[1]
That borne was in Burgoyne, by buke and by belle.   30
He ledde that lady so lange by these landes sydys,[2]
Sythen so neir a lorere scho lyghte[3] lawe by a felle.
Schir Arthure, with his Erles, full ernestly rydis,
To teche thame to thaire tristis, trewely to telle:[4]
   To thaire tristis he tham taughte, who that righte trowes,[5]   35
      Ilke a lorde, with owttyn lett,
      At his triste was he sett,[6]
      With bewe and with barcelett,
   Vndir these bewes.

IV.

Vndir these bewes thay bade, these beryns so bolde,   40
To bekire at those baryaynes,[7] in bankis so bare;
Thay keste of thaire copulls, in clyffes so calde;
Thay recomforthes thaire kenettis, to kele tham of care;

---

[1] 'And that barne on his blonke with the quene bidis.'
[2] 'By the lawe sides.'
[3] 'Under a lorre they lyghte.'
[4] 'The trouth for to telle.'   [5] 'Who the trouth trowes.'
   'To an oke he hem sett.'   [7] 'These baryanes.'

Thare myght hirdmen hendaly forsothe herdis by holde,¹
Herkyn huntyngis² with hornnes, in holtis so hare,
Thay fellede downe the ffemmalls, full thikke folde,
With fresche hundis and felle, felonosly thay fare;³
    They questys and quellys,⁴
    By frythis and fellis,⁵
    The dere in the dellys,⁶
Thei droupen and dare.⁷

V.

Alle darkis the dere in the dim schowys,⁸
And for drede of the dede⁹ drowpys the daa,
And by the stremys so strange, that swythly swoghes,¹⁰
Thay wery the wilde swyne, and wyrkkis tham waa;
Thay hunte and halowes, in hurstis and huwes,¹¹
And till thaire riste, raches relyes on thaire raye;¹²
Thay gafe [to] no gamen no grythe, that one grownde growes,
Grehundis in the green greues full gladly gan gaa.

---

  ¹ 'There might hatheles in high, herdes be holde.'
  ² 'Huntyng in haste.'   ³ 'Thei folowen her fare.'
  ⁴ 'With gret questis and quellis.'
  ⁵ 'Both in frithis and fellis.'
  ⁶ 'All the dere in the delles.'
  ⁷ 'Thei durken and dare.'
  ⁸ 'Thei durken the dere in the dyme skuwes.'
  ⁹ 'That for drede of the deth.'
  ¹⁰ This line omitted in MS. D.
  ¹¹ 'In hurstis and huwes.'—MS. L. reads 'in holttis and hillys.'
  ¹² 'And bluwe rechas, ryally thei ran to ro.'

Thus thies gomes thay ga in greuys so grene, 60
    And boldly blawes[1] rechayse,
    And folowes faste one the trase,
    With many seriandis a-mase,
Swylk solauce to sene.

VI.

Thus with solauce they semeledde, the prowdeste in palle,[2] 65
And soʒt to ther soueraygne, undur the schaschene:[3]
Alle bot[4] Schir Gawane, graythest of alle,
Hy leuys with dame Gaynoure in those greues grene:
Vndir a lorere scho laye, that lady so smalle,
Off boxe and of barborane,[5] byggit full bene; 70
Faste by fore vndrone, this ferly gan falle,
And this meikill mervelle, that I of mene.
    Now will I of this mervele mele, ʒif I mote,[6]
    The daye woxe als dirke,
    Als it were mydnyghte mirke: 75
    Ther of Schir Gawane was irke,[7]
    And lyghte one his fote.

VII.

Thus one fote are thay lyghte, those frekis vnfayne,[8]
And fledde faste to the foreste fro the fawe fellis;[9]

---

[1] 'The King blew.'
[2] 'They sembled.'
[3] 'Within schaghes schene.'
[4] 'Al bot.'
[5] 'And of barber.'
[6] 'Meve if I mote.'
[7] 'Thereof the King.'
[8] 'Thus to fote ar thei faren.'
[9] 'And fleen fro the fforest to the fewe fellis.'—MS. L. reads 'faste to the foreste, and to.'

Thay rane fast to the roches, for reddoure of the rayne,¹ 80
Ffor the slete and the snawe, that suappede tham so snelle : ²
Thare come a lawe one the loughe, in lede is noȝt to layne,³
In the lyknes of Lucyfere, lauyst in helle,
And glyddis to dame Gaynoure, the gatis full gayne,⁴
ȝolland [ful] ȝamyrly, with [a] many lowde ȝelle ; ⁵ 85
  It ȝellede, it ȝamede with vengeance full wete ; ⁶
    And said, aftre syghande full sare,
    I bann the body that me bare,⁷
    Allas ! now kyndyls my kare,
  I gloppyn and I grete ! 90

VIII.

Thane gloppenyde and grett dame Gaynoure the gay,
And askede Schir Gawayne, whatt was his beste rede ?—
It es the clippus of the sune I herde a clerke saye ; ⁸
And thus he comforthede the Qwene, with his knyghthede.

---

    ¹ Lines 3 and 6 are omitted in MS. D.
    ² 'For the sueterand snawe suartly hem snelles.'
    ³ 'A lede of tha lawe, in land is.'
    ⁴ 'And glides to Schir Gawayne the gates to gayne.'
    ⁵ 'ȝauland and ȝomerand.'
    ⁶ 'Hit ȝaules, hit ȝamers with waymeyngis wete.'
    ⁷ 'I ban the body me bare.'
    ⁸ 'The clippes of the Son.'

Schir Cadore, Schir Caduke, Schir Costantyne,
　　Schir Kaye,[1]　　　　　　　　　　　　　95
Thir knyghtes are vn curtayse by crose and by
　　crede,
That thus me hase lefte in this Erthe at my dede
　　daye,
With the gryselyeste gaste, that euer herde I
　　grete !—
　　At this gaste, quod Schir Gawayne, greue ȝowe
　　　　no more,[2]
　　　　I salle speke with ȝone sprete,　　　　100
　　　　In ȝone wayes so wete,
　　　　If I maye the bales bete,
　　Of ȝon body bare.

IX.

Bare was hir body, and blake to the bane,
Alle by claggede in claye, vn-comlyly clede :　105
It weryit, it wayemettede, lyke a Woman,
That nowther one hede, ne one hare, hillynge it
　　hade ;[3]
It stottyde, it stounnede, it stode als a stane,[4]
It menet, it memerede, it moyssed for made.
Vn to that grysely gaste Schir Gawane es
　　gane,　　　　　　　　　　　　　　　110
He raykede to it one a rase, for he was neuer
　　·rade :[5]

---

　[1] 'Schir Cador, Schir Clegis, Schir Costardyne, Schir
Cay.'
　　[2] 'Of the goost, quod the grome.'
　　[3] 'But on hide, ne on huwe, no helling.'
　　[4] 'Hit stemered, hit stounade.'
　　[5] 'Neuer drade.'

For rade was he¹ neuer ʒett, who that ryghte redis,
  One the chefe of the cholle,²
  A tade pykit one hir polle,³
  Hir eghne ware holkede full holle,   115
Glowand als gledis.

X.

Alle glowede als gledis, the gaste whare scho glydis,
Vmbeclosut in a clowde,⁴ with clethynge vn-clere;
Cerkelytt with serpentes that satt by hir sydes,⁵
To tell the tadis ther one with tongue wer to tere.
The beryn brawndeche owte his brande, and the body bydis,   121
Therefore that chevalrous knyghte thoghte it no chere;⁶
The hundes hye to the hillys⁷ and ther hedus hydus
  The grewhundes were agayste, for that grym bere,
  The birdes on the bewes,   125
  That one that gaste gewes,
  Thay scryken in the clewes,⁸
That herdus myʒten hom here.⁹

---

¹ 'Drade was he.'
² 'Chef of the clolle.'   ³ 'The gooste glowes.'
⁴ 'Vmbe clipped with a cloude.'
⁵ 'Skeled with serpentes all aboute the sides.'
⁶ 'Charged no chere.'
⁷ 'The houndes higher to the wode.'
⁸ 'Thei skryke in the skowes.'
⁹ 'That hatheles may here.'

XI.

Alle the herdus myȝtest here, the hindeste of alle,[1]
How hir cholle chatirede, hir chaftis, and hir chyne;[2]   130
Thane coniurede hir that knyghte, and one Criste gun he calle,
Alls thou was crucyfyede one croyse, to sauc ws fra syn!
Thou spirette saye me the sothe, whedir that thou sall,
And whi that thow walkes thies woddis with inn?
—I was of Fegure, and of flesche,[3] the fayereste of alle,   135
Christenede and krysmede, with kynges in my kyn:[4]
  I hafe kynges in my kyn, knawen for kyde full kene,
    God hase sent me this grace,
    To dre my paynes in this place,
    And nowe am I commen one a pase,[5]   140
  To speke with ȝoure Qwene.

XII.

Qwene was I whilome, wele bryghtere of browes
Than Beryke or Brangwayne,[6] the byrdis so balde;
Of any games or gudis, that one the grownde growes,
Wele grettere than Gaynoure of garsomes and of golde,   145

---

[1] 'Hathelesse might here so fer into halle.'
[2] 'How chatered the cholle, the challus, on the chyne.'
[3] 'Figure and face.'   [4] 'And knowen.'
[5] 'I am comen in this cace.'   [6] 'Than berell.'

Of pales, of powndis, of parkis, of plewes,
Of tounes, of towris, of tresoures vn-tolde ;
Of contres, of castells, of cragges, of clewes ;
And now am I cachede owte of kythe, in carys so
    colde :
    In care am I cachede, and cowchede in claye ;
        Loo ! curtayse knyghte,   151
        How that dede hase me dyghte,[1]
        Now gyffe me anes a syghte [2]
    Of Gayenour the gaye.

XIII.

Nowe to Gayenour the gaye Schir Gawayne es
    gane,   155
And to that body hase he broghte that birde then
    so bryghte :
Welcome, Waynoure ![3] scho says, thu worthye in
    wane !
Loo! howe that dulefull dede hase thi dame
    dyghte,
I was reddare in rode than rose in the rayne ;
My lyre als the lely, lufely to syghte,[4]   160
And nowe I am a gresely gaste, and grymly I grane,
With Lucefere in a lake lawe ame I lyghte ;
    Thus am I lyke to Lucefere, takis witnes by mee,
        For all ȝoure fresche fauoure,
        Now meyse one this mirroure,   165
        For bothe Kynge and Emperoure,
    Thus sall ȝe bee.

---

[1] 'How delfulle deth hath me dight.'
[2] 'Lete me onys haue a sight.'
[3] It is curious that in this stanza in all the MSS. we have *Gaynour* and *Waynour*, two variants of the same name ; and the latter frequently occurs afterwards, as does *Wawayn* for *Gawayn*.   [4] 'Lonched on hight.'

XIV.

And thus dede will ȝow dyghte, take thare of no dowte,[1]
And there one hertly takis hede, while that thu es here,
When thou es richely arrayed, and rydes in a rowte, 170
Hafe than peté, and mynd one the pore, for thu arte of powere.
Beryns and byrdis are besye the abowte,
When thi body is bawmede, and broghte appone bere,
Than will thay leue the lyghtely, that nowe will lowte,
And than helpes the no thynge, bot halye prayere :
   The prayere of the pore, purchases the from helle,[2] 176
      Of thase that ȝellis at the ȝate,
      When thu sittis in thi sete,[3]
      With all mirthes at thi mete,
   Some dayntethis on dese. 180

XV.

With dayntethis one dese, thi dyetes are dyghte ;
And I in dawngere and dole am dowme for to duelle,[4]
Naxty and nedfull, and nakede one nyghte
There ffolowes me a ferde of ffendis ffull ffell :[5]

---

[1] 'Takis witness by mee.'—MS. L.
[2] 'Than lit wyn the light.' [3] 'May purchas the pes.'
[4] 'In dongon I dwelle.' [5] 'Fendes of helle.'

Thay harle me vnhendely, and hewys me one
    hyghte;   185
In brasse and in bromstane I birne als a belle:
Was neuer wroghte in this werlde a wafullere
    wyghte,
It were tere till any tonge my tourmenttis to telle!
   Bot now will I of my tourment talke, or I gaa;
      Thynke hertly on this,   190
        Now fonde to mende of this mys;
        For thou arte warnede I wysse,
     Be warre now be my waa!

XVI.

Now wo es me! for thi waa, sayd Waynour, I
    wysse,
Bot a worde wolde I wete, and thi will ware: 195
Gyff matyns or messes myghte oghte menden thi
    mysse,
Or any mobylls on molde, my myrthis ware the
    mare;
Or bedis of bechopes myghte brynge the to
    blysse;
Or conuentis in cloysters myghte kere the of care;
For if thou be my modir, grete mervelle it es,   200
That thi burlyche body es bakenede so bare![1]—
   I bare the of my body; whate bote es to lye?[2]
      Be that takenynge thou trewe,
      I make a solempne a vowe,
      That none wyste bot I, and thowe,[3]   205
   And ther fore dole I dye.[4]

---

    [1] 'Is brought to be so bare.'
    [2] 'What bote is hit I layn.'
    [3] 'And no man wist h^t but thowe.'
    [4] 'That sothely I sayn.'

XVII.

Telle me now sothely, what may safe thi sytis,[1]
And I sall garre seke sayntes for thi sake;[2]
Bot of thase balefull bestis, that one thi body bytys,
All blendis my blode, thi blee es soo blake;[3]   210
This es it to luffe paramoures, and lustys, and litys,
That gerse me lyghte and lenge so lawe in this lake;
For alle the welthe of this werlde, thus awaye wytis;
This werlde is wandrethe, that wirkes me wrake:[4]
  For wrake it me wirkes, now Waynoure, I wysse!   215
    Were thritty trentalls done,
    By twyxen vndrone and none,
    My saule were saluede full sone,[5]
  And broghte in to blysse.

XVIII.

To blysse brynge the that barne, 'that boghte the on rode.'[6]   220
That was crucyfiede one croyse, and crownnede with thorne;

---

[1] 'What may the sauen y wis.'
[2] 'And I sall make sere men to singe for thi sake.'
[3] 'Al bledis my ble, thi bones.'
[4] 'With the wilde wormis that worche me wrake.'
[5] 'Socoured with son.'
[6] 'That barne that brought the on rode.'—'that dere has the boghte.'—MS. L.

Crystynnede and krysemmede with candills and
    coude,
Fullede in funstane, full frely by forne;[1]
Mary, that es myghty, and myldest of mode,
That bare that blysschede [barne], in Bedleme was
    borne,   225
Gyffe me grace for to grete thy saule with some
    gude;
And mene the with messes and matynes one
    morne;
   For hym, that ryste on the rode,[2]
   Gyffe nowe fast of thy gude,
   To folke that fayles the fude,   230
Whylls that thou erte here.

XIX.

Now here hertly one hande I heste the to halde,
With a melyone of messes to make thy menynge.
Bot one worde, saide dame Waynoure, now wiete
    that I walde,   234
What greues God moste[3] of any kyns thynge?—
Pride, with apparementis,[4] als prophetis haue tolde
By fore the pople appertly in thaire prechynge;
The 'bowes' is full bittire, thare of be thou balde,
It makis beryns full balde,[5] to breke his byd-
    dynge;
   Who so his byddyng brekis, bare he es of blysse;
   Bot thay saluen hom[6] of ther sare,   241
   Certis, or thay hethyn fare,
   Thay mon wiete of calde care,
Waynoure, I wys.

---

[1] 'Ffolowed in fontestone.'   [2] 'Grete myster.'
[3] 'What wrathed God most.'   [4] 'With appurtennance.'
[5] 'Burnes so bly.'   [6] 'Be salued.'

XX.[1]

Telle me, sayde Waynoure, a worde ʒif thou woste,
Whate bedus that myghte beste in to blys the
    brynge?— 210
Mekenesse and mercy, scho saide, tho are the moste,
Hafe peté on the pore, thane plesys thou owre
    Kynge;
Sythen after that do almous dedis of alle other
    thynge,
Thies aren the gud gyftis of the Haly Goste, 250
That enspyres alle sperites, withowttyn spyllynge;
For to come to that blysse, that euer more sall
    laste,
  Of thies sperituale thinges, spyre me na mare.[2]
    Whills thou arte Qwene in this quarte,
    Halde thies wordis in thyn herte, 255
    For thou sall lyffe bot a starte;
  Hethyn sall thu ffare.

                    A Fytte.

XXI.

How sall we fare, said the freke, that fowndis to
    fyghte,
That ofte foundis the folkes,[3] in fele kyngis landis;
That riche rewmes ouer rynnes agaynes the ryghte,
And wynnes wirchippis[4] and welthis by wyghtenes
    of handis, 261

---

  [1] This stanza in the Lincoln MS. is misplaced, as it is there introduced as the 18th.
  [2] 'Spute thou na mare.'
  [3] 'And thus defoulen the folke.'
  [4] 'Wynnen worshipp in werre thorgh.'

—ȝowre Kynge es to covetous, I tell the, Schir knyghte;
May no man stere hym of strenghe,[1] whills thou whale standis,
When he es in his mageste hegheste, and maste es of myghte,
He sall lighte full lawe appone the see sandis: 265
 Thus ȝowre cheualrous Kynge[2] chefe schalle a chawnce,
  False fortune in fyghte,[3]
  That wondirfull whele wryghte,[4]
  'Makis'[5] lordis lawe for to lyghte;
Takis witnes by Fraunce.   270

XXII.

Fraunce hafe ȝe frely with ȝour fyghte wonnen;
The Ffrolo and the Ffarnaghe es frely by leuede;[6]
Bretayne and Burgoyne es bothe to ȝow bownnen.[7]
And alle the Dugepers of Fraunce with the dyn dreuede:
Gyane may gretyn that the werre was by gounnen; 275
Es noghte a lorde in that lande, appon lyfe leuede;
ȝete sall the riche Romaynes with ȝow ben ouer ronnen,
And alle the Rownde Tabill thaire rentis be reuede.

---

[1] 'May no man stry him with strength, while his whole stondes.'
[2] 'Chiualrous knight.'   [3] 'Falsely fordone in fight.
[4] 'With a wonderfull wight.'   [5] 'Mase.'—MS. L.
[6] 'Freol and his folke fey ar they leued.'
[7] 'To ȝow bowen.'

Thay sall ȝitt be Tybire tymbire ȝow tene,[1]
  Gete the Schir Gawayne   280
  Turne thou to Tuskayne,
  For [Iese] thu sall Bretayne,
With a knyghte kene.

XXIII.

A knyghte sall kenly closen the crowne,[2]
And at Carelyone be crownede for kynge:[3]   285
That sege sall be sesede at a sesone,[4]
That mekill bale and barete till Ynglande[5] sall brynge;
ȝe sall in Tuskane be tallde of that tresone,
And torne home aȝayne for that tydynge;
And ther sall the Rownde Tabille losse the renowne,   290
Be syde Ramessaye, faill ryghte[6] at a rydynge,
  And at Dorsett sall dy the doghetyeste of alle.
  Gette the Schir Gawayne,
  The baldest of Bretayne;
  For in a slake thu sall be slayne,   295
Swylke ferly sall falle.

XXIV.

Siche ferly sall falle with owtten any fabille,
Appone Cornewayle coste, with a knyghte kene:
Arthure the auenance that honeste es and abill,
Sall be wondid I wysse full wathely I wene: 300

---

[1] 'Thus shall a Tyber vn true tymber with tene.'
[2] 'This knight shal be clanly enclosed with a crowne.'
[3] 'At Carlele shal that comly.'
[4] 'A sege shal he seche with a cession.'
[5] 'To Bretayn.'
[6] 'Beside Ramsey full rade.'

'And al the rial rowte of the Rounde Tabille
Thei shullen dye on a day, the doughty by dene'¹
Supprysede with a sugette that beris of sabille,²
A sawtire engrelede of Siluer full schene ;
 He beris 'it' of sabille, sothely to saye, 305
  In kyng Arthures haulle
  The childe playes hym at the balle
  That fall owttraye ȝow alle,
 Full derfely a daye.³

XXV.

Hafe gude daye, dame Gaynoure, and Gawane the
 gude ; 310
I hafe no langare tyme, mo tales to telle,
For I mun wende one my waye, thorowte this wode,
Vn to my winnynge wane, in waa for to welle :
For him that rewfully rase, and rente was one rude,
Thynke one the dawngere, and the dole, that I in
 duelle; 315
And fede folk, for my sake, that fawte the fude,⁴
And mene me with messes, and matyns in melle :
 ' Messes are medecynes to vs that bale bides '⁵
  Vs thynke a messe als swete,
  Als any spyce that euer thu ete :' 320
  And thus with a grysely grete
  The gaste awaye glydis.

---

¹ Instead of these two lines, taken from MS. D., the third and fourth lines of this stanza are repeated in MS. L. They occur correctly, but with literal variations, in the Ireland MS.
² 'Supprisset with a surget, he beris hit in sable.'
³ 'Delfully that day.' ⁴ 'That failen the fude.'
⁵ The last four lines of Stanza xix. are here repeated by mistake in MS. L., followed, however, by the lines in the text, except the 9th, which is given from MS. D. In the Ireland MS. the sequence is correct, but the text differs in the literal readings, which are inferior to those of the Douce MS.

XXVI.

With a grisly grete the gaste away glydis;
And goes with gronyng sore, thorgh the greues
    grene:'[1]
The wynde and the wedyre, 'the' welkyn vn hydis,
Than vnclosede the clowddis, the sone schane
    schene.
The kynge his bogill has blowen, and on the bent
    bydis,
His fayre folk in firthes, flokkes in fere;[2]
All that royalle rowte, to the Qwene rydys
And melis to hir mildely, one thaire manere;[3]
    The wyes[4] on swilke wondirs, a wondirde thaire
        were;
        The prynces prowdeste in palle,
        Dame Gaynoure, and alle,
        Wente to Rendolfe sett haulle[5]
    To thaire sopere.

XXVII.

The Kynge was sett to the supere, and serued in
    sale,[6]
Vndir a Seloure of silke, full daynetyuousely dyghte;
With alle the wirchipe to welde, and wyne for to
    wale,[7]
Birdis in brede, of brynt golde bryghte.[8]

---

[1] These lines are wanting in MS. L. They are found with changes in the Ireland MS.
[2] 'In the frith thei flokken by dene.'
[3] 'She sayis hem the selcouthes that thei hadde thair scene.'   [4] 'The wise of the weder.'
[5] 'Went to Rondoles halle.'   [6] 'Serued in halle.'
[7] 'Worshipp and wele, mewith the walle.'
[8] 'Briddes branden and brad in bankers bright.'

Ther come two sotolers in with a symbale, 340
A lady, lufesome of late, ledande a knyghte;
Scho rydes vp to the heghe[1] desse by fore the royalle;
And ask'd[2] Schir Arthure, full hendely one highte,
Scho saide[3] to that souerayne, wlonkeste in wedis,
Mane moste of myghte,[4] 345
Here es comyn ane armede knyghte,[5]
Now do him resone and ryghte,
For thi manhede.

XXVIII.

The mane in his mantyll, syttis at his mete, 349
In paulle purede with pane, full precyously dyghte,[6]
Trofelyte and trauerste, with trewloues in trete;[7]
The tasee was of topas that ther to was tyghte:
He glyfte vpe with hys eghne, that gray ware, and grete,
With his burely berde,[8] one that birde bryghte.
He was the Soueraynste Sir, sittande in sette, 355
That euer any segge saughe, or sene with syghte.
Thus the kyng, crowned in kythe, carpis hir till;[9]
Welcome worthyly wyghte!
Thou sall hafe resone and ryghte;
Whythen es this comly knyghte, 360
If it be thi will?

---

[1] 'Ho raykes up in a res.'   [2] 'And halsed.'
[3] 'Ho said.'   [4] 'Mon makles.'
[5] 'An errant knight.'
[6] 'Pured to pay prodly pight.'
[7] This line is omitted in MS. D. The Ireland MS. reads—'Trowlt with trulufes and tranest be-tuene.'
[8] 'With his beueren berde.'   [9] 'Talkis hir tille.'

XXIX.

Scho was the worthilieste wyghte, that any wy
    myghte weld [1]
Hir gyde was gloryous, and gaye, alle of gyrse
    grene;
Hir belle was of plonkette,[2] with birdis full baulde,
Botonede with besantes, and bokellede full bene;[3]
Hir faxe in fyn perrye frette was in fowlde,   366
The conterfelette in a kelle colourede full clene,[4]
With a crowne of crystalle, and of clere golde:
Hir courchefes were coryouse, with mony prowd
    pyn,
  'Her perre was praysed, with prise men of
    might.'[5]   370
    The bryghte byrde, and balde,
    Had note ynoghe to by halde
    One that freely to fawlde,
And one that hende knyghte.

XXX.

That knyghte in his coloures, was armede 'full'
    clene,   375
With his comly creste, full clere to by holde;
His brenyes, and his basnett, birneschet full
    bene,
With a bourdoure abowte, alle of brynte golde;

---

[1] 'That eny wede wolde.'
[2] 'Here belle was of blunket.'
[3] 'Branded with brende golde.'
[4] 'With a crowne craftly al of clene golde.'
[5] Omitted in MS. L. Ireland MS. reads—'Har anparel was a-praysut, with princes of myȝte.'

His mayles was mylk whytte, enclosede so clene;¹
His horse trapped with the same, als it was me
    taulde;²
The schelde one his schuldir, of syluere full schene,
With bare heuedis of blake, burely, and baulde;³
  His horse with sendale was teldade, and trap-
    pede⁴ to the hele
  And, his cheuarone by forne,
  Stude als dois vnycorne,⁵
  Als so scharpe as any thorne
And mayles of stele.⁶

XXXI.

In stele was he stuffede, that steryn was one stede,
Alle of sternys of golde; that stekillede was one
    straye;⁷
He and his gambesouns, 'glowede als a glede,'⁸
With graynes of rubyes, that graythede were gaye,
And his schene schynbandes,⁹ scharpe fre to
    schrede;
'His polans with pelicocus were pondred to pay:'¹⁰
Thus with a lance appon lofte that lady gun he
    lede;
A swayne one a fresone,¹¹ folowede him on faye.

---

  ¹ 'Were mylke white .... many hit seen.'
  ² 'Trapped of that ilke as true men me tolde.'
  ³ 'Of brake browed ful bolde.'
  ⁴ 'In fyne sandel was trapped.'   ⁵ 'Stodr as an.'
  ⁶ 'An anlas of stele.'   ⁷ 'His pencell displaied.'
  ⁸ 'His gloves, his gamesouns glowed as a glede.' The end of this line in MS. L. seems to be 'glomede als stedie.'
  ⁹ 'Schynbandes.'
  ¹⁰ This line is wanting in MS. L. and also the 9th in this stanza. In the former the Douce copy reads *polemus*.
  ¹¹ 'A freke, on a freson.'

'The ffreson was afered, for drede of that fare;'
  He was seldom wounte [1]
  To see a tablet at his frounte,[2]
  Swilke gammens was he wonte,[3]
'Saghe he neuer are.'[4]   400

XXXII.

Arthure askede in hye, one herande tham alle,
Whate woldest thu, Wy, ȝif it were thi wille?
Telle me whate thu sekis, and whedir that thu schalle?
And why thu stonyes on thi stede, and stondis so stille?[5]
He lyfte vpe his visare[6] fro the ventalle;   405
And with a knyghtly contenance he carpis hym till.
Be thu kaysere or kynge, here I the be calle
To fynde me a freke, to fyght one my fill:
  For fyghtynge to frayste, I fowndede fra hame.
    The kynge carpede on heghte,[7]   410
    'Lyghte, and lenge alle nyghte:
    If thou be curtayse knyghte,
  And tell me thi name.'

XXXIII.

My name es Schir Galleroun, with owttyn any gyle;   414
The gretteste of Galowaye, of greues and of gyllis,

---

[1] 'For he was selden wonte to see.'
[2] 'This tablet floure.'   [3] 'Siche gamen ne gle.'
[4] 'Full seldome to see.'—MS. L.
[5] 'Sturne on thi stede.'   [6] 'He wayned up his viser.'
[7] 'Then said the King vppon hight.'

Of Konynge; of Carryke; of Connygame;[1] of
    Kylle :
Of Lomonde;[2] of Lenay; of Lowthyane hillis.
Thou hase wonnen thaym one werre with owtt-
    rageouse will;[3]
And gyffen tham Schir Gawayne, and that myn
    herte grilles.
'But he shall wring his honde, and warry the
    wyle'[4]   420
Or he welden my landes at myn vn thankes :[5]
    By alle the welthe of this werlde, he sall them
        neuer welde,
        Whills I my hede may bere ;
        Bot he wyn tham one werre,
        Bothe with schelde and with spere,   425
    Appone a fair felde.

XXXIV.

I will feghte on a felde, and ther to make I my
    faythe,
With any freke one the faulde, that frely es
    borne :
To lose swilke a lordschipe me thynke it full
    laythe;
And ilke a leueande lede wolde laughe me to
    skorne.[6]—   430

---

  [1] 'Of Connok, of Conyngham, and also Kyle.'
  [2] 'Of Lomand of Losex.'
  [3] 'With a wrange wille.'
  [4] This line is wanting in MS. L. It occurs in the Ireland MS.; but the readings are inferior.
  [5] 'Er he weld hem Y wys agayn myn umwylles.'
  [6] 'And sicke lede opon lyve.'

We aren here in the wode walkand one our
    wathe,¹
We hunte at the herdis with hundes and with
    horne ;
We aren one owre gamen, we ne hafe no gude
    graythe ; ²
Bot ȝitt thu sall be machede by middaye to morne.
  And for-thi I rede the, thu rathe mane, thu risté
      the all the nyghte.   435
    Than Gawayne, gayest of alle,³
    Ledis hym owte of the haulle,
    Vn till a paveleone of paulle,
  That prowdely was pyghte.   439

XXXV.

Pighte was it prowdely with purpure and paulle,
With dossours and qweschyns, and bankowres full
    bryghte ; ⁴
With inn was a chapelle, a chambir, and ane
    haulle ; ⁵
A chymneye with charecole, to chawffen that
    knyghte,
His stede was sone stabillede, and lede to the
    stalle,
And haye hendly heuyde in hekkes one hyghte.⁶
Sythen he brayde⁷ vp a burde, and clathes gun
    calle ;   445
Sanapes, and salers, full semly to syghte,

---

¹ 'Went to walke.'
² 'Gome graithe.'   ³ 'Grathest of alle.'
⁴ 'Birdes branden above, in brend gold bright.'
⁵ 'Inwith was a.'
⁶ 'Hay hertly he had in haches on hicht.'
⁷ 'Thei braide.'

Preketes, and broketis, and standertis by
    twene:¹
  Than thay seruede that knyghte,²
  And his worthy wyghte,   450
  With full riche daynteths dyghte,
In Siluere full schene.

XXXVI.

In Siluer sa semly thay serue tham of the beste,
With vernage in verrys and cowppys sa clene:
And thus thase gleterande gommes gladdis thaire
    gestis,³   455
With riche dayntethe, endorred, in dysches by
    dene.
When the ryalle renke was gone to his ryste,
The Kynge in to concelle hase callede his knyghtis
    so kene;
Sayes: luke nowe, ʒe lordyngs, oure loos be noghte
    lost,
W[h]o sall enconter with ʒone knyghte, cast ʒo
    by twene.⁴   460
  Thane said Schir Gawayne,⁵ he sall vs noghte
    greue,
  Here my trouthe I ʒow plyghte,⁶
  I sall feghte with ʒone knyghte,
  In the defence of my ryghte,
My Lord, with ʒowre leue.   465

---

¹ 'Torches.'   ² 'Thus thei.'
³ 'And thus Schir Gawayn the good.'
⁴ 'Kestis ʒou bitwene.'
⁵ 'Then said Gawayn the goode.'
⁶ 'Here my honde I you highte.'

XXXVII.[1]

I leue wele, quod the kynge, thi latis are 'light,'
'But I nolde for no Lordeshippe se thi life lorne.'
Late gaa, quod Schir Gawayne, Gode stond with
    the right,
If he skape skatheles, 'hit were a foule skorne.'
In the dawynge of the day, the doughti were
    dight;   470
Thaye herde matyns 'and masse erly on morne.'
In myd Plumtun lone hor paueluns were piȝte,
Whare neuer freke opon folde had foughten
    biforne;
    Thei setten listes by lyue on the logh lande:
        Thre soppus of [pain-]mayn   475
        Thei brought to Schir Gawayn,
        For to comfort his brayn,
    The King gared commaunde.

XXXVIII.

The King commaunded kindeli the Erle of Kente,[2]
For his meculle curtasy to kepe tother knygte,   480
With riche dayntethe, 'or that day he dynede in
    his tente,
With birdes baken in brede, of brynte golde
    bryghte;[3]

---

[1] The greater part of this and the two first lines of the next stanza are torn away in MS. L. The 7th line is taken from the Ireland MS., the rest from the Douce.

[2] The Douce MS. reads *Kindely, the Erlis son of Kent*. A few other literal improvements have been borrowed from the Ireland text.

[3] 'After buskis him in a brene that burneshed was bright.'

And sythen vn to dame Waynour full warly he
    wente;
And lefte with hir in warde¹ that wurlyche
    wyghte:
And than thies hachells full hendely thaire horsses
    hase hent² 485
At the lycence of the lorde that lordely gun lyghte,³
  Alle bot thir 'two' beryns,⁴ bouldeste of blode.
    The kynges chere was sette,
    Abowne on a chasselett:⁵
    And many a gaylyarde grett 490
  For Gawayne the gude.
                              A Fytte.

XXXIX.

Gawayne and Galleron dyghtis thaire stedis,⁶
Alle of gleterande golde full gaye was thaire
    gere;
Twa lordes be lyfe to thaire lystes thaym ledis,
With many sergeauntes of mace, it was the
    manere; 495
The beryns broches thaire blonkes to thair sydes
    bledis.
Aythir freke appon felde hase fichede thaire
    spere,⁷
Schaftis of schene wode thay scheuerede in
    schides;⁸
So jolyly those gentill men justede one were; 499

---

¹ 'He in here.'
² 'After aither in high hour horses thei hent.'
³ 'And at the listes on the lande.'
⁴ 'Bothe thes two burnes.'
⁵ 'Quene on a chacelet.'   ⁶ 'Gurden her stedes.
⁷ 'Has fastned his spere.'   ⁸ 'Thei shindre.'

Schaftis thay scheuer in schydes full schene :[1]
  Sythen with brandes full brygthe,
  Riche mayles thay richte;
  Thus enconterde the knyghte
With Gawayne one grene.

XL.

Gawayne was graythely graythede on grene,[2]   605
With griffons of golde, engrelede full gaye,
Trayfolede with trayfoles [3] and trewluffes by twene,
'On' a stertande stede he strykes one straye.[4]
'That other in' his turnaynge he talkes tille him in tene;
'Whi drawes thou the one dreghe, and makis swilke delay?   610
'He swapped him then at the squyre' with a swerde kene:
'That greued Schir Gawayn to his dede day.
  The dyntes of that doughty were dowttous by dene.
    Fyftè mayles and mo
    The swerde swapt in two,   615
    The canel bone also,'
  And clef his schelde schene.[5]

XLI.

He keruet of the cantel, that couurt the kny3te,
Thro his shild and his shildur, a schaft-mun he share;

---

[1] 'Shaftes thei shindre in sheldes so shene.'
[2] 'Gaily grathed in grene.'
[3] 'Trifeled with traues.'   [4] 'On a stargand stede.'
[5] These lines, partly destroyed in MS. L., are filled up from MS. D.

Then the latelest lord loghe opon he3te, 520
And Gauan grechut ther with, and greuut wundur sore:
Sayd, "he should rewarde thè this route, and I con rede o-ry3te."
He foundes into the freke with a fresche fare;
Thro3t basynet and breny, that burnyschet wos bry3te, 524
With a bytand brand euyn throghe he him bare;
He bare thru3e his breny, that burneyst were bry3te.
 Then gloppunt that gaye,
 Hit was no ferly, in faye,
 His stedes startun on straye,
With steroppus fulle stry3te.[1] 530

XLII.

Thenne with steroppus fulle stre3te stifly he strikes,
Waynes atte Sir Wawane, ry3te as he were wode;
Thenne his lemmon on lofte scrilles and scrykes,
Quenne the balefulle birde blenked on his blode.[2]
Other lordus and ladès thayre laykes welle likes,
Thonked God of his grace for Gawan the gode.
With a swappe of his squrde squeturly him strykes,
Smote of Gauan stede heued, in styd quere hestode;
 The fayre fole foundret, and felle bi the rode;
 Gauan was smyther and smerte, 540
 Owte of his steroppus he sterte,
 As he that was of herte,
Fro Greselle the gode.

---

[1] A leaf in the Lincoln MS. appears unfortunately to be lost. This and the next five stanzas, and part of the 47th which it seems to have contained, are therefore printed from the Ireland copy.

[2] 'Burne,' here and elsewhere in MS. D. for 'barne' or 'beryn.'

XLIII.

"Greselle," quod Gauan, "gone is, God ote !
He wos the burlokke[st] blonke, ther euyr bote
    brede ! 645
By him that inne Bedelem wasse borne for oure
    bote,
I schalle reuenge thè to day, and I con ryʒt rede."
"Foche thè my fresun," quod the freke, "is fayrest
    on fote,
He wulle stond thè in stoure, in-toe so mycul
    styd."—
"No more for thi fresun, then for a rysche rote,
Butte for dylle of a dowmbe best, that thus schuld
    be ded ; 651
  I mowrne for no matyttory, for I may gete more."
    And as he stode bi his stede,
    That was gud in iche nede,
    Neʒehond Syr Wauan wold wede, 655
  So wepputte he fulle sore.

XLIV.

Sore wepput for woe, Syr Wauan the wiʒte,
Bouun to his enmy, that woundut was sore ;
The tother droʒghe him o-dreghe, for drede of the
    knyʒte,
Then he brochet his blonke, opon the bente bare.
"Thus may we dryue furthe the day," quod Gauan,
    "to the dirke nyʒte, 661
The sun is past the merke of mydday and more,"
In myddes the lyist on the lawunde, this lordes
    doun lyʒte ;
A-gayn the byrne with his brand, he busket him
    ʒare :

Thus to batelle thay boune with brandis so bry3te;
   Shene schildus thay shrede,
   Welle ryche mayles wexun rede,
   And mony du3ty hadun drede,
So fursely thai fo3tun.   669

XLV.

Thus on fote con thai fe3te, opon the fayre fildus,
As fresch as ij lions, that fawtutte the fille:
Witturly ther weys, thayre weppuns thay weld;
Wete 3e wele, Sir Wauan, him wontut no wille,
He berus to him with his brand, vndur his brode shild,
Thro the wast of the body wowundet him ille;   675
The squrd styntet for no stuffe, he was so wele stelet,
The tothur startes on bakke, and stondus stone stille;
   If he were stonit in that stouunde, 3ette strykes he sore;
   He girdus to Syr Gauane,
   Thro3he ventaylle and pusane,   680
   That him lakket no more to be slayne,
Butte the brede of hore.

XLVI.

And thus the hardy on heyte, on helmis thai heuen,
Betun downe berels, in bordurs so bry3te,   684
That with stones iraille were strencult and strauen,
Frettut with fyne gold, that failis in the fi3te.
With schildus on ther schildurs, schonely thay shewen,
Stythe stapuls of stele, thay striken doune stre3te.
Thenne byernes bannes the tyme, the bargan was bruen,
That euyr these du3ti with dyntus, so dulfuly were di3te.   690

Hit hurte King Arther in herte, and mengit his mode;
Bothe Sir Lote, and Sir Lake,
Meculle menyng con make;
Thenne Dame Gaynor grette for his sake,
For Gawan the gode!

XLVII.

Thenne grette Dame Gaynour, with hur gray een,
For grefe of Sir Gauan grimliche wouundes;
Thenne the kny3te, that was curtase, cruail, and kene,
With a stelun brand, he strikes in that stounde;
Alle the cost of the kny3te, he keruys doune clene,
Thro the riche mayles, that ronke were and rouunde;
Suche a touche in that tyde, he ta3te hym in tene,[1]
And gurdes one Sir Gallerun, euyn grouelinge[2] on grounde.
 Alle grouelinge in grounde, gronet on grene,
  Als wowundut as he wasse,
  Wundur rudely he rose,[3]
  Fast he foundes atte his face,
 With a squrd kene.[4]

XLVIII.

Clenly that crewelle couerde hym on highte,
And with a caste of the carhonde, in kantelle he strykis;

---

[1] 'With a teneful touche.'
[2] Robson printed 'grouelonges.'
[3] 'Sone buredely he ras.'
[4] 'Schene.'—MS. L.

Full ȝerne he wayttis Schir Wawayne [1] the wighte,
Bot hym lympede the werse; and that me wele lykis;
He etyllde with a slynge [2] hafe slayne hym with slighte,
The swerde sleppis on slante, [3] and one the mayle slykys,
And Schir Gawayne by the colere clekis the knyghte, [4] 615
Than his leman so lowde skremes and skrykis. [5]
  Scho grete one dame Gaynour, with granes so grylle,
  And saide, lady! makles of myghte,
  Hafe now mercy one ȝone knychte,
  That es so dulefully dyghte, 620
Giffe it be thi will.

XLIX.

Than wilfully dame Waynour [6] son to the kynge went;
Scho caught of hir coronalle, and knelyd hym till:
Als thu erte Roye ryalle, and recheste of rent,
And I thyn wyfe, weddid at myn awen will, [7] 625
ȝone beryns in ȝone batelle that bledis one ȝone bent,
Thay are wery, I wysse, and wondide full ille,
Thurgh 'thaire' schene schildis thaire schuldirs are schent;
'The granes of Schir Gawayne dois my hert grille.' [8] 629

---

[1] 'And waynes at Schir Wawayn.'
[2] 'He atteled with a slenk.'
[3] 'The swerde swapped on his swange.'
[4] 'Keppes the knight.'
[5] 'Skrilles and skrikis' . . . 'skykis.'—MS. L.
[6] 'Wisly dame Waynour.'   [7] 'At thi awen wille.'
[8] This line is omitted in MS. L.

The grancs of Schir Gawayne greuys me full fare:
  Wolde thu, lufly lorde,[1]
  Gare the knyghtis accorde,
  It ware grete comforde,
Till alle that here ware.   634

L.

Bot than hym spake Galleron to Gawayne the gude:
" I wende no wy in this werlde, were haluendelle so wyghte,
Here I make the relese of my rentis, by the rode;
And by fore thiese ryalle, resynge the my ryghte;[2]
And sythen I make the manreden with a mylde mode,   639
Als to mane in this medil erthe makles of myghte."
He talkes to warde the knyghte, one heghte there he stode,
He bedde that burely his brande, that birneschede was bryghte:
  Of renttis and reches I make the relese.
    Downe knelis that knyghte,
    And carpis thies wordes one highte: 645
  " The kyng send me vp ryghte,[3]
And commandis the pese."

LI.

The kynge commandis the pese, and cryes one highte;
And Gawayne was gudly, and lefte for his sake.   649

---

[1] 'Woldest thou leve lorde.'
[2] Probably, ' waive my right to ransom.'
[3] 'The kyng stode vp right.'

And than to the lystis the lordis leppis full lyghte,
Schir Owayne, Schir Vryene, and Arrake full
 rathe:[1]
Marrake, and Menegalle, that maste were of
 myghte,[2]
Bathe thase truelde knyghtis trewly thay taghte:
Vnnethes myghte those knyghtes stande vp
 ryghte,
Thay were for bett, and for blede thaire wedis
 wexe bleke:[3]   655
 Hir blees were brosed, for beting of brondes[4]
 With owtten more lettynge,
 Was dighte there thayre saȝtenynge;[5]
 By fore that comly kynge,
 Thay helde vpe thair hondes.   660

LII.

I gyffe to the Schir Gawayne, quode the kynge,
 tresoure, and golde,[6]
Glamorgans landis,[7] with greuys so grene:
The wirchipe of Wales, to welde and to wolde;
With Gryffons castelle, kirnelde so clene;   664
And the husters haulle,[8] to hafe and to holde;
Wayfurthe, and Waturforthe, wallede I wene;[9]

---

[1] 'Schir Ewayn, Schir Erian, and Arrak, Schir Lake.'
[2] 'Schir Dowrelat and Moylard that most wer of might.'
[3] 'What for buffetes and blode, her blees wex blake.'
[4] This line is omitted in MS. L.
[5] 'Dight was here saughtlying.'
[6] 'With gerson and golde.'
[7] 'All the Glamorgan lande.'
[8] 'Eke Ulstur halle.'
[9] 'Wayford and Waterforde in Wales I wene.'

Twa baronryse in Bretan,¹ with burghes so balde,
That are moted abowte,² and byggede full bene :
  I sall endowe the als a duke, and dub the with
     myn hande,   669
    That thu saȝtun with yone gentill knyghte,
    That es so hardy and wyghte,
    And relese hym thi ryghte,
  And grante him his lande.

LIII.

Now, and here I gyffe hym, quod Gawayne,³
    withowttyn ony gyle,
Alle the landes, and the lythes, fra Lowyke to
    Layre ;⁴   675
Commoke, and Carrike ;⁵ Connynghame ; and
    Kylle ;
Als the cheualrous knyghte, hase chalandchede
    als Ayere ;
The Lebynge, the Lewpynge, the Leveastre I lee,⁶
Bathe frythes, and forestes, frely and faire :⁷
Vnder⁸ ȝour lordeship to lenge heren while,   680
And to the Rounde Table to make repaire ;
  I shall reseff him in felde, in forestis so faire :'
    Than the Kynge, and the Quene,
    And alle the doghety by dene,
    Thorow the greuys so grene,   685
  To Carlele thay kayre.

---

¹ 'Two baronrees in Bretane.'
² 'That arn batailed about.'
³ 'Here I gif Schir Galeron, quod G.'
⁴ 'Fra Lauer.'   ⁵ 'Connok and Carlele.'
⁶ 'The Lother, the Lemok, the Loynak, the Lile.'
⁷ 'Forestes and fosses so faire.'
⁸ This and the next two lines are not in MS. L.

LIV.

The Kyng to Carelele es comen, with knyghttis
   so kene,
To halde his Rownde Tabill[1] one ryalle array:
These knyghtes, that were[2] wondede full wathely,
   als I wene,
Surgeons sone sanede thaym, sothely to saye;   690
Bothe comforthede thaym than the Kynge,[3] and
   the Qwene;
Thay ware dubbyde Dukes bothe one a daye.
And ther Schir Galleron weddid his wyfe,[4] that
   semly and schene,
With gyftis, and gersonis, of Schir Gawayne the
   gaye.[5]   694
   And thus those hathells[6] with haldis that hende:
   And when he was saned, and sownde,
      Thay made hym sworne, to Schir Gawane in
         that stownde,[7]
      And sythen a knyghte of the Tabille
         Rownde,[8]
Vn till his lyues end.   699

LV.

Dame Gaynour garte besyly[9] wryte in to the weste,
To alle manere of relygeous, to rede and to synge;

---

    [1] 'And al the rounde table.'
    [2] 'The wees that were.'
    [3] 'Bothe conforte the knyghtis.'
    [4] 'There he wedded his wife, slonkest I wene.'
    [5] 'Schir Galeron the gaye.'
    [6] 'Thus that hathel in high.'
    [7] 'Thei made Schir Galeron that stonde.'
    [8] 'A knight of the Table Ronde.'
    [9] 'Waynour gared wisely.'

Priestes with processyons, to pray were full prest,[1]
With a mylion of messis, to make hir menynge ;
Dukes, Erles, Barouns, and bechoppes of the
    beste,[2]   704
Thurghe alle Ynglande scho garte make menynge.[3]
And thus this ferlyes by felle in a fforeste,[4]
Vndir an holte so hare, at an hunttynge ;
  Swylke hunttynge in holtis,[5] culde noghte ben
    hyd :—
    Thus to the fforestes thay fure,[6]
    Steryn knyghtes and sture :[7]   710
    And in the tym of Arthure
This awntyr by tyd.

This ferly by felle, full sothely to say[n]e,
In Yggillwode fforeste, at the Ternwathelayne.[8]

Explicit.

---

[1] Part of this line and the next is wanting in MS. L.
[2] 'Buke lered men ; bisshops the best.'
[3] 'Thorgh al Bretayne besely the burde gared rynge.'
[4] 'This ferly bifelle in Englond forest.'
[5] 'A holte so hore.'
[6] 'Thay fore.'
[7] 'And store.'
[8] Tern Wathelayne, or Tearne Wadling, the name of a small lake near Hesketh in Cumberland. It is celebrated in several old ballads and romances. Yggilwoode, Englewood, or, as it is sometimes called, the English wood, was an extensive forest in Cumberland, sixteen miles in length, and reached from Penrith to Carlisle. It is intimately associated with the story of *Adam Bel* (Hazlitt's "Popular Poetry of England," 1864-6, ii. 131 *et seq.*, and present work, *infra*).

The Pystyl of Swete Susan.

HUCHEON of the Awle Ryale, as we learn from Wyntoun's "Metrical Chronicle," was the author of this very ancient and curious relique of Scotish poetry on the story of Susanna and the Elders. His great work was the "Gest Historiale," in which, according to the same authority, Hucheon

    ——" has tretyd curyously
  In Gest of Broyttys auld story,"

and the Prior of Lochleven defends him and "the Auctore," from whom his work was perhaps translated, against the exceptions that in his time had been made to some of the statements which it contained. Wyntoun, to whom we owe all the information we possess respecting Hucheon and his writings, says,

    ——Men of gud discretyowne
  Suld excuse and lovē Huchowne
  That cunnand wes in Literature.
  He made the gret Gest of Arthure,
  And the Awntyre of Gawane,
  The Pystyl als of Swete Susan ;
  He wes curyws in hys style,
  Fayre of facund, and subtile,
  And ay to plesans and delyte,
  Made in metyre mete his dyte,
  Lytil or nowcht nevyr the les
  Waverand fra the suthfastnes.
      B. V. xiv. 300-312.

From Hucheon's being thus called of "the Awle Ryale," or royal hall or palace, the learned editor of Wyntoun's Chronicle supposes he may have been the King's Poet. It seems, however, agreed among our poetical antiquaries that this Hucheon was one and the same person with the Sir Hugh of Eglynton, a Scotish poet of the fourteenth century, who is mentioned by Dunbar in his "Lament for the Death of the Makaris." "He flourished," says Mr. George Chalmers, in a letter to the Editor, "under David II. and died under Robert II. I think there cannot be any doubt whether Sir Hugh de Eglynton were not Hucheon of the Awle Ryale. He is supposed to have died about the year 1381. As he was a busy knight in his day, so are there many notices about him."

No other production by our author is known to be extant, unless, on the authority of Wyntoun, we should attribute to him one or other of the curious metrical romances of the adventures of Arthur and Gawane.

Of the "Pystill of Susan" there are various ancient manuscripts. It was, indeed, included by Ritson in his "Caledonian Muse," printed about the year 1803 and not published till 1821, and then in the incomplete state in which the original editor had left it at his death. The care and fidelity exhibited in what he has done is beyond all praise, and might have served as a guide to editors who have since been engaged in similar publications. We owe much to the zeal which Ritson showed towards the remains of our ancient poetry at a time when they were disregarded and overlooked by our countrymen.

The copy followed by Ritson is contained in the very large collection, or *ingens volumen*, as it is properly enough styled, in the Bodleian Library: it is called, from its donor, the Vernon Manuscript, and was probably compiled about the end of the fourteenth century. In a volume of old metrical romances in the Cotton Library, written about the middle of the fifteenth century, is another copy, wanting, however, the first eight stanzas; and a third copy forms part of a volume once in Mr. Heber's possession. This last, which had successively belonged to Sir Henry Spelman, Dr. Taylor, (the editor of Demosthenes,) and Richard Gough, Esq., is described by Dr. Whitaker, the learned editor of "Piers' Plouhman's Visions," as a manuscript, which, "from the handwriting, might probably be assigned to the reign of Richard the Second." He considers the poem to be nearly as ancient as "Piers' Plouhman;" and, from the alliteration being combined with rhyme, and a very complicated stanza, (he adds,) it is not to be wondered at that it has had no imitators.

The Pistill of Susan.

I.

HER was in Babiloine a bern, in that borw riche,
That was a Jeugh jentil, and Joachim he hiht;
He was so lele in his lawe, there lived non him liche,
Of all riches that reuke arayes he was riht:
His innes, and his orchardes, weren withinne a dep dich, 5
Halles and herbergages, hey uppon height;
To seche thoru that cité ther nas non sich,
Of erbes, and of erberi, so avenauntliche idiht,
      That day.
    Withinne the sercle of sees, 10
    Of erberi and alees,
    Of alle maner of trees,
      Sothely to say.

II.

He had a wif hight Susan, was sotil and sage,
Heo was Elches doughter, eldest and eyre, 15
Lovelich and lilie-whit, on of that lynage,
Of alle fason of foode frelich and feire:
Thei lerned hire lettrure of that langage,
The maundement of Moises, thei marked to that deire,
To the mount of Synai that went in message, 20
That the Trinité bitok of tables a peire,
      To rede;
    Thus thei lerne hire the lawe,
    Cleer clergye to knawe
    To God stod hire gret awe, 25
      That wlonkest in weede.

III.

He hedde an orchard newe, that neighed wel nere,
Ther Jewes with Joachim preveliche gon playe;
For he real and riche of rentes ever were,
Honest, and avenaunt, and honorablest aye. 30
I wis, ther haunted til her hous hende, ȝe mai here,
Two domes of the lawe, that dredde were that day,
Preostes and presidens preised als peere,
Of whom ur soverein lord sawes gan say,
    And tolde,   35
  How heor wikkednes comes
  Of the wrongwys domes
  That they have gyve to gomes,
    Theis juges of olde.

IV.

Thus theis dredful domes [-men] on daie thider drewe; 40
Al for gentrise and joye of that Juwesse,
To go in hir gardeyn, that gayliche grewe,
To fonge floures and fruit, thought thei no fresse:
And whon they seigh Susan, semelich of hewe,
Thei weor so set uppon hir, might thei not sesse; 45
Thei wolde enchaunte that child: hou schold heo eschewe?
And thus th[e]is cherles unchaste in chaumbre hir chesse,
    With chere,
  With two maidenes alon,
  Semelyche Suson,   50
  On daye in the merion,
    Of murthes wol here.

V.

Whon theos perlous prestes perceyved hire play,
Tho thoughte the wretches to bewile that worly in wone,
Heore wittes wel waiwordes thei wrethen awai, 55
And turned fro his teching, that teeld is in trone.
For siht of here soverayn, sothli to say,
Heore hor hevedes fro hevene thei hid apon one,
Thei caught for heor covetyse the cursyng of Kai,
For rightwys jugement recordet thei none, 60
    They two.
  Every day bi day
  In the pomeri thei play,
  While thei mihte Susan assay,
    To worchen hire wo. 65

VI.

In the seson of somer, with Sibell and Jone,
Heo grethed hir til hir gardin, that growed so grene,
Ther lyndes and lorers wer lent upon lone,
The savyne and sypres, selcouth to sene,
The palme, and the popler, the pirie, the plone, 70
The juniper jentel, jonyng bitwene,
The rose ragged on rys, richest on rone,
Ipeuwed with the thorn trinaunt to sene,
    So tiht;
  Ther weore popejayes prest, 75
  Nihtyngales uppon nest,
  Blithest briddes o the best,
    In blossoms so briht.

VII.

The briddes in blossoms thei beeren wel loude
On olyves, and amylliers, and al kynde of trees, 80
The popejayes perken and pruynen for proude,
On peren and pyn-appel they joyken in pees;
On croppes of canel keneliche thei croude,
On grapes the goldfinch thei gladen and glees;
Thus schene briddes in schawe schewen heore schroude, 85
On figges and fygers thei fongen heore sees,
    In fay;
  Ther weore growyng so grene
  The date, with the damesene,
  Turtils troned on trene, 90
    By sixti, I saygh.

VIII.

The fyge and the filbert were fodemed so fayre,
The chirie and the chestein, that chosen is of hewe,
Apples and almaundes that honest are of ayre,
Grapes and garnettes gayliche thei grew, 95
The costardes comeliche in cuylthes thei cayre,
The britouns, the blaunderers, [the] braunches, the bewe,
Fele floures and fruit, frelich of flayre,
With wardons winlich and Walshe notes newe,
    They wald 100
  Over heor hedes gon hyng,
  The wince and the wederlyng,
  Spyces speden to spryng,
    In erbers enhaled.

IX.

The chyve, and the chollet, the chibolle, the cheve, 105
The chouwet, the cheverol, that schaggen on niht,
The parsel, the passenep, poretes to preve,
The pyon, the peere, wel proudliche ipiht;
The lilye, the louache, launsyng with leve,
The sauge, the sorsecle, so semeliche to siht; 110
Columbyne and charuwé clottes thei creve,
With ruwe and rubarbe, ragget ariht,
   No lees;
 Daysye, and ditoyne,
 Ysope, and averoyne, 115
 Peletré, and plantoyne,
   Proudest in prees.

X.

Als this schaply thing ȝede in hire ȝerde,
That was hir hosbondes and hire, that holden with hende:
"Now folk be faren from us, thar us not be ferde 120
Aftur myn oynement, warliche ȝe wende.
Espieth now specialy, the ȝates ben sperde
For we wol wassche as i-wis bi this welle strende.
For-thi the wyf werp of hir wedes unwerde,
Under a lorere ful low that ladi gan lende, 125
   So sone:
 By a wynliche well,
 Susan caste of hir kelle,
 Bote feole ferlys hir bifelle,
   Bi midday or none. 130

XI.

Now wer this domes-men derf drawen in derne,
Whiles thei seo that ladi was laft al hire one,
For to heilse that hende thei highed ful ʒerne,
With wordes thei worshipe that worliche in wone:
Wolt thou, ladi, for love, on ure lay lerne,   135
And under this lorere ben ur lemmone?
The ne tharf wonde for no wight ur willes to werne,
For alle gomes that scholde greve of gardin ar gone
   In feere.
  ʒif thou this neodes deny,   140
  We schall telle trewely
  We toke the with avourti;
    Under this lorere.

XII.

Then Susan was serwful, and seide in hire thought:
I am with serwe biset on everiche syde,   145
ʒif I assent to this sin, that theis segges have sought,
I be bretenet and brent in baret to byde:
And, ʒif I nikke hom with nai, hit helpeth me nought:
Such toret and teone taketh me this tyde.
[W]ar I that worthlich[est] wrech, that all this world wrought,   150
Beter is wemles [to] wende of this world wyde.
   With this
  Tho cast heo a careful cri,
  This loveliche ladi,
  Hir servauns hedde selli,   155
    No wonder, i-wis.

XIII.

Whon kene men of hir court comen till her cri,
Heo hedde cast of hir calle ann hire kever-cheve
In at a privé posterne thi passen in hi,
And findes this prestes wel prest her poyntes
    preve   160
Tho seid the loselle aloud to the ladi,
Thou hast gon with a gome, thi God to greve,
And ligge with thi lemon in avoutri.
Bi the lord and the lawe that we onne leeve,
            They swere,   165
    Alle hire servauns, thei shont,
    And stelen away in a stont;
    Of hire weore thei never wont
            Such wordes to here.

XIV.

Hir kinrede, hir cosyns and al that hire knewe,   170
Wrong handes, i-wis, and wepten wel sare,
Sykeden for Susan, so semeliche of hewe,
Al onwyse of that wyf, wondred thei were.
Thei dede hire in a dungon, ther never day
    dewe,
While domes-men were dempt this dede to
    clare;   175
Marred in manicles, that made wer newe;
Metelés, whiles the morwen to middai and mar,
            In drede.
    Ther com hir fader, so fre,
    With al his affinitè;   180
    The prestes sauns pitè,
            And ful of falshede.

XV.

Tho seide the justises on bench, to Joachim the Jewe,
That was of Jacobes kynde, gentil of dedes,
Let senden after Susan, so semelych of hewe,   185
That thou hast wedded to wyf, wlonkest in wedes;
Heo was in trouthe, as we trowe, tristi and trewe;
Hir herte holliche on him that the hevene hedes.
Thus thei brought hir to the barr, hir bales to brewe,
Nouther dom ne deth that day heo ne dredes,   190
  Als thare.
 Hir hed was ʒolow as wyre
 Of gold fyned with fyre;
 Hire scholdres schaply and schire;
  That bureliche was bare.   195

XVI.

Nou is Susan in sale, sengeliche arayed,
In a selken schert, with scholdres wel schene.
Tho ros up with rancour the reukes reneyed,
This comelich accused, with wordes wel kene;
Homliche on her heved heor hondes thei leyed: 200
And heo wepte for wo, no wonder, i-wene.
We schul presenten this pleint, hou thou ever be paied,
And sei sadliche the soth, right as we have sene,
  On sake.
 Thus with cauteles waynt,   205
 Preostes presented this playnt,
 ʒit schal trouthe hem ataynt.
  I dar undertake.

XVII.

Thorw-out the pomeri we passed us to play,
Of preier and of penaunce was ur purpose,   210
Heo com with two maidens, al richeli that day,
In riche robes arayed, red as the rose;
Wylyliche heo wyled hir wenches away,
And comaunded hem kenely the ȝates to close;
Heo rode to a ȝoung mon, in a valay,   215
The semblaunt of Susan wolde non suppose,
      For soth:
  Be this cause that we say,
  Heo wyled hir wenches away,
  This word we witnesse for ay,   220
      With tonge and with toth.

XVIII.

Whon we that semblant seigh, we siked wel sare,
For sert of hir sovereyn, and for hir owne sake,
Ur copes weore cumberous, and cundelet us care,
But ȝit we trinet a trot, that traytur take;   225
He was borlich and bigge, bold as a bare;
More mighti mon then we his maistris to make:
To the ȝate ȝaply thei ȝeoden wel ȝare,
And he lift up the lach, and leop over the lake,
      That ȝouthe.   230
  Heo ne schunte for no schame,
  But bouwed aftur for blame,
  Heo nolde cuythe us his name,
      For craft that we couthe.

XIX.

Now heo is dampned on deis, with deol thaigh
    hir deve,   236
And hir domes-men unduwe do hir be withdrawen.
Loveliche heo louted, and latched hir leve,
At kynred and cosyn, that heo had ever i-knawen,
Heo asked merci with mony, in this mischeve :
I am sakeles of syn, heo seide in hir sawen,   240
Grete God of his grace ȝor gultus forȝive,
That doth me derfliche be ded and don out of
    dawen,
        With dere.
    Wolde God that I micht
    Speke with Joachim a nicht,   245
    And sithen to deth me bediht ;
        I charge hit not a pere.

XX.

Heo fel doun flat in the flore, hir feer whom heo
    fand,
Carped to him kyndeli, as heo ful wel couthe :
I wis I wraththed the nevere, at my witand,   250
Neither in word, ne in werk, in elde, ne in ȝouthe.
Heo kevered upon hir kneos, and cussed his hand :
For I am dampned, I ne dar disparage thi mouth.
Was never more serwful segge, bi se, nor bi sande,
He never a sorioure siht, bi north, ne bi south,   255
        Tho thare.
    Thei toke the feteres of hire feete,
    And evere he cussed that swete :
    In other world schul we mete.—
        Seide he no mare.   260

XXI.

Then Susan, the serwfol, seide uppon hight,
Heef hir hondes on high, biheld heo to hevene :
Thou maker of middelert, that most art of miht,
Bothe the sonne and the see, thou sette uppon sevene ;
Alle my werkes thou wost, the wrong, and the riht,   265
Hit is nedful nou thy names to neven.
Seththe I am deolfolich dampned, and to deth diht,
Lord, herteliche tak hede, and herkne my stevene.
          Se fre !
     Seththe thou maight not be sene,   270
     With no fleschliche eyene,
     Thou wost wel that I am clene,
          Have merci now on me !

XXII.

Now thei dresse hir to deth withouten eny drede,
And lede forth that ladi, lovesum of lere ;   275
Grete God, of his grace, of gultes unguede,
Holp with the Holi Gost, and herde hir preyere.
He directed this dome, and this delful dede
To Danyel, the prophete, of dedes so dere.
Such ȝiftes god him ȝaf in his ȝouthehede,   280
ȝit failed hit a fourtenight, ful of the ȝere,
          Nought sayne.
     Tho criede that freoly fode,
     Why spille ȝe innocent blode ?
     And alle thei stodeyd and stode,   285
          This ferlys to frayne.

XXIII.

What signefyes, gode sone, these sawes that thou seeth,
Thus these maisterful men mouthes can mele,
Thei be fendes all the frape, I sei hit in feith,
And in folk of Israel be foles wel sele.   290
Umbiloke ȝou, lordes, such lawes ben leith,
Methinketh ȝor dedes unduwe such domes to dele,
Aȝein to the ȝildhalle, ȝe gomes ungreith,
I schal, be proces apert, disprove this apele,
      For nede.   295
  Lat twinne hem in two,
  For now wakneth heor wo,
  Thei schal graunte, as thei go,
      Al heore falshede.

XXIV.

Thei disevered him sone, and sette hem sere,   300
And sodeynly askede, thei brought into the sale,
Bifore this ȝonge prophete this preost go apere,
And he him apeched sone, with chekes wel pale :
Thou hast I bè presedent, the peple to steere,
Thou dotëst nou on thin olde tos, in the dismale ;   305
Now schal thi conscience be knowen that ever was unclere,
Thou hast in Babiloygne on benche brewed much bale,
      Wel bolde :
  Now schal ȝor synnes be seene,
  Of fals domes bideene,   310
  For theose in Babiloyne han bene
      Jugget of olde.

XXV.

Thou seidest thow seighe Susanne sinned in thi siht,
Tel nou me trewly, under what tre?—
Mon, bi the muche God, that most is of miht,   315
Under a cyne, sothli, myselven I hir se.—
Now thou lyest in thin hed, bi heven uppon hiht,
An angel with a naked swerd the neighes wel nei,
He hath brandist his brond, brennynde so briht,
To marke thi middel at a mase in more then in thre,
    No lese: 321
  Thou brak Godes comaundement,
  To sle such an innocent,
  With eny fols juggement,
    Unduweliche on dese.   325

XXVI.

Now is this domes-mon withdrawen withouten eni drede,
And put into prison aȝeyn into place,
Thei broughten the tother forth whom the barn bede,
To-fore the folk and the faunt, freli of face:
Cum forth, thou corsed caytif, thou Canaan, he sede,
Bi cause of thi covetise, thou art in this case,   331
Thou hast disceyvet thi self, with thi oune dede,
Of thy wit for a wyf biwiled thou wase,
    In wede.
  Thou sey now, so mote thou the,   335
  Under what kind of tre,
  Semeli Susan thou se
    Do that derne dede.

XXVII.

Thou gome of gret elde, thin hed is grei hored,
Tel hit me treweli, are thou thi lif tyne.
Tho that rothly cherl ruydely rored,
And seid bifore the prophet, thei pleied bi a prine.—
Now thou liest loude, so helpe me ur lorde;
For fulthe of thi falshed thou schalt ha evel pine,
Thou and thi cursed cumpere, ȝe mon not acorde;
ȝe schul be drawen to the deth, this dai ar we dine,
      So rathe.
    An angel is neih honde,
    Takes the domes of ȝor honde,
    With a ornneynge bronde,
        To byte you bathe.

XXVIII.

Then the folk of Israel felle upon knees,
And lowed that loveli lord, that hir the lyf lent;
All the gomes, that hir God wolde gladen and glees,
This prophete so pertli proves his entent,
Thei trompe bifore this traitours, and traylen hem on trees,
Thorw-out the cité, by comuyn assent;
He that leeveth on the lord, thar him not drede no lees,
That thus his servant saved that schold haue be schent,
      In sete.
    This ferly bifel
    In the days of Danyel,
    The Pistel witnesseth wel
        Of that Profete.

Explicit.

Orfeo and Heurodis;

OR

King Orfeo.

"Herken, lordyngys, that ben trewe,
And Y wol you telle of sir Orphewe."

THE fairy tale of "Orfeo and Heurodis" is possessed of a very distinct, though not less interesting character, from the numerous remains of early Romantic fiction. In the concluding lines it professes to be a lay of Bretaigne; but whether a translation or not, there can be no doubt that it was formed on the classical story of Orpheus and Eurydice. This tale was extensively known at an early period, owing to the circulation of the Latin poets and the works of other ancient authors in which it has been so beautifully narrated. In proof of this, Mr. Turner, in his valuable and instructive history, has shown that during the eleventh century King Alfred, when translating the Metrum to the "Consolations of Philosophy," in his Anglo-Saxon version of Boethius, where the incident is described in a general manner by that popular writer, has told "the story so completely in his own way, and with so many of his own little touches and additions, as to make his account an original tale."[1] In the present instance the narrative (as observed by a distinguished writer of our times, who in a felicitous manner has employed it to illustrate a highly interesting

---

[1] History of the Anglo-Saxons, vol. ii. p. 157, edit. 1820.

essay on "The Fairies of Popular Superstition"[1]) has been transformed into a beautiful romantic tale of faery, in which the Gothic mythology and the usages of chivalry are with singular skill engrafted on the fables of Greece.

Among the "pleysand storeis" enumerated in "The Complaynt of Scotland," 1549, as being popular, is "Opheus, Kyng of Portingal;" but no romance of this particular title is known; therefore it is more than probable that it might be some corruption of the present story, as we know how little stress should be laid on the geographical correctness or consistency of the minstrel-writers. Thus, in the following tale, we have Orfeo represented as King of Winchester, the ancient name of which "the romancer, with unparalleled ingenuity, discovers to have been Traciens or Thrace;"[2] and in the burlesque interlude of "the laying of a gaist," printed in this collection, "the Ghaist" is married to "the Spenzie flie"—

> And crownd him kyng of Kandelie:
> And thay gat them thame betwene
> *Orpheus* Kyng, and *Elpha* quene.

The story of Orpheus and Eurydice in the latter part of the fifteenth century was moralised by Robert Henryson, the Scotish poet. It was first printed at Edinburgh in the year 1508, with the title, "Heir begynnis the traitie of Orpheus kyng, and how he ʒeid to hewyn t to hel to seik his quene." After detailing, with minute fidelity to his classical authorities, the genealogy and history of the King of Thrace, Henryson introduces, in a different kind of measure, the "mone lamentable" of Orpheus, beginning—

> O dulfull harpe! with mony dolly string
> Turne all thi mirth and musik in murnyng
> And cess of all the subtell sangis sweit.

After this pathetic lamentation, the poet, having related his visit to the celestial spheres, conducts him to the infernal

---

[1] Minstrelsy of the Scottish Border, vol. ii. p. 174, edit. 1803.
[2] Minstrelsy of the Scottish Border, vol. ii. p. 203.

regions in search of Eurydice. From this part of Henryson's performance a few stanzas, by way of specimen, may be given.

> He passit furth the space of xx. dayis,
> Fer and full ferther than I can tell,
> And ay he fand stretis and redy wayis,
> Tyll at the last, vnto the yett of hell
> He com ; and thare he fand a portar fell
> With three hedis, was callit Cerberus ;
> A hund of hell, a monster meruailus !

He charms Cerberus, and then the "three sisters," Alecto, Megera, and Thesiphoné, whose employment was turning round the wheel on which Ixion was spread. "Syne," the poet says—

> Syne com he till a wonder grisely flud,
> Droubly and depe, that rathly doun can ryn,
> Quhare Tantalus nakit full thristy stude,
> And yit the water yede abone his chyn ;
> Thouch he gapit thare wald na drop cum in,
> Quhen he dulkit the water wald descend ;
> Thus gat he noucht his thrist to slake or mend.

> Before his face ane apill hang also
> Fast at his mouth apon a tolter threde,
> Quhen he gapit it rokkit to and fro
> And fled, as it refusit him to fede :
> Than Orpheus had reuth of his grete nede
> Tuke out his harp, and fast on it can clink,
> The water stude, and Tantalus gat drink.

The next object which presents itself in his progress is Theseus preyed on by a "grisely gripe" or vulture, which also excites the compassion of Orpheus. On entering "hydouse hellis house," he exclaims—

> O dolly place and groundles depe dungeoun !
> Furnes of fyre, with stynk intollerable,
> Pit of dispair, wythout remissioun,
> Thy mete venym, thy drynk is poysonable,
> Thy grete panis to compt vnnowmerabil ;
> Quhat creature cummys to duel in the
> Is ay deyand, and newir more may dee !

We must pass over the different personages whom he here beholds, in order to make room for the description of his meeting with Eurydice.

> Syn nethir mare he went quhare Pluto was
> And Proserpine, and thider ward he drewe,
> Ay playand on his harp as he coud pas,
> Till at the last Eurydice he knewe;
> Lene and dedelike pitouse and pale of hewe,
> Rycht warsch and wan, and walowit as a wede,
> Hir lily lyre was lyke vnto the lede.
>
> Quod he, my lady lele, and my delyte,
> Full wa is me, to se yow changit thus!
> Quhare is thy rude as rose with chekis quhite?
> Thy cristall eyne with blenkis amorouse?
> Thi lippis rede to kis deliciouse?—
> Quod scho, as now I dar noucht tell, perfay,
> Bot ye sall wit the cause ane other day.

The present tale has been justly admired no less for the harmony of its versification than for the beautiful description which it contains of fairyland. Heurodis is carried away by the king of the fairies, whose attendants are as numerous as his riches and magnificence are dazzling; and is recovered by Orfeo in the guise of a minstrel. The following lines, which occur in one of the ancient copies of this poem, (but apparently omitted by the transcriber of the manuscript that is followed,) may be quoted as illustrative of Orfeo's skill and love of minstrelsy:—

> "Orpheo most of ony thing,
> Lovede the gle of harpyng;
> Syker was every gode harpoure
> Of hym to have moche honour.
> Hymself loved for to harpe,
> And layde thereon his wittes scharpe;
> He lerned so, ther non was
> A better harper in no plas.
> In the world was never man born,
> That onus Orfeo sat biforn,
> And he myght of his harpyng her,
> He shulde thinke that he wer
> In one of the joys of paradys,
> Suche joy and melody in his harpyng is."

The reader will perceive that in this story the catastrophe is different; but if less pathetic, it certainly is more agreeable than that of the classical fiction.

At some later period this romantic legend appears to have been considerably altered and abridged. In such a state it is preserved in a manuscript in the Harleian Collection,[1] from which it was published by Ritson.[2] The present copy is taken from the more ancient volume in the Advocates' Library, called, from its donor, Sir Alexander Boswell of Auchinleck, the Auchinleck Manuscript. The period of its composition may be referred to the beginning of the fourteenth century, as the volume which contains it was evidently written during the minority of Edward III. From this early and precious record of ancient poetry the text is given literally, except that a few useless contractions are discarded, which might only have served to perplex the reader. As Ritson's Collection, which contains the story in its more recent and somewhat compendious state, is by no means of rare occurrence, it was thought unnecessary to point out any of the variations. The prologue that there accompanies it is not found in the Auchinleck MS., yet, as the leaf immediately before the first line,

"Orfeo was a king,"

has been torn out for the sake of the illumination, it is possible that it may not have begun so abruptly, even although the commencement of another poem in the volume is in substance the same with that of the "Sir Orfeo" in the Harleian MS., which in all consists of 510 lines.[3] The opening lines of the ensuing piece have been supplied from the Ashmole MS., which is fuller than the Auchinleck copy. A few readings necessary to the sense have been adopted from the same source. The Ashmole text is reprinted entire in Hazlitt's *Fairy Tales*, 1875.

---

[1] MSS. Harl., No. 3810.
[2] Ancient English Metrical Romances, vol. ii. pp. 248-269. 1802, 8vo.
[3] Lai le Fraine, printed in Weber's Collection.

Orfeo and Heurodis.

ERY tyme is in Aperelle
That mekyll schewys of mauys
wylle
In feldys ⁊ medews flow[r]ys
spryng
In grovys ⁊ wodes foulcs syng
Than wex ȝong men jolyffe 5
And þan prevyth man ⁊ wyffe

The brytans, as þe boke seys,
Off diuʳse thingę þⁱ made þʳ leys
Som þi made of harpyngę
And som of oþʳ diuʳse thingę 10
Som of werre ⁊ som of wo
Som of myrthe ⁊ joy also
Som of trechery ⁊ som off gyle
Som of happys þᵗ felle som whyle
And som be of rybawdry 15
And many þʳ ben of fary
Off all þe ventᵘrys men here ore se
Most off luffe for soth þi be
That in þe leys ben j-wrought
Ffyrst fond ⁊ forth brouȝt 20
Off aventoʳs þᵗ fell som deys
The bretonys þʳof made þʳ leys
Off kingę þᵗ be fore vs were
When þⁱ myȝt ony woundres here
They lete them wryte as it wʳ do, 25
And þʳ among is sir Orfew.
He was for soth a nobulle kyng
That most luffyd gle ⁊ herpyng;
Wele sekyr was euʳy gode herper
To haue off mekyll honoʳ 30

Hym selue he lernyd for to herpe
And leyd þʳ ō hys wytte so scherpe
He lernyd so wele wᵗ outen les
So gode herper neuʳ nō was
In all þˢ werld was no man bore   35
That had kyng Orfeo ben be fore
And he myʒt hys herpe here
Bot he wold wene þᵗ it were
A blyssed full note of peradẹ
Suche melody þʳ in is.   40

The kyng jorneyd in Tracyence
That is a cyte off grete defence
And wᵗ hym hys quen off price
That was callyd dame Heroudys :
A feyrer lady than sche was one   45
Was neuʳ made off flesch ne bone
Sche was full off lufe ⁊ godnes
Ne may no man telle hyr feyrnes.

¶ Bifel so in the comésing of May,
When miri and hot is the day,   50
And oway beth winter schours,
And eueri feld is ful of flours,
And blosme breme on eueri bough,
Ouer al wexeth miri anough,
This ich quen dame Heurodis   55
Tok with hyr maidens of priis,
And went in an vndren tide
To play bi an orchard side
To se the floures sprede and spring,
And to here the foules sing :   60
Thai sett hem doun al thre,
Vnder a fair ympe tre,
And wel sone this fair quene,
Fel on slepe opon the grene :

The maidens durst hir nought awake,
Bot lete hir ligge and rest take,
So sche slepe til after none,
That vnder tide was al y done;
Ac as sone as sche gan awake,
Sche crid and lothli bere gan make;
Sche froted hir honden and hir fet,
And crached her visage, it bled wete,
Hir riche robe hye al to rett,
And was remeyd out of hir witt:
The tvo maidens hir biside,
No durst with hir no leng abide,
But [t]ourn to the palays ful right
And told both squier and knight,
That her quen awede wold,
And bad hem go and hir be-hold.
Knightes rvn, and leuedis al so,
Damisels sexti and mo,
In the orchard to the quen thei come,
And her vp in ther armes nome,
And brought hir to bed atte last,
And held hir there fine fast;
Ac euer sche be-gan to cri
And wold vp and owy.
When Orfeo herd that tiding,
Neuer him nas wers for no thing;
He come with knightes tene,
To chaumber right bifor the quene.
And biheld and seyd with grete pite:
O life liif, what ayles the?
That euer ȝete hast ben so stille,
And now gredest wonder schille;
Thi bodi, that was so white y core,
With thine nailes is al to tore,
Allas! thi rod that was so red,
Is al wan as thou were ded;

```
              And also thine fingres smale,
              Beth al blodi and al pale;
              Allas! thi louesum eyghen to
              Loketh so man doth on his fo;
              A dame, Ich biseche merci,           105
              Lete ben al this reweful cri,
              And tel me, lady, for thy prow,
              What thing may the help now?
              Tho lay sche stille attelast,
              And gan to wepe swithe fast,         110
              And seyd thus the king to,
              Allas! mi lord sir Orfeo,
              Seththen we first to gider were,
              Ones wroth neuer we nere,
              Bot euer Ich haue y-loued the        115
              As mi liif, and so thou me,
              Ac now we mot delen a-tuo:
              Do thi best, for Y mot go.
              Allas! quath he, forlorn Ich am,
              Whider wiltow go and to wham?        120
              Whider thou gost ichil with the,
              And whider Y go thou schalt with me.
              Nay, nay, sir, that nought nis,
              Ichil the telle al how it is:
              As Ich lay this vnder tide,          125
              And slepe vnder our orchard side,
              Ther come to me tuo fair knightes
              Wele y-armed al to rightes,
              And bad me comen an heighing,
              And speke with her lord the king;    130
              And Ich answerd at wordes bold,
              Y durst nought, no Y nold:
              Thai priked oghain as thai might driue,
              Tho com her king also bliue,
              With an hundred knightes and mo,     135
              And damissels an hundred al so;
```

Al on snowe white stedes,
As white as milke were her wedes,
Y no seighe neuer ȝete bifore
So fair creatours y core!
The king hadde a croun on hed,
It nas of siluer, no of gold red,
Ac it was of a precious ston;
As bright as the sonne it schon:
And as son as he to me cam,
Wold Ich, nold Ich, he me nam,
And made me with him ride,
Opon a palfray bi his side,
And brought me to his pallays,
Wele atird in ich ways;
And schewed me castels and tours,
Riuers, forestes, frith with flours;
And his riche stedes ichon,
And seththen me brought oghain hom
In to our owhen orchard,
And said to me after ward:
Loke, dame, to morwe thatow be
Right here vnder this ympe tre;
And than thou schalt with ous go
And liue with ous euer mo,
And ȝif thou makest ous y-let,
Where thou be, thou worst y-fet
And to-tore thine limes al,
That nothing help the no schal,
And thoȝ thou best so to-torn,
Ȝete thou worst with ous y-born.

¶ When king Orfeo herd this cas,
O we! quath he, allas! allas!
Leuer me were to lete mi liif,
Than thus to lese the quen mi wiif,
He asked conseyl at ich man,
Ac no man him help no can.

A morwe the vnder tide is come,
And Orfeo hath his armes y-nome,
And wele ten hundred knightes with him, 175
Ich y-armed stout and grim;
And with the quen wente he
Right vnto that ympe tre:
Thai made scheltrom in ich a side,
And sayd thai wold there abide, 180
And dye ther euerichon,
Er the quen schuld fram hem gon:
Ac ʒete amiddes hem full right,
The quen was oway y-tvight,
With fairi forth y-nome, 185
Men wist neuer wher sche was bicome,
Tho was ther criing, wepe and wo,
The king in to his chamber is go,
And oft swoned opon the ston,
And made swiche diol and swiche mon, 190
That neighe his liif was y-spent;
Ther was non amendement.
He cleped to gider his barouns,
Erls, lordes of renouns,
And when thai al y-comen were: 195
Lordinges, he said, bifor ʒou here
Ich ordaine min heigh steward
To wite mi kingdom after ward,
In mi stede ben he schal,
To kepe mi londes ouer al, 200
For now Ichaue mi quen y-lore,
The fairest leuedi that euer was bore;
Neuer eft y nil no woman se,
Into wildernes Ichil te,
And liue ther euer more, 205
With wilde bestes in holtes hore;
And when ʒe vnder stond that Y be spent,
Make ʒou then a parlement,

And chese ȝou a newe king:
Now doth ȝour best with al mi thing. 210
¶ Tho was ther wepeing in the halle;
And grete cri among hem alle;
Vnnethe might old or ȝong
For wepeing speke a word with tong.
Thai kneled adoun al y-fere, 215
And praid him ȝif his wille were,
That he no schuld nought fram hem go.
Do way! quath he, it schal be so.
All his kingdom he forsoke
But a sclauin on him he toke; 220
He no hadde kirtel, no hode,
Schert, no nother gode,
Bot his harp he toke algate,
And yede him barfot out atte ȝate:
No man most with him go. 225
O way! what wepe ther was, and wo,
When he that hadde ben king with croun,
Went so pouerlich out of toun,
Thurch wode and ouer heth,
Into the wildernes he geth, 230
Nothing he fint that him is ays,
Bot euer he lieuth in gret malais;
He that hadde y werd the fowe and griis,
And on bed the purper biis,
Now on hard hethe he lith, 235
With leues and gresse he him writh:
He that hadde castels and tours,
Riuer, forest, frith with flours;
Now, thei it commenci to snewe and frese,
This king mot make his bed in mese: 240
He that had y-had knightes of priis
Bifor him kneland, and leuedis,
Now seth he no thing that him liketh,
Bot wild wormes by him striketh:

He that had y-had plenté 245
Of mete and drink of ich deynté,
Now may he al day digge and wrote,
Er he sinde his fille of rote;
In somer he liueth bi wild frut,
And berren, bot gode lite; 250
In winter may he no thing finde,
Bot rote, grases, and the rinde;
Al his bodi was oway duine
For missays, and al to chine,
Lord! who may telle the sore 255
This king sufferd ten ȝere and more:
His here of his berd, black and rowe,
To his girdel stede was growe;
His harp, where on was al his gle,
He hidde in an holwe tre; 260
And, when the weder was clere and bright,
He toke his harp to him wel right,
And harped at his owhen wille,
Into alle the wode the soun gan schille,
That alle the wilde bestes that ther beth, 265
For ioie abouten him thai teth;
And alle the foules that ther were,
Come and sete on ich a brere;
To here his harping a fine,
So miche melody was ther in. 270
And when he his harping lete wold,
No best bi him abide nold.

¶ He might se besides
Oft in hot vnder tides,
The king o' fairy, with his rout, 275
Com to hunt him al about:
With dynne, cri and bloweing,
And houndes also with him berking;
Ac no best thai no nome,
No neuer he nist whider thai bi-come. 280

And other while he might se
A gret oste bi him te,
Wele atourned ten hundred knightes,
Ich y-armed at all ryȝt;
Of cuntenaunce stout and fers,   285
With mani desplaid baners;
And ich his swerd y drawe hold:
Ac neuer he nist whider thai wold.
And other while he seighe other thing;
Knightes and leuedis com daunceing,   290
In queynt atire gisely,
Queyitt pas, and softly:
Tabours and trimpes ȝede hem bi,
And al maner menstraci.

¶ And on a day he seighe him biside   295
Sexti leudis on hors ride,
Gentil and iolif, as brid on ris;
Nought o man amonges hem ther nis;
And ich a faucoun on hond bere,
And riden on haukin bi o riuere,   300
Of game thai founde wel gode haunt,
Maulardes, hayroun, and cormeraunt;
The foules of the water ariseth,
The faucouns hem wele deuiseth,
Ich faucoun his pray slough: 305
That seighe Orfeo, and lough.
Par fay, quath he, ther is fair game!
Thider Ichil, bi Godes name,
Ich was y won swiche werk to se.
He aros, and thider gan te;   310
To a leuedi he was y-come,
Biheld, and hath wele vnder nome,
And seth, bi al thing, that it is
His owhen quen dam Heurodis:
ȝern he biheld hir, and sche him eke,   315
Ac noither to other a word no speke:

For messais that sche on him seighe,
That had ben so riche and so heighe,
The teres fel out of her eighe;
The other leuedis this y-seighe, 320
And maked hir oway to ride,
Sche most with him no lenger abide,
Allas! quath he, now me is wo!
Whi nil deth now me slo,
Allas! wroche, that Y no might 325
Dye now after this sight!
Allas! to long last mi liif,
When Y no dar nought with mi wiif,
No hye to me o word speke,
Allas! whi nil min hert breke! 330
Parfay, quath he, tide what bitide,
Whider so this leuedi ride,
The selue way Ichil streche,
Of liif no deth me no reche.
His sclauain he dede on, all so spac, 335
And henge his harp opon his bac;
And had wel gode wil to gon,
He no spard noither stub no ston:
In at a roche the leuedis rideth,
And he after, and nought abideth; 340
When he was in the roche y-go,
Wele thre mile other mo,
He com in to a fair cuntray,
As bright als sonne on somers day;
Smothe, and plain, and al grene, 345
Hille no dale nas ther non y sene;
Amidde the lond a castel he sighe,
Riche and real, and wonder heighe;
Al the vtmast wal
Was clere and schine as cristal; 350
An hundred tours ther were about,
Degiselich and bataild stout;

The butras com out of the diche,
Of rede gold y-arched riche;
The bonsour was amelyd al, 356
Of ich maner diuers amell;
With in ther wer wide wones,
Al of precious stones,
The werst piler on to biholde
Was al of burnist gold; 360
Al that lond was euer light,
For when it schuld be therk and night,
The riche stones light gonne,
As bright as doth at none the sonne,
No man may telle, no thenche in thought, 365
The riche werk that ther was wrought,
Bi al thing, him think that it is
The proude court of paradis.
In this castel the leuedis alight,
He wold in after, ʒif he might. 370

¶ Orfeo knokketh atte gate,
The porter was redi ther ate,
And asked, what he wold haue y do?
Parfay, quath he, Icham a minstrel, lo,
To solas thi lord with my gle, 375
ʒif his swete wille be.
The porter vndede the ʒate anon,
And lete him in to the castel gon.

¶ Than he gan bihold about al,
And seighe full ligʒeand with in the wal, 380
Of folk that were thider y-brought,
And thought dede and nare nought:
Sum stode with outen hade;
And sum armys nade;
And sum thurch the bodi hadde wounde; 385
And sum lay wode y-bounde;
And sum armed on hors sate;
And some astrangled as they ete;

And sum were in water adreynt;
And sum with fire al for-schreynt; 390
Wiues ther lay on child bedde;
Sum ded, and sum awedde;
And wonder fele ther lay besides,
Right as thai slepe her vnder tides;
Eche was thus in this warld y-nome, 395
With fairi thider y-come;
Ther he seighe his owhen wiif,
Dame Heurodis his liif liif
Slepe vnder an ymde tre;
Bi her clothes he knew that it was sche. 400

¶ And when he hadde bihold this meruails alle,
He went in to the kinges halle;
Then seighe he ther a semly sight,
A tabernacle blisseful and bright;
There in her maister king sete, 405
And her quen fair and swete;
Her crounes, her clothes, schine so bright,
That vnnethe bihold he hem might:
When he hadde biholden al that thing,
He kneled adoun bifore the king; 410
O Lord, he seyd, ȝif it thi wille were,
Mi menstraci thou schust y here.
The king answerd what man artow,
That art hider y-comen now?
Ich no non that is with me 415
No sent neuer after the,
Seththen that ich here regne i-gan,
Y no fond neuer so fole hardi man
That hider to ous durst wende,
Bot that Ichim walde offende. 420
Lord, quath he, trowe ful wel,
Y nam bot a pouer menstrel,

And, sir, it is the maner of ous,
To seche mani a lordes hous,
Thei we nought welom no be,
ȝete we mot proferi-forth our glé.
¶ Bifor the king he sat adoun
And tok his harpe so miri of soun,
And trempreth his harp as he wele can,
And blisseful notes he ther gan,
That al that in the palays were,
Com to him for to here,
And liggeth adoun to his fete,
Hem thenketh his melody so swete.
The king herkneth, and sitt ful stille,
To here his gle he hath gode wille;
Gode bourde he hadde of his gle,
The riche queu al so hadde sche;[1]
When he hadde stint his harping,
Then seyd to him the king,
Menstrel, me liketh wele thi gle,
Now aske of me what it be,
Largelich Ichil the pay,
Now spake, and tow might asay.
Sir, he seyed, Ich beseche the,
Thatow woldest ȝiue me,
That ich leuedi bright on ble,
That slepeth under the ympe tre.
Nay, quath the king, that nought nere,
A fori couple of ȝou it were,
For thou art lene, rowe, and blac,
And sche is louesome with outen lac;
A lothlich thing it were forthi,
To se hir in thi companyi.
¶ O sir, he seyd, gentil king,
ȝete were it a wele fouler thing

---

[1] 'He' p. 'she' MS.

To here a lesing of thy mouthe,
So, sir, as ȝe seyd nouthe,
What Ich wold aske haue Y schold ;
And nedes thou most thi word hold.　　460
The king seyd, seththen it is so,
Take hir bi the hand, and go ;
Of hir Ichil thatow be blithe.
He kneled adoun, and thonked him swithe.
His wiif he tok bi the hond,　　465
And yede him swithe out of that lond ;
And went him out of that thede,
Right as he come the way he ȝede.
So long he hath the way y-nome,
To Winchester he is y-come,　　470
That was his owhen cite,
Ac no man knewe that it was he,
No forther than the tounes ende,
For knoweleche no durst wende,
Bot with a begger y bilt ful narwe,　　475
Ther he tok his herbarwe,
To him, and to his owhen wiif,
As a minstrel of pouer liif ;
And asked tidinges of that lond,
And who the kingdom held in hond.　　480
The pouer begger, in his cote,
Told him euerich a grot,
Hou her quen was stole owy,
Ten ȝer gon with fairy,
And how her king en exile ȝede,　　485
Bot no man niste in wiche thede,
And how the steward the lond gan hold,
And other mani thinges him told.
　¶ A morwe oȝain none tide
He maked his wiif ther abide,　　490
The beggers clothes he borwed anon,
And heng his harp his rigge opon,

And went him in to that cite,
That men might him bihold and se.
Erls, and barouns bold, 495
Buriays and leuedis him gun bihold :
Lo ! thai feyd, swiche a man,
Hou long the here hougeth him opan !
Lo ! hou his berd hongeth to his kne,
He is y-clongen al so a tre : 500
And as he ȝede in the strete,
With his steward he gan mete,
And sonde he sett on him a crie,
Sir steward, he seyd, merci,
Icham an harpour of hethenisse, 505
Help me now in this distresse !
The steward seyd, com with me, come,
Of that Ichaue, thou schalt haue some ;
Euerich gode harpour is welom me to,
For mi lordes loue sir Orfeo. 510

¶ In the castel the steward sat atte mete,
And mani lording was bi him sete ;
There were trompours and tabourers,
Harpours fele, and crouders,
Miche melody thai maked alle, 515
And Orfeo sat stille in the halle,
And herkneth when thai ben al stille,
He toke his harp and tempred schille,
The blifulest notes he herped there,
That euer ani man y-herd with ere : 520
Ich man liked wele his gle ;
The steward biheld and gan y-se,
And knewe the harp als-bliue ;
Menstrel, he seyd, so mot thou thriue,
Where hadestow this harp, and hou ? 525
Y pray that thou me telle now.

¶ Lord, quath he, in vncouthe thede
Thurch a wildernes as Y ȝede ;

Ther Y founde in a dale
With lyouns a man to-torn smale,
And wolues him frete with teth so scharp;
Bi him Y found this ich harp,
Wele ten ʒere it is y-go.
O! quath the steward, now me is wo!
That was mi lord sir Orfeo!
Allas, wreche, what schall Y do,
That haue swiche a lord y-lore,
Owa, that Ich was y bore,
That him was so hard grace y ʒarked,
And so vile deth y-marked!
Adoun he fel aswon to grounde,
His barouns him tok vp in that stounde,
And telleth him hou it geth,
It nis no bot of mannes deth.

¶ King Orfeo knewe wel bi than,
His steward was a trewe man,
And loued him as he aught to do,
And stont vp, and seyt thus lo:
Steward, herkne now this thing,
ʒif Ich were Orfeo the king,
And hadde y-suffred ful ʒore
In wildernisse miche sore;
And hadde y-won m' quen owy
Out of the lond of fairy;
And hadde y-brought the leuedi hende
Right here to the tounes ende,
And with a begger her in y-nome,
And were mi self hider y-come,
Pouerlich to the thus stille,
For to asay thi gode wille;
And Ich founde the thus trewe,
Thou no schust it neuer rewe,
Sikerlich for loue, or ay,
Thou schust be king after mi day,

And ȝif thou of mi deth hadest ben blithe,
Thou schust haue voided al so swithe. 566
¶ Tho al tho that ther in sete,
That it was king Orfeo vnder ȝete,
And the steward him wele knewe,
Ouer that bord anone he threwe, 570
And fel adoun to his fet;
So dede euerich lord that ther sete,
And al thai sayd at o criing:
ȝe beth our lord, sir, and our king.
Glad thai were of his liue, 575
To chaumber thai ladde him als biliue,
And bathed him and schaued his berd,
And tired him as a king apert;
And seththen with gret processioun
Thai brought the quen in to the toun 580
With al maner menstraci;
Lord, ther was grete melody!
For ioie thai wepe with her eighe;
That hem so sounde y-comen seighe.
Now king Orfeo newe-coround is 585
And his quen dame Heurodis,
And liued long afterward;
And seththen was king the steward.
Harpours in Bretaine after than
Herd hou this meruaile bigan, 590
And made of her a lay of gode likeing,
And nempned it after the king:
That lay Orfeo is y-hote,
Gode is the lay, swete is the note.
Thus com sir Orfeo out of his care; 595
God graunt ous alle wele to fare! Amen.

Explicit.

Thomas of Ersyldoune and the Quene of Elf-land.

THERE are, perhaps, few poems now extant that may so well as the following beautiful and interesting tale of fairyland exemplify the practice of those whose employment it was to chant or rehearse the effusions of the minstrels. This legend of Thomas of Ersyldoune in its present state evidently owes much to that facility and readiness of composition, which at times might enable them to enlarge and amplify the productions of others, in order to suit existing circumstances, and serve for the amusement of their auditors. The exordium is professedly the work of an English reciter, anxious to draw the attention of the assembled company to the "mervelles" and predictions of which he was about to tell. Nor is it less evident, but that the prophetic parts, however obscure their object may now be, or uncertain from what materials they were constructed, were either added at a subsequent period, or so altered as to be instrumental to some political purpose. Of the poems or prophecies attributed to Thomas the Rhymer, we unfortunately have none but what are preserved in English manuscripts, in which they have lost much of their individuality, the orthography being uniformly accommodated to that of the transcriber.

This poem is preserved in three ancient manuscripts, each of them in a state more or less mutilated, and varying in no inconsiderable degree from the other. A portion of it was first printed in the "Border Minstrelsy" from the fragment in the British Museum among the Cotton MSS.;[1] and the one which Mr. Jamieson adopted in his collection of

---

[1] Cotton MSS. Vitellius, E. x.

"Popular Ballads and Songs" was carefully deciphered from a volume of no ordinary curiosity in the University Library, Cambridge,[1] written in a very illegible hand, about the middle of the fifteenth century. It is now printed from the third and earliest copy preserved in the Lincoln MS., the text of which is in every respect preferable to that of either of the other manuscripts. It had been supposed that another copy of this poem might be found in Peterborough; but the editor may state that, after a careful and satisfactory search, it appears that if ever such a manuscript was there deposited, it must have suffered the fate of the numerous collection, of which a list, drawn up at a remote period, is found in Gunton's history of that splendid cathedral.

Owing to the loose and careless manner in which the Lincoln MS. has at some former time been kept, this poem has suffered much, in common with most of the others which the volume contains, many of the leaves having been either mutilated or entirely lost. An endeavour has been made to fill up the defective parts from the Cambridge copy, though in some instances, as will be seen, without success.

After the copious illustrations of this poem by its former editors, in works which either are or ought to be in the hands of every possessor of this collection, little farther can be required. The reader will perceive the great beauty of the descriptive parts, and the fine vein of imagination that runs through nearly the whole of the first Fytt. "In the introduction to the prophecies," as Mr. Jamieson has well observed, "there is so much more fancy and elegance than in the prophecies themselves, that they can hardly be supposed to be the composition of the same person. Indeed, the internal evidence to the contrary almost amounts to a proof that they are not, and that the romance itself was of Scotish origin, although no indubitably Scotish copy is known to be in existence. It is remarkable," Mr. J. continues, "that in all the three copies the poet begins the story in the first person, and seems disposed to tell the incidents as if they had really happened to himself.

---

[1] Bishop More's MSS. Ff., v. 48. Printed in Hazlitt's *Fairy Tales, Legends, and Romances*, 1875, p. 100 *et seqq.*, from a collation of this and other MSS.

St. 1. "As *I me* went this Andyr's day,
　　　Fast on *my* way making *my* mone," &c.

St. 3. "Alle in a longyng as *I* lay,
　　　Undreneth a semely tre,
　　　Saw *I* wher a lady gay,
　　　Came ridand ouer a longe lee," &c.

"And although he afterwards, awkwardly and unnaturally enough, speaks of Thomas as a third person, yet even then he seems to insinuate that the story which he is garbling was told by another before him:

St. 14. "And certenly, *as the story sayse*,
　　　He hir mette at Eldyn tre."

"If he assumes the mask with a bad grace here, he shows still less address when he drops it again at stanza 52 of the First Fit:

"Ther was revell, game, and play,
　More than I you say, perdye,
　Till hit fell upon a day,
　My lufly lady said to *me:*
　Busk *the*, *Thomas*, for *thu* must gon;
　For here no longer mayst *thu* be,
　Hye *the* fast with mode and mone;
　I shall *the* bryng to the Eldyn tre."

"Would it not be pardonable, from such instances as these, to suppose it at least probable that Thomas Rymour was really the original author of this romance; and that, in order to give a sanction to his predictions, which seem all to have been calculated, in one way or other, for the service of his country, he pretended to an intercourse with the Queen of Elf-land, as Numa Pompilius did with the nymph Egeria? Such an intercourse, in the days of True Thomas, was accounted neither unnatural nor uncommon."[1]

The Huntly Bank on which Thomas is said to have met

---

[1] It will be remarked that although Thomas is taken to Fairyland by the Queen, and cautioned as to keeping counsel as to their amour if the King of Faëry presents himself, no description occurs of the latter personage, and a very meagre one of the place. The Queen and Thomas are the only real *dramatis personæ*.

the Queen of Faëry is situated on one of the Eldoun Hills, not far distant from the Eldoun Tree. Such a distinction, however, is claimed for another Huntly Bank, which, with a cleugh, that still retains the name of "The Rhymer's Glen," became the property of Sir Walter Scott, by whom, in the publication of the ancient metrical romance of "Sir Tristrem," formerly attributed to our author, it is almost unnecessary to observe, a degree of interest has been attached to the character of Thomas which even, as being the earliest of our poetical writers, he might not otherwise have enjoyed.

With respect to the prophetic character of Thomas, we have sufficient evidence in the testimony of such early writers as Barber and Wyntown. The latter, in describing the battle of Kylblene, in the year 1335, says:

> "Of this Fycht qwhilum spak Thomas
> Of Ersyldowne, that sayd in derne,
> Thare suld mete stalwartly stark and sterne:
> He sayd it in his Prophecy;
> Bot, how he wyst it, wes Ferly."

But whether or not this be one of the predictions contained in the following poem is uncertain—the prophetic parts of which might afford ample scope for illustration, were this the object of the editor; though, indeed, it would be no easy matter to reconcile them with any degree of satisfaction to the various national events that seem to have been foretold.

The reader will no doubt be glad to receive the following illustrations of the prophetical parts of this poem, coming as they do from one who is so well qualified to elucidate both the historical and literary remains of our country. Sir Walter Scott (in a letter to the editor) says, "I am much delighted, and considerably puzzled, with 'Thomas the Rhymer.' It seems to me made up of different patches, which have been added from time to time in the true spirit of English prophecy,—for you may remember Comines says, 'Le Chancelier d'Angleterre, commença par une prophetic *dont les Anglois ne sont jamais despourveus.*' Pinky Cleugh is in one place distinctly mentioned by name; in another, Black Agnes of Dunbar is spoken of as alive, and her captivity is prophetical. There must have been a lapse of more than two centuries betwixt the composition of these two different passages." (But, whatever credit we may be disposed to give, either to Thomas or the actual writer of these prophecies, it ought to be kept in view that the manuscript from which the poem is now given was written more than a century previous to the fulfilment of some of the predictions which it is supposed to contain.) "As well as I can without books," Sir Walter proceeds, "I will endeavour to guess at the different historical events which are obscurely or more directly alluded to :—

"Fytt 2nd, line 21. 'The Baliolfe—Comyns—Barlays (rather Barclays)—as well as the Fresells (Frasers)' were all distinguished during the wars of David II.'s minority, or shortly before, as probably were the Russells.

"Line 44. The fight at Eldone Hill here alluded to, may, perhaps, be that in which Oswin, a pretender to the throne of Northumberland, was defeated and slain by Ethelwold, about the middle of the eighth century. The field of battle is still called Corpse Cleugh, or some such name, and distinguished by barrows and other marks of ancient contest:—bones and remnants of armour are even yet turned up by the plough.

"Line 50. The battle of Falkirk is obviously that in which Wallace was defeated by Edward I.

"Line 70. Bannockburn is mentioned by name. The allusion to the defeat of the English chivalry by stratagem is worth remarking; it shows the country of the pseudo-prophet, who is naturally disposed to apologise for the defeat of the English at that memorable occurrence.

"Line 97. Dupplin Moor is distinctly mentioned; and the subsequent capture of Perth, line 102.

"The battle of Durham, and the captivity of David II. is alluded to from line 120 to line 135, and the three last lines of the Second Fytt seem to me a variation of the same passage; or it may relate to the previous battle of Halidon, where the Regent, Archibald Douglass, may be the 'full doughty that was slain.'

"All these personages and events hitherto noticed relate as distinctly as can well be expected to the middle of the fourteenth century, when, in the beginning of Fytt Third, we light all at once upon 'Spynkarde Cleugh,' being clearly our unlucky battle of Pinkie. I cannot help thinking this stanza much more modern than the rest of the poem.

"The battle of Pentland Hill, appears to be a wild guess at future events. In former times the prediction might have been deemed oracular, but now few will be disposed to allow that it hath any reference to the battle of Pentland, in Charles II.'s time, any more than the press of banners between Seton and the sea refers to the battle of Prestonpans. But Thomas, or more properly his imitator, has made a chance hit in both cases. In the latter especially, a staunch Jacobite would say, the rout of the dragoons was foretold, line 53,—only they did not stay for the *hewing*, mentioned line 57.

"The story of the Cross of stone is a favourite presage in Nixon's prophecy, and I know not how many besides.

"Line 125. The rivulet near to Flodden-field is called Sandyford, or something like it. Flodden is, therefore, probably alluded to in this and the following stanza.

"Line 150. Here the story returns to the fourteenth century, and to Black Agnes of Dunbar, which makes it probable that this part of the poem must have been written when she was in the height of renown.

"It is singular that Thomas should be represented as speaking of himself as one in disgrace with Agnes of Dunbar, though her bounden vassal. Unquestionably it is highly probable that Thomas of Ercildoune held his lands of the Earl of Dunbar, as he resided in the very village which took the name of Earls-town from its dependence on these great earls. An antiquary is tempted to guess that the obscure hint here thrown out may possibly allude to some dispute between Thomas and his superior, which, making a part of the remembered history of the former, was introduced by the English imitator who writes prophecies in his name."

After all, it may in general be admitted that the whole of the prophecies attributed to

"Thomas the true, that never spak false,"

in the corrupted and modernised state in which those bearing his name now appear, are little better than spurious.[1] If he attempted any such predictions, which cannot reasonably

---

[1] Predictions made after the events!

be doubted after the uniform tradition of more than five centuries, and the concurring testimony of so many ancient writers to his prophetical character, they were not, it is highly probable, committed to writing in his own time, but being circulated and handed down by tradition only, every person no doubt considered it lawful to alter or accommodate them to his own views. At least, we find occasionally the same prophecy, either by accident or design, bearing the most opposite construction. But if there be one exception, it is that which follows, given exactly as it occurs in a very ancient manuscript in the Harleian Collection (No. 2253, fol. 127), supposed to be of the time of Edward I., and which, as it approaches so near the period in which he flourished, may be considered as exhibiting a genuine specimen of the language of the author. This "Response" assuredly bears reference to the wars in Scotland during the time of Edward I. A contrary opinion, however, has long been held (see "Border Minstrelsy," vol. iii. pp. 282-5; "Sir Tristrem," p. xvi.), and Sir Walter Scott thinks that "the battle of Dupplin is distinctly referred to in line 16, and that line 11 alludes to the dreadful famine in the reign of David II. The only line of the prophecy still remembered and quoted is that of a hare kindling on the hearthstone—a prophecy which Thomas is said by tradition to have uttered concerning the desolation of his own house:

'The hare sall kittle litter on my hearth stane,
And there will never be a laird Learmont again.'"

Every circumstance, however, warrants us in referring the following lines to some time before the end of the thirteenth century, and their application to the wars of Edward I. just previous to the commencement of a long series of war and desolation (about which time Thomas appears to have died), is certainly more appropriate than conceiving him to overlook these in a foresight of what should take place more than half a century after his death. The erroneous supposition of this response having been addressed to Black Agnes, the heroic Countess of March, seems first to have given rise to the conjecture which has thrown discredit on the idea of its being uttered by the Poet of Ersyldoune. In his time the title of that powerful family had not been changed from Dunbar to March.

"La Countesse de Donbar demanda a Thomas de Essedoune, qᵃnt la guere descoce prendreit fyn/ e yl la respoundy et dyt.

When man as mad a kyng of a capped man/
When mon is leuere oþer mones þyng þen is owen/
When Loudyon ys forest and forest/ ys felde/
When hares kendles oþe herston/
When wyt ⁊ wille werres togedere
When mon makes stables of kyrkes ⁊ steles castles wyþ styes
When Rokesbourh nys no burgh ant market is at Fforwyleye
When þe alde is gan ant þe newe þᵘ don noþt
When Bambourne ys donged with dedemen
When men ledes men in ropes to buyen ⁊ to sellen/
When a qᵃrter of whaty whete is chaunged for a colt of ten marks/
When prude prikes ⁊ pees is leyd in prisoun,
When a Scot ne may hym hude ase hare in forme/
   þᵗ þe Englyssh ne shal hym fynde/
When ryþᵗ ant wronge astenteþ to gedere/
When laddes weddeþ louedis
When Scottes flen so faste þᵗ for faute of ship hy drouneþ hemselve/
  Whenne shal this be/
  Nouþer in þine tyme ne in myne,
  Ah comen ⁊ gone
  Wiþinne twenty wynter ant on/"

The prophecies attributed to Thomas the Rhymer in the common collection of "The Whole Prophecies of Scotland, England, France, Ireland," &c., have not the slightest marks of authenticity. They are, besides, too darkly veiled in allegory, or shadowed forth in obscure allusions, to interest any one. But the persons or events prefigured must have at one time been more intelligible than now, else it would be difficult to account for their extensive popularity, unless, on the idea which the common people may have entertained of their actually bearing reference to future national occurrences; as it is said, "though thir sayis be selcouth, they shall be sooth found." Without, therefore, being possessed either of historical value or poetic merit, they are now to be regarded merely as literary curiosities.

Thomas of Ersseldoune.

[The Prologue.[1]]

LYSTNYS, lordyngs, bothe grete and smale,
    And takis gude tente what I will say:
I sall ȝow telle als trewe a tale,
    Als euer was herde by nyghte or daye:
And the maste meruelle fforowttyn naye,   5
    That euer was herde by fore or syen,
And ther fore pristly I ȝow praye,
    That ȝe will of ȝoure talkyng blyn.
It es an harde thyng for to saye,
    Of doghety dedis that hase bene done;   10
Of felle feghtyngs and batells sere;
    And how that knyghtis hase wonne thair schone.
Bot Jhu Christ, that syttis in trone,
    Safe Ynglysche men bothe ferre and nere;
And I sall telle ȝow tyte and sone,   15
    Of Battells done sythen many a ȝere;
And of batells that done sall bee;
    In whate place, and howe and whare;
And wha sall hafe the heghere gree;
    And whethir partye sall hafe the werre;   20
Wha sall take the flyghte and flee;
    And wha sall dye, and by tene, thare:
Bot Jhu Christ, that dyed on tre,
    Saue Inglysche men whare so thay fare.

[The Fyrst Fytt.]

Als I me wente this Endres daye,
    Full faste in mynd makane my mone,
In a mery mornynge of Maye,
    By Huntle bankkes my selfe allone.

---

[1] Not in the Cambridge MS.

I herde the jaye, and the throstelle,[1] 5
    The mawys meuyde of hir songe,
The wodewale beryde als a belle,
    That alle the wode abowte me ronge.

Allone in longynge, thus als I laye,
    Vndre nethe a semely tre, 10
Saw I whare a lady gaye,
    Came ridand ouer a longe lee.

If I suld sytt to Domesdaye,
    With my tonge, to wrebbe and wrye,
Certanely that lady gaye, 15
    Neuer bese scho askryede for mee.

Hir palfraye was a dappill graye;
    Swilke one I saghe ne neuer none:
Als dose the sonne, on someres daye,
    That fair lady hir selfe scho schor.e. 20

Her sette it was of reuylle bone;
    Full semely was that syghte to see!
Stefly sett with precyous stone,
    And compaste all with crapoté.

Stones of Oryente grete plenté; 25
    Hir hare abowte hir hede it hange;
Scho rode ouer that lange lee,
    A whylle scho blewe, a nother scho sange.

Hir garthis of nobyll sylke thay were;
    The bukylls were of berelle stone; 30
Hir steraps were of crystalle clere,
    And all with perelle ouer by gone.

---

[1] Old copy erroneously reads *throstylle cokke*.

Hir payetrelle was of iralle fyne;
 Hir cropoure was of orfare;
And als clere golde hir brydill it schone; 35
 One aythir syde hange bellys three.

Scho led iij. grehoundis in a leeshe;
 And seuen raches by hir fete rone;—
Scho bare a horne abowte hir halse;
 And vndir hir belte full many a flone. 40

Thomas laye and sawe that syghte,
 Vnder nethe ane semly tree;
He sayd, ʒone es Marye most of myghte,
 That bare that childe that dyede for mee.

But I speke with ʒone lady bryghte, 45
 I hope myn herte will bryste in three;
Now sall I go with all my myghte,
 Hir for to mete at Eldone[1] tree.

Thomas rathely vpe he rase,
 And he rane ouer that mountayne hye; 50
Gyff it be als the storye sayes,
 He hir mette at Eldone tree.

He knelyde down appon his knee,
 Vndir nethe that grenwode spraye:—
And sayd, lufly ladye! rewe one mee; 55
 Qwene of heuen, als thu wele maye.

Than spake that lady milde of thoghte:—
 Thomas, late swylke wordes bee;
Qwene of heuenne am I noghte,
 For I tuke neuer so heghe degre. 60

---

[1] *i.e.*, Halydown or Halidon. See introductory matter and a note *infra*.

Bot I ame of ane other contree,
   If I be parellid moste of prysse;
I ryde aftyre this wylde fee:
   My raches rynnys at my devyse.

If thu be parelde moste of prysse,   65
   And here rydis thus in thy balye,
Of lufe, lady, als thu art wysse,
   Thou gyffe me leue to lye the bye.

Scho sayde: thu man, that ware folye;
   I praye the, Thomas, thu lat me bee;   70
For I saye the full sekirlye,
   That synne will for-doo all my beauté.

Now, lufly ladye, rewe on mee,
   And I will euer more with the duelle;
Here my trouthe I plyghte to thee.   75
   Wethir thu will in heuen or helle.

Man of molde, thu will me merre,
   But ȝitt thu sall hafe all thy will;
And trowe it wele thu chewys the werre,
   For alle my beauté will thu spylle.   80

Down than lyghte that lady bryghte,
   Vndir nethe that grene wode spraye;
And, als the storye tellis full ryghte,
   Seuen sythis by hir he laye.

Scho sayd: man, thu lykes thi playe: 85
   What byrde in boure maye dwelle with the?
Thou merrys me all this longe daye;
   I pray the, Thomas, late me bee.

Thomas stode vpe in that stede,
    And he by-helde that lady gaye;   90
Hir hare it hange all ouer hir hede,
    Hir eghne semede owte, that are were graye.

And all the riche clothynge was a waye,
    That he by-fore sawe in that stede;
Hir a schanke blake, hir other graye,[1]   95
    And all hir body lyke the lede.

Than sayd Thomas, allas! allas!
    In faythe this es a dollfull syghte;
How arte thu fadyde thus in the face,
    That schane by-fore als the sonne so bryght!   100

Scho sayd, Thomas, take leve at sone and mone,
    And als at lefe that grewes on tree;
This twelmoneth sall thu with me gone,
    And medill erthe thu sall non see.

He knelyd downe appon his knee,   105
    To Mary mylde he made his mone;
Lady, but thou rewe on mee,
    All my games fro me are gon.

Allas! he sayd, and wa es mee,
    I trewe my dedis will wirke me care;   110
My saulle, Jhu, by-teche I the,
    Whedir come that euer my banes sall fare.

---

[1] The Lincoln MS. inserts after this line two others, which appear to be redundant:—

    Thomas laye, and sawe that syghte,
        Vndir nethe that grenewod tree.

Scho ledde hym in at Eldone birke,
   Vndir nethe a derne lee;
Whare it was derk als mydnyght myrke,   115
   And euer the water till his knee.

The montenans of dayes three,
   He herd bot swoghyne of the flode,
At the laste, he sayde, full wa es mee!
   Almaste I dye, for fawte of fude.   120

Scho lede hym in till a faire herbere,
   Whare frwte was growyng gret plentee:
Pere and appill, bothe rype thay were,
   The date, and als the damasee.

The fygge, and als so the wyneberye;   125
   The nyghtyngales lyggande on thair neste;
The papeioyes faste abowte gan flye;
   And throstylls sange, wolde have no reste.

He presed to pulle the frwte with his hande;
   Als man for fude that was nere faynt.   130
Scho sayd, Thomas, thu late tham stande,
   Or ells the fende the will atteynt.

If thu it plokk, sothely to say,
   Thi saule gose to the fyre of helle;
It comes neuer owte or Domesdaye,   135
   Bot ther in payne ay for to duelle.

Thomas, sothely I the hyghte,
   Come lygge thyn hede down on my knee,
And thou sall se the fayreste syghte,
   That euer sawe mon of thi contree.   140

He did in hye als scho hym badde;
   Appone hir knee his hede he layde,
For hir to paye he was full glade,
   And than that lady to hym sayde :

Seese thu nowe ȝone faire waye,   145
   That lyggis ouer ȝone heghe montáyne?—
ȝone es the waye to heuen for aye,
   When synfull sawles have duryd ther payne.

Seese thu nowe ȝone other waye,
   That lygges lawe by nethe ȝone rysse? 150
ȝone es the waye, the sothe to saye,
   Vnto the joye of paradyse.

Seese thu ȝitt ȝone thrid waye,
   That ligges vnder ȝone grene playne?
ȝone es the waye, with tene and traye,   155
   Whare synfull saulis suffirris thare payne.

Bot seese thu nowe ȝone fourt waye,
   That lygges ouer ȝone depe delle?
ȝone es the way, the sothe to say,
   Vnto the brennande fyre of hell.   160

Seese thu ȝitt ȝone faire castelle,
   That standes vpone ȝone heghe hill?
Of towne and towre it beris the belle;
   In mydul erthe es non lyk ther-till.

For sothe, Thomas, ȝone es myn awen,   165
   And the kyngus of this countree;
Bot me ware leuer hanged and drawen,
   Or that he wyste thou laye by me.

When thu commes to ȝone castelle gay,
   I pray the curtase man to bee; 170
And whate so any man to the saye,
   Luke thu answere none bott mee.

My lorde es seruede at ylk a mese
   With thritty knyghttis faire and free;
I sall saye, syttande at the dese, 175
   I tuke thi speche by ȝonde the see.

Thomas still als stane he stude,
   And he by-helde that lady gaye;
Scho come agayne als faire and gude,
   And al so ryche one hir palfraye. 180

Hir grehundis fillide with dere blode;
   Hir rachis couplede by my faye;
Scho blewe hir horne with mayne and mode,
   Vn to the castelle scho tuk the waye.

In to the haulle sothely scho went; 185
   Thomas foloued at hir hande;
Than ladyes come bothe faire and gent,
   With curtesy to hir knelande.

Harpe and fethill bothe thay fande,
   Getterne and als so the sawtrye; 190
Lutte and rybybe bothe gangande,
   And all manere of mynstralsye.

The most meruelle that Thomas thoghte,
   When that he stode appon the flore;
For feftty hertes in were broghte, 195
   That were bothe large, grete and store.

Raches laye lapande in the blode,
    Cokes come with dryssynge knyfe;
They bryttaned tham als thay were wode;
    Reuelle amanges thame was full ryfe.   200

Knyghtis dawnsede by three and three,
    Thare was revelle, gamen, and playe,
Lufly ladyes faire and free,
    That satte and sange one riche araye.

Thomas duellide in that solace,   205
    More than I ȝowe saye, perdé;
Till one a daye, so hafe I grace,
    My lufly lady sayde to mee:

Do busk the, Thomas, for thu must gon,
    For thu may here no lengare be;   210
Hye the faste with mode and mone;
    I sall the brynge till Eldone tree.

Thomas sayde than with heuy chere:
    Lufly lady, nowe lat me be;
For certis, lady, I hafe be here   215
    Bot the space of dayes thre.

For sothe, Thomas, als I the telle,
    Thou hase bene here seven ȝere and more;
Bot langere here thu may noghte duelle,
    The skylle I sall the telle where fore.   220

To morne of helle the foulle fende
    Amange this folke will seche his fee;
And thu arte mekill man and hende;
    I trowe full wele he wolde chese the.

For all the gold that euer may bee, 225
    Fro hethyn vn to the worldis ende,
Thou bese neuer be trayede for mee;
    There fore with me I rede thou wende.

Scho broghte hym agayne to Eldone tree,
    Vndir nethe the grenewode spraye, 230
In Huntlee bannkes es mery to bee,
    Whare foulis syng bothe nyght and daye.

Ferre owtt over ȝone mountane graye,
    Thomas, a fawkon byggis a neste;—
A fawcoun is an yrons praye; 235
    For-thi in na place may he reste.

Fare wele, Thomas, I wend my waye;
    For me by-houys ouer thir benttis brown.
—Loo here a fytt : more es to saye
    Of THOMAS OF ERSELLDOWN. 240

[The Second Fytt.]

Fare wele, Thomas; I wend my waye;
    I may no lengare stande with the.
Gif me a tokynynge, lady gaye,
    That I may saye I spake with the.

To harpe or carpe, whare so thu gose, 5
    Thomas, thu sall hafe the chose sothely;
And he said, harpynge kepe I none;
    For tonge es chefe of mynstralsye.

If thou will spelle, or tales telle,
    Thomas, thu sall neuer lesynge lye : 10
Whare euer thu fare, by frythe or felle,
    I pray the speke none euyll of me.

Fare wele, Thomas,[1] with owttyn gyle;
   I may no lengar duelle with the.
Lufly lady, habyd a while,
   And telle thu me of some ferly.

Thomas, herkyn what I the saye,
   When that a tree rote es dede,
The leuis fal and wyce a waye;
   And froyte it beris nodur whyte ne rede.

Of the Baylliolse blod so sall it falle,
   It sall be lyke a rotyn tre;
The Comyns and the Barlays alle,
   The Russells, and the Fresells free.

All sall thay fade and wyce a waye;
   Na wondur if the rote drye;
And mekill bale sall after spraye,
   Whare joy and blysse was wonte to bee.

Fare wele, Thomas, I wende my way;
   I may no lenger stand thee by.
Now, lufly lady, gude and gay,
   Telle me gitt of some ferly.

What kyne ferlys, Thomas gode,
   Suld I thee telle, and thi wille bee?
Telle me of this géntill blode,
   Wha sall thrife, and who sall thee.

Wha sall be kynge, wha sall be nane,
   And wha sall welde this North contré;
Wha sall flee, and wha sall be tane,
   And whare thir batells donne sall bee.

---

[1] How human the lady is made in this production! Always turning on her heel to go, like a jade, and persuaded to remain and tell more.

Thomas, of a Batelle I sall the telle,
  That sall be done righte sone at wille:
Beryns sall mete bothe fers and felle,
  And freschely fighte at Eldone¹ hille.

The Bretans blode sall vndir fete; 45
  The Bruyse blode sall wyn the spraye;
Sex thowsande Ynglysche, wele thu wete,
  Sall there be slayne that ilk day.

Fare wele, Thomas, I wende my waye;
  To stande with the me thynk full irke— 50
Of a batell I will the saye,
  That sall be done at Fawkirke.

Baners sall stande, bethe large and leng,
  Trowe this wele, with mode and mayne;
The Bruysse blood sall vndir gane, 55
  Seuen thowsande Scottis ther sall be slayne.

Fare wele, Thomas; I pray the sesse;
  No lengar here thu tarye mee;
My grehundis thay brek thaire lesse,
  And my raches thaire copills in three; 60

Loo! whare the dere by twa and twa
  Haldis ouer ʒone montane heghe—
Thomas said, God schilde thu gaa,
  Bot tell me ʒitt of some ferly.

Holde thi greyhundis in thi honde; 65
  And cupull thi raches to a tre;
And lat the dere reyke ouer the londe;—
  Ther is a herd in Holteby.²

---

¹ The MSS. vary in this place, some reading *Ledyn*, others *Halydowne* and *Eldone*. But it may be questioned whether these are not all differing forms of the same word—Haly-doun, the holy height or down. See *suprâ*.

² ? Holte by.

Off a batelle I sall the saye,
    That sall gare ladyes morne in mode: 70
At Banokis borne bothe water and claye
    Sall be mengyde with mannis blode.

Stedis sall stombill with tresoune,
    Bothe baye and broun, grysselle and graye;
Gentill knyghtis sall stombill downe,   75
    Thorowe takynge of a wykkide waye.

The Bretans blode sall vndir falle;
    The Bruysse blode sall wynn the spraye;
Sex thowsand Ynglysche, grete and smale,
    Sall there be slane that ilk a daye.   80

Than sall Scottland kyngles stande;
    Trow it wele that I the saye;
A tercelet of the same lande
    To Bretane sall take the redy waye.

And take tercellettis grete and gaye,   85
    With hym owte of his awen contree;
Thay sall wende on an ryche arraye,
    And come agayne by land and see.

He sall stroye the North contree
    Mare and lesse hym by-forne;   90
Ladyes sall saye, alas and waloway!
    That euer that royalle blode was borne!

He sall ryse vpe at Kynkehorne,
    And tye the schippis vn to the sande;
At Dipplynge more, appon the morne,   95
    Lordis will thynke full lange to stande.

By twix Dipplynge and the dales
    The watir that rynnes on rede claye,
Thare sall be slayne for sothe, Thomas,
    Eleuen thowsande Scottis that nyght and daye.   100

Thay sall take a townn of grete renowne,
    That standis nere the water of Taye,
The fadir and the sone sall be dongen downe,
    And with strakis strange be slayne awaye.

When thay hafe wone that wallede towne,   105
    And ylke man hase cheuede thayre chaunce,
Than sall thir Bretans make them bown,
    And fare forthe to the werre of Fraunce.

Than sall Scotland kynglesse stande,
    And be lefte, Thomas, als I the saye;   110
Than sall a kyng be chosen so ȝynge,
    That kane no lawes lede, perfaye.

Dauid with care he sall be-gynn,
    And with care he sall wende a waye;
Lordis and ladyes, more dois myn,   115
    Sall come appon a riche araye;
And croune hym at the town of Skynne,[1]
    Appon ane certane solempne daye.

---

[1] Scone. According to the Cambr. MS. they read—

    'Robert with care he shall reng,
        And also he shalle wynd awaye;
    Lordys and ladys, both olde and yeng,
        Shall draw to hym with owtyn naye.'

Beryns balde, both ȝonge and alde,
    Sall till hym drawe with owttyn naye;   120
Euyn he sall to Yngland ryde,
    Este and weste, als lygges the waye.

Be-twixe a parke and an abbaye,
    A palesse and a paresche kyrke,
Thare sall ȝour kynge faill of his praye,   125
    And of his lyfe be wondir irke:

He sall be tane so wondir sare,
    So that a waye he sall noghte flee;
Heys nebbe sall ryne, or he thethyn fare,[1]
    The rede blode trykelande vn to his knee.   130

He sall than be with a false - - -
    Be trayede of his awen - - -
And whether it come - - - -
    He sall byde - - - -

That ran -   - - - - 135

    [About six lines seem to be wanting.]
- - - - - -
    In the Northe to do owttraye.

And when he es man moste of mayne,
    And hopis beste than for to spede,
On a ley lande sall he be slayne   145
    Be syde a waye, for owttyn drede.

Sythen sall selle Scotland, per ma faaye,
    Fulle and fere full many ane,
For to make a certane paye,
    But ende of it sall neuer come nane.   150

---

[1] 'His nek shall rife.'—MS. Cambr.

And than sall Scotland kyngles stande,
    Trowe this wele, that I telle the;
Thre tercelettis of the same lande
    Sall stryfe to bygg and browke the tree;

He sall bygg, and browke the tree;   155
    That hase no flyghte to fley a waye;
Thay fall with pryde to Ynglande ryde,
    Este and weste, als lygges the waye.

Haly kyrke bese sett be syde,
    Relygyous byrnede on a fyre;   160
Sythen sall thay to a castelle ryde,
    And schewe tham thare with   . .

By syde a wyth .   .   .   . .
    A why .   .   .   .   . .

[Be [1] twene a myckul way and a water,   165
    A parke and a stony way then,
Ther shal a cheften mete in fere;
    A ful dughty ther shalbe slayn.[2]

The toder cheftan shalbe tane,
    A presans of blode hym shal slee,   170
And lede hym a way in a wane,
    And cloyse hym in a castell hee.

---

[1] The conclusion of the Second Fytt (evidently consisting of about twelve lines), which is wanting, is here added from the Cambridge MS.

[2] This stanza in the Cotton MS. is here added, as it varies from that given above.

      'Betwys a wethy and a water,
        A wel and a haly staine,
      Ther sal two cheftans met in fer;
        The Douglas ther sall be slaine.'

Fare wel, Thomas; I wende my way;
   For I most over ȝone bentis brown.
Here ar two fytts, Thomas, to say,   175
   Off THOMAS OF ERSELDOWN.]

[The Third Fytt.]

Now, luffy lady, gente and hende,
   Tell me, ȝif it thi willis bee,
Of thyes batells, how thay schall ende,
   And whate schall worthe of this Northe contre.

This worlde, Thomas, sothely to telle,   5
   Es noghte bot wauerethe and woghe;
Of a batelle I will the telle,
   That schall be done at Spynkerde cleughe.

The Bretans blode schall vndir falle;
   The Bruyse blode schalle wyn the spraye; 10
Sex thowsande Ynglysche grete and smalle
   Salle thare be slayne that nyghte and daye.

The rerewarde sall noghte weite, perfaye,
   Of that ilke dulfulle dede;
Thay sall make a grete journaye   15
   Dayes tene with owttyn drede.

And of a batelle I will the telle,
   That sall be done now sone at will;
Beryns sall mete, both ferse and felle,
   And freschely fyghte at Pentland hyll.   20

By-twyx Sembery[1] and Pentlande,
   The haulle that standis appone the rede claye,
There schall be slayne Eleuen thowsande
   Off Scottis men that nyghte and daye.

They sall take a towne of grete renown,   25
   That standis nere the water of Taye,[2]
.   .   .   .   .

   The tother este at Barbeké.   40

Foryours furthe sall flee [a mayne]
   On a Sonondaye by fore the messe;
Seuen thowsande sothely sall be slayne,
   One aythir pertye, more and lesse.

For ther sall be no banneres prese,   45
   Bot ferre in sondir sall they bee;
Carefull sall be the after mese,
   By-twixe Seton and the see.

Schippes sall stande appon the sande,
   Wayffande with the see fame;   50
This ȝere and mare than sall thay stande,
   Or any beryn come for tham hame.

Stedis awaye masterles sall flynge,
   Ouer the mountans too and fra;
Thaire sadills one thaire bakkis sall hynge,   55
   Vn to the garthe be rotyn in twa.

Ȝitt sall thay hewe one other aye,
   Vnto the sone be sett nere weste;
Bot thare es no wighte that ȝitt wete maye,
   Whether of thaym sall hafe the beste.   60

---

[1] Instead of 'Sembery,' the Cambridge MS. reads 'Edynborow.'

[2] About thirteen lines are torn away.

Thay sall plante down thaire baners thare,
    Worthi men all nyghte sall dye;
Bot one the morne ther sall be care,
    For nowther syde sall hafe the gree.

Than sall thay tak a truce and swere,
    For thre ʒere and more, I vnderstande;
That nane of tham sall other dere,
    Nouther by see ne ʒitt by lande.

Be twene the twoo seynt Mary dayes,[1]
    When the tyme waxis nere long,
Then sall thei mete and baners rese,
    In Gleydis-more that is so long.

Gladys-more, that gladis us all;
    This is beginning of oure gle;
Grete sorow there sall fall,
    Where rest and peese were wont to be.

Crowned kyngus ther shalbe slayn,
    With dynts sore and wonder to se,
Out of a more a raven shal cum,
    And of hym a schrew shall flye,

And seke the more with owten rest,
    After a crosse is made of ston,
Hye and lowe, both est and west;
    But up he shal spede anon.

---

[1] This and the three following stanzas are supplied from the Cambridge MS.

He sall lyghte whare the crose sulde bee, 85
   And holde his nebbe wp to the skye;
And drynke of gentill blode and free;
   Then ladys waylowaye sall crye.

Then sall a lorde come to that werre,
   That sall be of full grete renowne; 90
And in his benere sall he bere,
   Triste it wele, a rede lyone.

Ther sall another come to that werre,
   That sall fyghte full fayre in molde;
And in his banere sall he bere 95
   A schippe with an ankyre of golde.

ȝit sall another come to that werre
   That es noghte knawen by northe [ne weste,]
And in his banere sall he bere
   A wolfe with a nakede childe in his [brest.] 100

ȝitt sall the forthe lorde come to that werre
   That sall grete maystree after men
And in his   .   .   .   .
   The bere   .   .   .   .   .

Then[1] shal they fight with helm and spere, 105
   Un to the sun be set nere west;
Ther is no wyght in that fyld ther
   That wots qwylke side shall have the best.

A bastard shall cum fro a forest,
   Not in Yngland borne shall he be,— 110
And he shal wyn the gre for the best,
   Of alle men leder in Bretan shal he be.

---

[1] This and the next sixteen stanzas are supplied from the Cambridge MS.

And with pride to England ride,
    Est and west in certayn;
And holde a parlement with pride,
    Wher never non be-fore was seyn.

All false lawes he shalle lay doune,
    That are begune in that cuntré;
Truly to wyrke he shalbe boune,
    And leder of all Bretans shal he be.

The bastard shal get hym power strong,
    And all his faes he shall down dyng;
Of alle the v. kingys londis
    Ther shal non bodword home bryng.

The bastard shalle go in the Holy land;
    Trow this wel y the say:
Tak his soule to his hande,
    Jhu Christe that mycull may!

Thomas, truly I the say,
    This is trewith ylke worde;
Of that last batel I the say,
    That shalbe don at Sandeforde.

Nere Sandyforth ther is a wro,[1]
    And nere that wro is a well;
A ston there is the wel even fro,
    And nere the wel truly to tell,

On that grounde ther groeth okys thre,
    And is called Sandyford;
Ther the last batel done shalbe;
    Thomas, trow thu ilke a worde—

---

[1] In MS. Cotton it is 'broo.'

This[1] she said with hevy chere;
  The terys ran out of her een gray—
Lady, or thu wepe so sore,
  Take thi houndis, and wende thi way.

I wepe not for my way-walkyng,   145
  Thomas, treuly I the say;
But for ladys shal wed laddys ȝing,
  When ther lordis are dede away.

He shall have a stede in stabul fed,
  A hauke to beyre upon his hond;   150
A bright lady to his bed,
  That before had non in londe.

Fare wel, Thomas, I wende my way;
  Alle the day thu wil me marre.—
Lufly lady, tel thu me   155
  Of Black Agnes of Dunbar.

And why she have gyven me the warre,
  And put me in her prison depe;
For I walde dwel with her ever marre,
  And kepe hir plaes and hir shepe. 160

Of black Agnes cum never gode,
  Wher for, Thomas, she may not the;
For al hir welth and hir worldly gode,
  In London cloysed shal she be.

Ther prevys never gode of hir blode; 165
  In a dyke than shall she dye;
Houndis of hir shall have ther fode,
  Margrat of all hir kyn and she.

---

[1] MS. Then.

Then Thomas a sory man was he,
    The terys ran out of his een gray :   170
Lufly lady, ȝet tell to me,
    If we shall parte for ever and aye ?

Nay, when thou sitts at Erseldown,]
    To Huntlee bankkis take thi waye,
There sall I sikirly be bowne,   175
    To mete the, Thomas, if that I maye.

. . .ll the kene whare euer thu gaa
    . . . the pryce of our taysye ;
A tunge es wele, a tunge es waa,
    The tunge es chefe of mynstralsye.   180

She blewe hir horne on hir palfraye,
    And lefte Thomas at Eldoune tre ;
Till Helmesdale scho tuke the waye,
    And thus depertede scho and hee.

Of such a woman wolde I here   185
    That couth telle of swilke ferly ;
Jhu crownde with a crown of brere,
    Brynge vs to thy halle on hye.
                      Amen.   Amen.

Explicit Thomas of Erseledownn.

The Fermorar and his Dochter.

THIS lively and spirited dialogue between a farmer and his daughter, on the subject of her marriage, is apparently of English composition, although the editor found it written on the fly-leaf of an ancient copy of Wyntoun's "Chronicle," which appears to have formerly belonged to the Abbey of Cambuskenneth. The date of the manuscript itself is the earlier part of the fifteenth century; that of the poem is certainly not later than the reign of James V.

In a foolish and vulgar English song of the last century, not worth preserving, entitled "The Maid's Resolution to Marry a Rake," we find reasons nearly similar to those expressed in the following dialogue, for choosing a gentleman, instead of a ploughman or farmer, as her husband:—

> My Mother would have me to marry a Clown
> That hedges and ditches all week for a crown;
> But to marry a Rake is all my delight;
> If he rambles all day, he will please me at night.
>
> The name of a Clown I highly disdain,
> My Father and Mother they love the same:
> A Clown is a Clown both at home and abroad,
> When a Rake he is comely, and sweet in his bed.
>
> A Ploughman I own is good in his kind,
> But I'm resolv'd to alter my mind;
> For a Rake dress'd in scarlet and trimm'd with gold
> Is handsome and pleasant, and lovely to behold.

The sixth stanza of this poem is defective of three lines; but possibly we have no great cause to regret the loss which it has sustained.

'𝕮𝖍𝖊 𝕱𝖊𝖗𝖒𝖔𝖗𝖆𝖗 𝖆𝖓𝖉 𝖍𝖎𝖘 𝕯𝖔𝖈𝖙𝖍𝖊𝖗.'

AS I did walk onys be ane medo side,
    In ane symmer sessoun, quhen men wynnis thair hay,
    I hard ane riche fermorar with his dochter chide,
Tuiching hir merriage, and thus he did say:
Here duellis Symkin my nychtbour, ourthort ȝone way,   5
    He hes thre welthy childering, choise the one of thoise ;—
    Thow sall haue one of thame, with myche of my poise.

Fader, quoth the dochter, that gois aganis my hart,
Sen I haue bene ȝour drevill this xx. ȝeris and more,
Now wald ȝe gar me go at pleuch and at cart,   10
And leiff my liff in sklavary, as I haue done to fore ;
Tak it for ane ansuer, I will do so no more :
    ȝe can nocht compell me to mary one of thois,
    For I will haue ane gentill man, with pleasand cloise.

Dochter, quoth the fader, quhy dois thou thaim refuse,   15
Sen thai be gudlie ȝemen that be in all this land ?—
In all this cuntre, I think, thou can not chuse,
More nymlar fallowis of fute, nor of hand ;
More panefullar, more thrifty, I lat the vnderstand :
    Thou can nocht do better than mary on of thoise :   20
    No ! thou sall mary one of thame, in spite of thy noise.

VOL. I.   H

Fader, quoth the dochter, I put ȝou out of dout,
I rak nocht of thare manheid, nor thair thriftynes
    at all;
I am nocht disposit to mary Hob Klout,
To leif like my mothir, in messarie and thrall,   25
Servand the swyne, and the oxin in thare stall,
    With ane pare of clamper kynnis clowtit to my
        hoise,
    No! I will haue ane gentill man, in spyte of
        ȝour noise.

Gif I gett ane gentill man, I can nocht lychtly
    myse
Of doctouris of phesik and necessary fude;   30
Gif I say bot onys, gude husband, gett me this,
I can nocht lychtly laik it, and it will do me gude;
Sic qualities hes ane gentill man that is cum of
    gentill blude:
    How mony of this cuntre dois laik one of thoise?
    No! I will haue ane gentill man, in spite of
        ȝour noise.   35

  .   .   .   .   .   .

Ane gentill man is lusty, luvand, and faithfull of
    fay,
He is worthy to be lovit, he is plesand and gay:—
    Fader, content ȝou, in spite of ȝour noise,
    And euir I maryt be, I will haue one of thoise.

Giff I get ane gentill man, his sycht will do me
    gude   40
He will halse me, and braise me, and lufe me out
    of mesour;
So sall I haue my silkan gowne, with my franche
    hude,
I sall haue aboundance and infinite tressour,
And I salbe accumpanyit with ladeis of plesour,

And I sall haue my schois of veluot, to my fine
   hoise, 45
So will I haue ane gentill man, in spite of ȝour
   noise.

Ane gentill man is lusty, and will lay on the laid,
With ane swerde, and ane dagar glitterand by his
   side,
Quhen Symkin standis quhisling with ane quhip
   and ane gaid,
Prickand and ȝarkand ane ald ox hide, 50
With one pare of stro buskynis he gois to ride,
   Moist like ane spittell man :—suld I haue ane
      of thoise !
   No ! I will haue ane gentill man, in despite of
      your noise.

The Battle of Harlaw.

THE exact age of this historical song or poem has not been ascertained, and has given rise to some discussion, on which it is not necessary at present to enter at large. Lord Hailes suspected "that it will be found to be as recent as the days of Queen Mary or James VI." Mr. Sibbald concurs in this opinion; but, on the other hand, Mr. Ritson, Mr. Pinkerton, and Mr. Finlay maintain that, "from its manner, it might have been written soon after the event."

That this poem in its original form is of considerable antiquity cannot be doubted, the "battle of Hayrlau" being named amongst the popular songs of the time by the author of the "Complaynt of Scotland," 1549; and it may be considered as the original of rather a numerous class of our historical ballads. No copy of an earlier date than that in Ramsay's "Evergreen," 1724, is known; and he has evidently taken serious liberties with the text. An edition, printed in the year 1668, was in the curious library of Robert Myln.

The Battle of Harlaw. Foughten upon Friday, July 24, 1411, against Donald of the Isles.

I.

FRAE Dunideir as I cam throuch,
    Doun by the hill of Banochie,
    Allangst the lands of Garioch;
    Grit pitie was to heir and sé
    The noys and dulesum hermonie,   5
That evir that dreiry day did daw;
    Cryand the corynoch on hie,
Alas! alas! for the HARLAW.

II.

I marvlit quhat the matter meint,
    All folks war in a fiery fairy:
I wist nocht quha was fae or friend;
    Yit quietly I did me carrie.
    But sen the days of auld King Harry,
Sic slauchter was not hard nor sene,
    And thair I had nae tyme to tairy,
For bissiness in Aberdene.

III.

Thus as I walkit on the way,
    To Inverury as I went,
I met a man, and bad him stay,
    Requeisting him to mak me quaint
    Of the beginning and the event,
That happenit thair at the Harlaw;
    Then he entreited me tak tent,
And he the truth sould to me schaw.

IV.

Grit Donald of the Yles did claim
    Unto the lands of Ross sum richt,
And to the Governour he came,
    Them for to haif, gif that he micht:
    Quha saw his interest was but slicht;
And thairfore answerit with disdain;
    He hastit hame baith day and nicht,
And sent nae bodword back again.

V.

But Donald richt impatient
   Of that answer Duke Robert gaif,
He vowd to God Omnipotent,
   All the hale lands of Ross to haif,
   Or ells be graithed in his graif.
He wald not quat his richt for nocht,
   Nor be abusit lyk a slaif,
That bargin sould be deirly bocht.

VI.

Then haistylie he did command,
   That all his weir-men should convene,
Ilk ane well harnisit frae hand,
   To meit and heir quhat he did mein;
   He waxit wrath, and vowit tein,
Sweirand he wald surpryse the North,
   Subdew the brugh of Aberdene,
Mearns, Angus, and all Fyfe, to Forth.

VII.

Thus with the weir-men of the Yles,
   Quha war ay at his bidding bown,
With mony maid, with forss and wyles,
   Richt far and neir baith up and doun:
   Throw mount and muir, frae town to town,
Allangst the land of Ross he roars,
   And all obey'd at his bandown,
Evin frae the North to Suthren shoars.

VIII.

Then all the Countrie men did yield;
 For nae resistans durst they mak,
Nor offer battill in the feild,
 Be forss of arms to beir him bak; 60
 Syne they resolvit all and spak,
That best it was for thair behoif,
 They sould him for thair chiftain tak,
Believing weil he did them loife.

IX.

Then he a proclamation maid, 65
 All men to meet at Inverness,
Throw Murray Land to mak a raid,
 Frae Arthursyre unto Spey-ness.
 And further mair he sent express,
To schaw his collours and ensenȝie, 70
 To all and sindry, mair and less,
Throchout the boundis of Boyn and Enȝie.

X.

And then throw fair Strathbogie land,
 His purpose was for to pursew,
And quhasoevir durst gainstand, 75
 That race they should full sairly rew.
 Then he bad all his men be trew,
And him defend by forss and slicht,
 And promist them rewardis anew,
And mak them men of mekle micht. 80

XI.

Without resistans, as he said,
    Throw all these parts he stoutly past,
Quhair sum war wae, and sum war glaid,
    But Garioch was all agast.
    Throw all these feilds he sped him fast, 85
For sic a sicht was never sene;
    And then, forsuith, he langd at last
To sé the Bruch of Aberdene.

XII.

To hinder this prowd enterprise,
    The stout and michty Erle of Marr 90
With all his men in arms did ryse,
    Even frae Curgarf to Craigyvar;
    And down the syde of Don richt far;
Angus and Mearns did all convene
    To fecht, or Donald came sae nar 95
The ryall bruch of Aberdene.

XIII.

And thus the martial Erle of Marr
    Marcht with his men in richt array,
Befoir the enemie was ware,
    His banner bauldly did display. 100
    For weil enewch they kend the way,
And all their semblance weil they saw,
    Without all dangir or delay,
Came haistily to the HARLAW.

XIV.

With him the braif Lord Ogilvy,
   Of Angus Sherriff principall,
The constabill of gude Dundé,
   The vanguard led before them all.
   Suppose in number they war small,
Thay first richt bauldlie did pursew,
   And maid thair faes befoir them fall,
Quha then that race did sairly rew.

XV.

And then the worthy Lord Salton,
   The strong undoubted Laird of Drum,
The stalwart Laird of Lawristone,
   With ilk thair forces all and sum.
   Panmuir with all his men did cum,
The Provost of braif Aberdene,
   With trumpets and with tuick of drum,
Came schortly in thair armour schene.

XVI.

These with the Erle of Marr came on,
   In the reir-ward richt orderlie,
Thair enemies to sett upon;
   In awfull manner hardilie,
   Togither vowit to live and die,
Since they had marchit mony mylis
   For to suppress the tyrannie
Of douted Donald of the Yles.

XVII.

But he in number ten to ane,
  Richt subtilie alang did ryde,
With Malcomtosch and fell Maclean,
  With all their power at thair syde,
  Presumeand on thair strength and pryde,
Without all feir or ony aw,
  Richt bauldlie battill did abyde,
Hard by the town of fair HARLAW.

XVIII.

The armies met, the trumpet sounds,
  The dandring drums alloud did touk,
Baith armies byding on the bounds,
  Till ane of them the feild sould bruik.
  Nae help was thairfor, nane wald jouk,
Ferss was the fecht on ilka syde,
  And on the ground lay mony a bouk
Of them that thair did battill byde.

XIX.

With doutsum victorie they dealt,
  The bludy battil lastit lang,
Each man his nibours forss thair felt;
  The weakest aft-tymes gat the wrang.
  Thair was nae mowis thair them amang,
Naithing was hard but heavy knocks,
  That eccho maid a dulefull sang,
Thairto resounding frae the rocks.

XX.

But Donalds men at last gaif back;
    For they war all out of array.
The Earl of Marris men throw them brak,   155
    Pursewing shairply in thair way,
    Thair enemys to tak or slay,
Be dynt of forss to gar them yield,
    Quha war richt blyth to win away,
And sae for feirdness tint the feild.   160

XXI.

Then Donald fled, and that full fast,
    To mountains hich for all his micht;
For he and his war all agast,
    And ran till they war out of sicht:
    And sae of Ross he lost his richt,   165
Thocht mony men with him he brocht,
    Towards the Yles fled day and nicht,
And all he wan was deirlie bocht.

XXII.

This is, (quod he,) the richt report
    Of all that I did heir and knaw,   170
Thocht my discourse be sumthing schort,
    Tak this to be a richt suthe saw.
    Contrairie God and the Kings law,
Thair was spilt mekle Christian blude,
    Into the battil of HARLAW;   175
This is the sum, sae I conclude.

XXIII.

But yit a bony quhyle abyde,
   And I sall mak thé cleirly ken
Quhat slauchter was on ilkay syde,
   Of Lowland and of Highland men,   180
   Quha for thair awin haif evir bene.
These lazie lowns micht weil be spaird,
   Chessit lyke deirs into thair dens,
And gat thair waiges for rewaird.

XXIV.

Malcomtosh of the clan heid cheif,   185
   Macklean with his grit hauchty heid,
With all thair succour and releif,
   War dulefully dung to the deid.
   And now we are freid of thair feid,
They will not lang to cum again;   190
   Thousands of them without remeid
On Donald's syd that day war slain.

XXV.

And on the uther syd war lost,
   Into the field that dismal day,
Chief men of worth, (of mekle cost,)   195
   To be lamentit sair for ay.
   The Lord Saltoun and Rothemay,
A man of micht and mekle main;
   Grit dolour was for his decay,
That sae unhappylie was slain.   200

XXVI.

Of the best men amang them was,
    The gracious gude Lord Ogilvy,
The Sheriff-Principal of Angus;
    Renownit for truth and equitie,
    For faith and magnanimitie;   205
He had few fallows in the feild,
    Yit fell by fatall destinie,
For he nae ways wad grant to yield.

XXVII.

Sir James Scrimgeor of Duddap, Knicht,
    Grit constabill of fair Dundé,   210
Unto the dulefull deith was dicht,
    The Kingis cheif banner-man was he,
    A valʒiant man of chevalrie,
Quhais predecessors wan that place
    At Spey, with gude King William frie,   215
Gainst Murray and Macduncan's race.

XXVIII.

Gude Sir Allexander Irvine,
    The much renownit Laird of Drum,
Nane in his days was bettir sene,
    Quhen they war semblit all and sum,   220
    To praise him we sould not be dumm,
For valour, witt, and worthyness,
    To end his days he ther did cum,
Quhois ransom is remeidyless.

XXIX.

And thair the Knicht of Lawriston 225
    Was slain into his armour schene:
And gude Sir Robert Davidson,
    Quha Provest was of Aberdene;
The Knicht of Panmure, as was sene,
A martiall man in armour bricht, 230
    Sir Thomas Murray stout and kene,
Left to the warld thair last gude nicht.

XXX.

Thair was not, sen King Keneths days,
    Sic strange intestine crewel stryf
In Scotland sene, as ilk man says, 235
    Quhair mony lichtlie lost thair lyfe;
    Quhilk maid divorce twene man and wyfe,
And mony children fatherless,
    Quhilk in this realme has bene full ryfe;
Lord help these lands, our wrangs redress! 240

XXXI.

In July, on Saint James his even,
    That four and twenty dismall day,
Twelve hundred, ten score and eleven
    Of yeirs sen Chyrst, the suthe to say:
    Men will remember as they may, 245
Quhen thus the veritie they knaw,
    And mony a ane may murn for ay,
The brim battil of the HARLAW.

Finis.

The Thrie Tailes of the Thrie Priests of Peblis.

THE only printed edition of the "Tales of the Priests of Peblis," of which any trace now appears, is that produced at Edinburgh in 1603.[1] From this source these Tales were published by Mr. Pinkerton in 1792,[2] and a considerable portion of them by Mr. Sibbald in 1801.[3] It was thought advisable, however, to include these Tales in this collection, as meriting to be better known, and more accessible than at present they can be said to be.

The title of the original edition is as follows:—

The thrie Tailes of the thrie
Priests of Peblis.

Contayning many notabill examples and sentences and (that the paper sould not be voide) supplyit with sundrie merie tailes very pleasant to the Reader and mair exactlie corrected than the former Impression.[4]

OVID.

Expectanda dies homini est, dicique beatus
Ante obitum nemo supremaque funera debit.

IMPRINTED AT EDINBURGH
be Robert Charteris 1603.

CVM PRIVILEGIO REGALI.

---

[1] At the end is an advertisement, stating that the printer had set forth with the King's Majesties license "sundrie uther delectabill discourses,—sic as are *David Lindsayes Play; Philotus; and the Freirs of Berwick and Biblo.*" It has been asked, but in vain, if any one ever heard of *Biblo*. The other "discourses" are better known.

[2] Scotish Poems, &c. 1792, vol. i. p. 1–49.

[3] Chronicle of Scotish Poetry, vol. ii.

[4] The *merie tailes* mentioned in the above title-page are

In "The Complaynt of Scotland" (1549) there is an allusion to these Tales. "*The Priests of Peblis* (says the author) speiris an questioun in ane beuk that he compilit, quhy that burgis aryis thryuis nocht to the thrid ayr," &c. From this passage we might almost infer that "the beuk" had been but recently compiled. Mr. Pinkerton, however, observes, that the Tales "appear, from internal evidence, to have been written before the year 1492, because the kingdom of Grenada is mentioned as not yet Christian. Conjecture (he shrewdly adds) may well suppose that they were intended to chastise the weak government of James III., slain in 1488." With regard to the author, not the slightest hint is to be discovered; and, therefore, it were idle to have recourse to such suppositions as those in which Mr. Sibbald indulged;—who at length seemed to have settled the matter to his own conviction, by fixing their date between 1533 and 1540, and attributing them to John Rolland, the author of a metrical version of the "Sevin Sagis," which passed through several editions; and of a long dull moral poem, under the title of "The Court of Venus," printed at Edinburgh in 1575, of which one copy alone is known to be preserved. In answer to all Mr. Sibbald's conjectures, it is enough to state that a portion of these Tales, with the title, "*Heir begynnis the buke of the thre prestis of Peblis how thai told thar Tales*," is contained in a MS. which appears to have been transcribed at least twenty years previous to the date he assigns for their composition, and probably before Rolland was born.

Mr. Pinkerton says, "It is hardly necessary to remark, that these Tales of the Priests are more moral than facetious, and that their chief merit consists in a *naif* delineation of ancient manners." In like manner, the biographer of the Scotish Poets has said: "The three priests of Peebles, having met on St. Bride's day for the purpose of regaling themselves, agree, that each in his turn shall endeavour to entertain the rest by relating some story. They acquit

---

in prose, and printed in a "small letter on the margin: they are taken from George Peele's *Jests*," of which the earliest known impression seems to be that of 1607, although it was licensed in 1605, and might be supposed, from the above reference, to have been in existence in or before 1603.

themselves with sufficient propriety. The tales are of a moral tendency, but, at the same time, are free from the dulness which so frequently infests the perceptive compositions of our earlier poets."[1]

The Preface.

IN Peblis town sumtyme, as I heard tell,
The formest day of Februare, befell
Thrie Priests went unto collatioun,
Into ane privie place of the said toun.
Quhair that they sat, richt soft and unfute sair; 5
They luifit not na rangald nor repair:
And, gif I sall the suith reckin and say,
I traist it was upon Sanct Bryd's day.
Quhair that they sat, full easily and soft;
With monie lowd lauchter upon loft. 10
And, wit ye weil, thir thrie thay maid gude cheir;
To them thair was na dainties than too deir:
With thrie fed capons on a speit with creische,
With monie uthirsindrie dyvers meis.
And them to serve thay had nocht bot a boy; 15
Fra cumpanie thay keipit them sa coy,
They lufit nocht with ladry, nor with lown,
Nor with trumpours to travel throw the toun;
Both with themself quhat thay wald tel or crak;
Umquhyle sadlie; umquhyle jangle and jak; 20
Thus sat thir thrie besyde ane felloun fyre,
Quhil thair capons war roistit lim and lyre.
Befoir them was sone set a Roundel bricht,
And with ane clene claith, finelie dicht,
It was ouirset; and on it breid was laid. 25
The eldest than began the grace, and said,

---

[1] Irving's Lives of the Scotish Poets, vol. i. p. 372.

And blissit the breid with Benedicite,
With Dominus, Amen, sa mot I the.
And be they had drunken about a quarte,
Than spak ane thus, that Master was in Arte, 30
And to his name their callit Johne was he;
And said, sen we ar heir Priests thrie,
Syne wants nocht, be him that maid the mone,
Til us wee think ane tail sould cum in tune.
Than spake ane uther, to name hecht M. Archebald,
Now, be the hiest Hevin, quod he, I hald 36
To tel ane tail, methink, I sould not tyre,
To hald my fute out of this felloun fyre.
Than spak the thrid, to name hecht S. Williame,
To grit clargie I can not count nor clame; 40
Nor yet I am not travellit, as ar ye,
In monie sundrie land beyond the see.
Thairfoir me think it nouther shame nor sin,
Ane of yow twa the first tail to begin.
Heir I protest, than spak maister Archebald, 45
Ane travellit Clark suppois I be cald,
Presumpteouslie I think not to presume,
As I that was never travellit bot to Rome.
To tel ane tail bot eirar I suppone,
The first tail tald mot be Maister Johne: 50
For he hath bene in monie uncouth land,
In Portingale, and in Civile the grand;
In fyve kinrikis of Spane al hes he bene;
In foure christin, and ane heathin, I wene.
In Rome, Flanders, and in Venice toun; 55
And other Lands sundrie up and doun.
And for that he spak first of ane tail,
Thairfoir to begin he sould not fail.
Thein speiks maister Johne, Now be the Rude,
Me to begin ane tail sen ye conclude, 60
An I deny than had I sair offendit,
The thing begun the soner it is endit.

The first taile tald be maister Johne.

A KING thair was sumtyme, and eik a Queene ;
As monie in the land befoir had bene.
This king gart set ane plane parliament,　　　　65
And for the Lords of his kinrik sent :
And, for the weilfair of his Realme and gyde,
The thrie Estaits concludit at that tyde.
The king gart cal to his palice al thrie,
The estaits Ilkane in thair degrie.　　　　　　70
The Bishops first, with Prelats and Abbotis,
With thair Clarks servants, and Varlottis :
Into ane hall, was large, richt hie, and hudge,
Thir Prelats all richt lustelie couth ludge.
Syne in ane hal, ful fair farrand,　　　　　　75
He ludgit al the Lords of his Land.
Syne in ane Hal, was under that ful clene,
He harbourit all his burgessis, rich and bene.
Sa of thir thrie Estaits, al and sum,
In thir thrie Hals he gart the wysest cum.　　80
And of thair mery cheir quhat mak I mair?
They fuir als weil as onie folk micht fair.
THE King himself come to this Burgessis bene ;
And thir words to them carps I wene,
And says, Welcum burgessis, my bield and
　　bliss!　　　　　　　　　　　　　　　　85
Quhen ye fair weil I ma na mirths mis.
Quhen that your ships halds hail and sound,
In riches gudes and weilfair I abound.
Ye are the caus of my life, and my cheir,
Out of far Lands your Marchandice cums heir.　90
Bot ane thing is, for short, the cause quhy
Togidder heir yow gart cum have I.
To yow I have ane questioun to declair,
Quhy Burges bairns thryves not to the thrid air?

Bot casts away it that thair eldars wan. 95
Declair me now this questioun, gif ye can ;
To yow I gif this questioun, al and sum,
For to declair againe the morne I cum.
VNTO his Lords that cumen is the king,
Dois gladlie al he said baith old and ying: 100
My lustie Lords, my Leiges, and my lyfe,
I am in sturt quhen that ye ar in stryfe.
Quhen ye have peace, and quhen ye have pleasance,
Than I am glade, and derflie may I dance.
Ane heid dow not on bodie stand allane, 105
Fourout memberis, to be of micht and mane ;
For to uphald the bodie and the heid ;
And sickerlie to gar it stand in steid.
Thairfoir, my Lords, and my Barrouns bald,
To me alhail ye ar help and uphald. 110
And now I will ye wit, with diligence,
Quhairfoir that I gart cum sic confluence :
And quhy ye Lords of my Parliament,
I have gart cum, I will tell my intent.
Ane questioun I have, ye mon declair, 115
That in my minde is ever mair and mair ;
Quhairfoir, and quhy, and quhat is the cais,
Sa worthie Lords war in myne elders dayis ;
Sa full of fredome, worship, and honour,
Hardie in hart, to stand in everie stour. 120
And now in yow I find the hail contrair ?
Thairfoir this dout and questioun ye declair.
And it declair, under the hiest pane ;
The morne this tyme quhen that I cum agane.
THAN till his Clergie come this nobil king ; 125
Welcum bishops, he said, with my blissing ;
Welcum my beidmen, my blesse, and al my beild ;
To me ye ar baith Helmeit, Speir, and Scheild.
For richt as Moyses stude upon the Mont,
Prayand to God of Hevin, as he was wont ; 130

And richt sa, be your devoit orisoun,
Myne enemies sould put to confusioun.
Ye ar the gainest gait, and gyde, to God;
Of al my Realme ye ar the rewl and rod.
It that ye dome think it should be done; 135
Quhen that ye shrink, I have ane sunyie sone.
Thus be yow ay ane example men tais:
And as ye say than al and sundrie sayis:
It that ye think richt, or yit ressoun,
To that I can nor na man have chessoun. 140
And that ye think unressoun, or wrang,
Wee al and sundrie sings the samin sang.
Bot ane thing is I wald ye understude,
The cause into this place for to conclude,
Quhairfoir and quhy I gart yow hidder cum, 145
My Clargie, and my Clarks, al and sum;
To yow I have na uther tail, nor theame,
Exceptand to yow Bishops a probleame;
Quhilk is to me ane questioun and dout;
Out of my mind I wald ye put it out. 150
That is to say, Quhairfoir and quhy
In auld times and days of ancestry,
Sa monie Bishops war, and men of kirk,
Sa grit wil had ay gude warkes to wirk.
And throw thair prayers, maid to God of micht, 155
The dum men spak; the blind men gat their sicht;
The deif men heiring; the cruikit gat thair feit;
War nane in bail bot weill thay culd them beit.
To seik folks, or in sairnes syne,
Til al thay wald be mendis, and medecyne. 160
And quhairfoir now in your tyme ye warie;
As thay did than quhairfoir sa may not ye;
Quhairfoir may not ye as thay did than?
Declair me now this questioun, gif ye can.

To the Burgessis.

VPON the morne, efter service and meet, 165
The King came in, and sat doun in his sait,
Into the hal, amang the Burges men;
With him ane Clark, with ink, paper, and pen.
And bad them that they sould, foroutin mair,
His questioun reid, assolye, and declair. 170
Aud the Burgessis, that this questioun weil knew,
Hes ordaned ane wyse man, and ane trew,
The questioun to reid foroutin fail.
And he stude up, and this began his tail.

The answeir to the first questioun.

EXCELLENT, hie, richt michty prince and
    King! 175
Your hienes heir wald faine wit of this thing,
Quhy burges bairnis thryvis not to the thrid air;
Can never thryve bot of al baggis is bair.
And ever mair that is for to say,
It that thair eldars wan thay cast away? 180
This questioun declair ful weill I can:
Thay begin not quhair thair fathers began.
Bot, with ane heily hart, baith doft and derft,
Thay ay begin quhair that thair fathers left.
Of this mater largelie to speik mair, 185
Quhy that thay thryve not to the thrid air;
Becaus thair fathers purelie can begin;
With [a] hap, and [a] halfpenny, and a lambs skin.
And purelie run fra toun to toun on feit;
And that richt oft wetshod, werie, and weit. 190
Quhilk at the last of monie smale couth mak
This bonie pedder ane gude fute pak.
At ilkane fair this chapman ay was fund;
Quhil that his pak was wirth fourtie pund.
To beir his pak, quhen that he feillit force, 195
He bocht ful sone ane mekil stalwart hors.

And at the last so worthelie up wan,
He bocht ane cart to carie pot and pan;
Baith Flanders coffers, with counters and kist;
He wox ane grand rich man, or anie wist.   200
And syne into the town, to sel and by,
He held a chop to sel his chaffery.
Than bocht he wol, and wyselie couth it wey.
And efter that some saylit he the sey;
Than come he hame a verie potent man;   205
And spousit syne a michtie wyfe richt than.
He sailit ouer the sey sa oft and oft,
Quhil at the last ane semelie ship he coft.
And waxe sa ful of warldis welth and win;
His hands he wish in ane silver basin.   210
Foroutin gold or silver into hurde,
Wirth thrie thousand pund was his copburde.
Riche was his gounis with uther garments gay;
For sonday silk, for ilk day grene and gray.
His wyfe was cumlie cled in scarlet reid.   215
Scho had no doubt of derth of ail nor breid.
And efter that, within a twentie yeir,
He sone gat up ane stelwart man and steir.
And efter that this burges we of reid
Deit, as we mon do al indeid.   220
And fra [that] he was deid than come his sone,
And enterit in the welth that he had wone.
He steppit not his steps in the streit,
To win this welth; nor for it was he weit.
Quhen he wald sleip, he wantis not a wink   225
To win this welth: na for it sweit na swink.
Thairfoir that lichtlie cums wil lichtlie ga.
To win this welth he had na work, nor wa.
To win this gude he had not ane il houre;
Quhy sould he have the sweit, had not the soure?   230
Upon his fingers with riche rings on raw,
His mother not tholit the reik on him to blaw.

And wil not heir, for very shame and sin,
That ever his father sald ane sheip skin.
He wald him sayne with Benedicite, 235
Quha spak of onie degrading of his degrie.
With twa men and ane varlot at his bak;
And ane libberly ful lytil to lak.
With ane wald he baith wod and wraith,
Quha at him speirit how sald he the claith? 240
At hasard wald he derflie play at dyse;
And to the taverne eith he was to tyse.
Thus wist he never of wa, bot ay of weil,
Quhil he had slielie slidden fra his seil;
Syne to the court than can he mak repair, 245
And fallow himsyne to ane Lordis air.
He weips nocht for na warldis welth, nor win,
Quhil drink and dyce have pourit him to the pin.
He can not mak be craft to win ane eg;
Quhat ferlie is, thoch burges bairnes beg? 250
And, Sir, this is the caus, as I declair,
Quhy burges bairnis thrives not to the thrid air.
Weil, quod the King, thow servis thy rewaird;
For wyselie hes thow this questioun declaird.
Sir Clark, tak ink, with pen on paper wryte; 255
And as he said thow dewlie put on dyte.

'To the Lordis.'

THAN to his Lords cum is this nobil king,
Desyrand for to wit the solyeing
Of this questioun, this probleame, and this dout;
The quhilks lords had al round about, 260
Advysetlie, as weil it sould accord,
Thair language laid upon ane agit Lord.
The quhilk stude up, and richt wyselie did vail
Unto the King, and this began his taill:

The answere to the second questioun.

EXCELLENT, hie, richt mighty Prince and
    sure!   265
Ay at your call we ar, under your cure.
And now sen ye have gart us hither cum,
This dout for to declair, baith al and sum,
That is to say, the cause quhairfoir and quhy
Sic worthie Lords war in dayis gane by;   270
Sa ful of fredome, worschip, and honour,
Hardie in hart, to stand in everie stour:
And now in us ye meine ay mair and mair
Into your tyme ye find the hail contrair?
Sir, this it is the caus, quhairfoir and quhy: 275
Your Justice ar sa ful of surquedry;
Sa covetous and ful of avarice,
That thay your Lords impairis of thair pryce.
Thay dyte your lords, and heryis up your men:
The thief now fra the leillman quha can ken?   280
Thay wryte up leill and fals, baith al and sum;
And dytes them under ane pardoun.
Thus, be the husbandman never sa leil,
He dytit is, as ane thief is, to steil.
Thay luke to nocht bot gif ane man have
    gude;   285
And it I trow man pay the Justice sude:
The thief ful weill he wil himself overby;
Quhen the leill man into the lack will ly.
The leil man for to compone will nocht consent,
Because he waits he is ane innocent.   290
Thus ar the husbands dytit al but dout;
And heryit quyte away al around about.
Sumtyme, quhen husbandmen went to the weir,
Thay had ane jack, ane bow, or els ane speir:
And now befoir quhair they had ane bow,   295
Ful faine he is on bak to get ane fow.

And for ane jak ane raggit cloke hes tane;
Ane sword, sweir out, and roustie for the rane.
Quhat sould sic men to gang to ane hoist,
Lyker to beg than enemies to boist? 300
And your Lords, fra thair tennantes be puir,
Of gold in kist na koffer has na cuir.
Fra thay be al puir that ar them under;
Thoch tha be puir your Lords, is na wonder:
For ritch husbands and tenants of grit micht 305
Helps ay thair Lords to hald thair richt.
And quhen your Lords ar puir, thus to conclude,
Thay sel thair sonnes and airs for gold and gude;
Unto ane mokrand carle, for derest pryse,
That wist never yit of honour, nor gentryse. 310
This worship, and honour of linage,
Away it weirs thus for thair disparage.
Thair manheid and thair mense this gait thay murle;
In mariage thus unyte with ane churle.
The quhilk wist never of gentrie, na honour, 315
Of fredome, worship, vassalage, nor valour.
This is the caus dreidles, for withoutin dout,
Fra al your Lords how honour is al out.
And thus my Lords bade me to yow say,
How honour, fredome, and worship, is away. 320
   THAN spak the King, Your conclusion is quaint;
And thairattour ye mak to us a plaint:
And in your sentence thus ye meine to say,
Leil men ar hurt, and theifis gets away.
And thus methink ye meine justice is smuird; 325
Your tennants and your leill husbands ar puird:
And, quhan that thay ar puird, than ar ye puir.
The quhilk to yow is baith charge and cure;
That ye for gold baith wed and wage;
Ye sel your sones and aires in mariage 330

To cairls of kynde; and, bot for thair riches,
In quhom is na nurture, nor nobilnes,
Fredome, worschip, manheid, nor honour,
The quhilk to us and yow is dishonour.
In samekil this shortly I conclude, 336
As ye that are discendand of our blude,
For the quhilk thing I will ye understand,
With Gods grace, wee tak it upon hand,
To se for this, as ressoun can remeid;
In tyme to cum thairof thair be na pleid. 340
With our Justice thair sal pas ane Doctour,
That lufis God, his saul, and our honour.
The quhilk sal be ane Doctour in the Law,
That sal the faith and veritie weil knaw:
And frae hence furth he sal baith heir and se 345
Baith theif puneist, and leil men live in lie.
For weil I wait thair can be na war thing
Than covetyce in Justice or in King.
    Efter this tail in us ye sal not taint;
Nor yit of our Justice to mak ane plaint. 350
And afterward sa did this King but chessoun;
On him micht na man plenie of ressoun.
Syne bad his Clark, but onie variance,
Wryte this in his buik of rememberance.

'To the Clergie.'

THAN to the Clergie come this nobill king 355
Of his questioun to heir the absolving.
And thay, as men of wisdome in al wark,
Had laid thair speich upon ane cunning clark.
The quhilk in vane in scule had not tane
    grie;
In al science[s] sevin he was an *A per se*: 360
And in termis short and sentence fair
The questioun began for to declair.

That is to say quhairfoir and quhy,
In auld times and dayes of ancestry,
Sa monie Bishops war and men of kirk 365
Sa grit wil had ay gude warkes to wirk;
And throw thair prayers, maid to God of micht,
The dum men spak; the blind men gat thair sicht;
The deif men heiring; the cruiket gat thair feit;
Was nane in bail bot weil thay could them beit. 370
And quhairfoir now al that cuir can warie,
Methink ye mene quhairfoir sa may not we?
And thus it is your quodlibet and dout,
Ye gave to us to reid, and gif it out.

The answer to the thrid questioun.

THIS is the caus, richt michtie King! at short, 375
To your Hienes as we sal thus report.
The lawit folkes this law wald never ceis
But with thair use, quhen Bishops war to cheis,
Unto the kirk they gadred, auld and ying,
With meik hart, fasting and praying; 380
And prayit God, with word[i]s not in waist,
To send them wit doun be the halie Gaist,
Quhan them amang was onie Bishop deid,
To send to them ane Bishop in his steid.
And yet amang us ar fund wayis thrie 385
To cheis ane Bishope, after ane uthir die.
That is to say the way of the Halie Gaist,
Quhilk takin is of micht and vertue maist.
The second is, by way of electioun,
Ane Parsone for to cheis of perfectioun, 390
In that cathedral kirk, and in that se,
In place quhair that Bishope suld chosen be:
And gif thair be nane abil thair that can
That office weil steir, quhat sal thay than

Bot to the thrid way to ga forthi? 395
Quhilk is callit (via[m] scrutavi)
That is to say, in al the realme and land,
Ane man to get for that office gainand.
Bot thir thrie wayis, withoutin ony pleid,
Ane sould we cheis after ane uthers deid, 400
Bot, Sir, now the contrair wee find,
Quhilk puts al our heavines behind.
Now sal thair nane, of thir wayis thrie,
Be chosen now ane Bishope for to be;
Bot that your micht and Majestie wil mak 405
Quhatever he be, to loife or yit to lak;
Than heyly to sit on the rayne-bow.
Thir Bishops cums in at the north window;
And not in at the dur, nor yit at the yet:
But over waine and quheil in wil he get. 410
And he cummis not in at the dur,
Gods pleuch may never hald the fur[w].
He is na Hird to keip thay sely sheip;
Nocht bot ane tod in ane lambskin to creip.
How sould he kyth mirakil, and he sa evil? 415
Never bot by the dysmel, or the devil.
For, now on dayes, is nouther riche nor puir
Sal get ane kirk, al throw his literature.
For science, for vertew, or for blude,
Gets nane the kirk, bot baith for gold and gude. 420
Thus, greit excellent King! the Halie Gaist
Out of your men of gude away is chaist:
And, war not that doutles I yow declair,
That now as than wald hail baith seik and sair.
Sic wickednes this world is within, 425
That symonie is countit now na sin.
And thus is the caus, baith al and sum,
Quhy blind men sicht, na heiring gets na dum.
And thus is the caus, the suith to say,
Quhy halines fra kirkmen is away. 430

Than, quod the King, well understand I yow.
And heir to God I mak ane aith and vow,
And to my crown and to my cuntrie to,
With kirk-gude sal I never have ado,
It to dispone to lytil or to large; 435
Kirkmen to kirk sen they have al the charge.

Than had this nobil King lang tyme and space;
And in his tyme was mekil luk and grace.
His Lordis honourit him efter thair degrie;
The Husbands peice had and tranquilitie; 440
The Kirk was frie quhil he was in his lyfe;
The Burges sones began than for to thryfe.
And eftir long was never king more wyse:
And levit and deit, and endit in Gods servise.
And than spak all that fellowship but fail: 445
God and Sanct Martyne quyte yow of your tail.
And than spak Maister Archebald: falliswe
Gude tail or evil, quhider that ever it be.
Thus, as I can, I sal it tel but hyre,
To hald my fute out of this felloun fyre. 450

The second taill tald be M. Archebald.

A KING thair was sumtyme, and eik a Queene,
As monie in the land befoir had bene.
The king was fair in persoun, fresh and fors;
Ane feirie man on fute, as yit on hors.
And nevertheles feil falts him befell: 455
Hee luifit over weil yong counsel:
Yong men he luifit to be him neist;
Yong men to him thay war baith Clark and Preist.
Hee luifit nane was ald, or ful of age;
Sa did he nane of sad counsel nor sage. 460
To sport and play quhyle up and quhylum doun,
To al lichtness ay was he redie boun.

Sa ouir the sey cummin thair was a clark
Of greit science, of voyce, word, and wark.
And dressit him with al his besynes 465
Thus with this king to mak his recidens.
Weil saw he with this king micht na man byde,
Bot thay that wald al sadnes set on syde.
With club and bel, and partie cote with eiris,
He feinyeit him ane fule, fond in his feiris. 470
French and Dutche, and Italie yit als,
Weil could he speik, and Latine feinye fals.
Unto the kirk he came, befoir the king,
With club and cote, and monie bel to ring.
Dieu gard, sir King, I bid nocht hald in hiddil ; 475
I am to yow als sib as seif is to ane riddil.
Betwixt us twa mot be als mekil grace,
As frost and sna fra Yule is unto Pace.
Wait yee how the Frenche man sayis syne,
Nul bon, he sayis, *monsieur sans pyne.* 480
With that he gave ane loud lauchter on loft :
Honour and eis, sir, quha may have for nocht?
Cum on thy way, sir king, now for Sanct Jame,
Thow with me, or I with the, gang hame.
Now, be Sanct Katherine, quod the king, and smyld, 485
This fule hes monie waverand word and wyld.
Cum hame with mee : thow sal have drink ynouch.
Grand mercy, quod the fuill agane, and leuch.
Now, quod the king, fra al dulnes and dule
Wee may us keip, quhil that wee have this fuil. 490
He feinyeit him a fuil in deid and word ;
The wyser man the better can be bourd.
Quhil at the last this fuil was callit alway
Fuil of fuiles, and that ilk man wald say,
Thus was this fuil ay stil with the King, 495
Quhil he had weil considderit in al thing

The conditiouns, use, manner, and the gyse,
And coppyit weil the King on his best wyse.
 Sa fel it on a day this nobil King
Unto ane cietie raid for his sporting : 500
This fuil persavit weil the King wald pas,
Unto ane uther cietie as it was,
He tuke his club, and ane table, in his hand,
For to prevene the tyme he was gangand.
Sa be the way ane woundit man fande he ; 505
And with this fuil war runners, twa or thrie,
Sum of the court, and sum cf the kitchene,
And saw ane man but Leiche or Medycene
Sa sair woundit micht nouther ga nor steir :
At him this fuil con al the caus speir. 510
He answered, and said, Rever and thief,
Thou hes me hurt, and brocht me in mischeif.
With that his wounds war fillit ful of fleis,
As ever in byke theair biggit onie beis.
Than ane of them, that had pitie, can pray 515
That he mot skar they felloun fleis away.
Than spak the fuil and said, lat them be now, man ;
For thay ar ful ; the hungry wil cum than.
For thir dois nocht bot sit, as thou may se ;
For thay ar als ful as thay may be : 520
Be thir away, it is evil, and na gude,
The hungrie fleis wil cum and souk his blude.
The ofter that thir fleis away be cheist,
The new fleis will mair of his blude waist :
And draw his blude, and souk him sine sa sair ; 525
Thairfoir lat them alane ; skar them na mair.
The sair man him beheld, and him he demes,
And said he was not sik a fuil as he semes.
 Sone after that ane lytil came the King,
With monie man can gladelie sport and sing ; 530
Ane cow of birks into his hand had he,
To keip than weil his face fra midge and fle.

For than war monie fleand up and doun,
Throw kynd of yeir, and hait of that regioun.
Sa lukit he ane lytil by the way,   635
He saw the woundit man, quhair that he lay.
And to him came he rydand, and can fraine,
Quhat ailit him to ly and sairly graine?
The man answered, I have sik sturt,
For beith with theif and rever I am hurt.   640
And yit, suppois I have all the pyne,
The falt is yowris, sir King, and nathing myne.
For, and with yow gude counsal war ay cheif,
Than wald ye stanche weill baith rever and theif.
Have thow with thé, that can weil dance and sing,   645
Thow taks nocht thocht thi realms weip and wring.
With that the King the bob of birks can wave,
The fleis away out of his woundis to have:
And than began the woundit man to grane,
Do nocht sa, Sir, allace! I am slane.   650
How sayis thow, thow tell me? quod the King,
Quhy thow sayis sa, I ferly, of this thing?
And sa said al his men, that stude about,
Thow wald be haill and thay war chasit out.
The sair can say, be him that can us save,   655
Your fule, sir King, hes mair wit than ye have.
And weil I ken, be his phisnomie,
He hes mair wit nor al your cumpanie.
My tung is sweir, my bodie hes na strenth,
Frane at your fule he can tel yow at lenth;   660
I am but deid, and I may speik na mair,
Adew, sir, for I have said: weil mot ye fair.

   Fra this sair man now cummin is the King,
Havand in mynd great murmour and moving;
And in his hart greit havines and thocht,   665
Sa wantonly in vane al thing he wrocht;
And how the cuntrie throw him was misfarne,
Throw yong counsel, and wrocht ay as a barne.

And yit, as he was droupand thus in dule,
Of al and al he ferleit of his fule : 570
Quhat kynde of man this fuil with him sould be ;
And quhat this sair man be this fuil micht se.
And quhat it is the caus, quhairfoir and quhy,
He was wyser than al his cumpany.
Quhan cummin was the King to that citie,
Full fast than for his fule frainit he.
And quhan the King was set doun to his meit,
Unto his fuil gart mak ane semely seit ;
Ane Roundel with ane cleine claith had he,
Neir quhair the King micht him baith heir and se. 580
Than, quod the King a lytil wie, and leuch :
Sir fuil, ye ar lordly set aneuch :
Quhan ye ar fuil, quhat cal thay yow and how,
Sa hamely as ye ar with me now ?
Sir to my name thay cal me fule Fictus, 585
Befoir yow as ye may se me sit thus ;
And of this cuntrie certes am I borne,
With luk, and grace, and fortoun me beforne.
Schir fuill, tell me gif that ye saw this day
Ane woundit man ly granand by the way ? 590
Ye, sir, forsuith sik ane man couth I sie :
And in his wound was monie felloun flie.
Now, quod the King, Sir fuill, to me ye say
Quhy skarrit ye not thay flies al away ?
Thocht ye it was ane deid of charitie 595
In seik mans wound for to leife ane flie ?
Sir, trow me weill, full suith it is I say,
Better was stil thay fleis, than skarrit away ;
For gif sa be the fleis away ye skar ;
Than efter them cums hungriar be far. 600
Thairfoir war better let them be, but dout,
For the full fleis halds the hungrie out.
The hungrie flie, that never had been thair,
Scho souks the mans wound sa wonder sair ;

And quhen the fleis ar ful than byde thay stil, 605
And stops the hungrie beis to come thairtil.
Bot, sir, allace, methink sa do not ye;
Ye ar sa licht and full of vanitie:
And sa weil lufis al new things to persew;
That ilk sessioun ye get ane servant new. 610
Qnhat wil the ane now say unto the uther?
Now steir thy hand, myne awin deir brother;
Win fast be tyme, and be nocht lidder:
For wit thou weil, Hal binks ar ay slidder.
Thairfoir now, quhither wrang it be or richt, 615
Now gadder fast, quhil we have tyme and micht.
Sé na man now to the King eirand speik,
Bot gif we get ane bud; or ellis we sal it breik.
And quhan thay ar ful of sic wrang win,
Thay get thair leif: and hungryar cums in. 620
Sa sharp ar thay, and narrowlie can gadder,
Thay pluck the puir, as thay war powand hadder.
And taks buds fra men baith neir and far;
And ay the last ar than the first far war.
Justice, Crounar, Sarjand, and Justice Clark, 625
Removes the auld, and new men ay thay mark.
Thus fla thay al the puir men belly flaucht;
And fra the puir taks many felloun fraucht,
And steirs them, and wait the tide wil gang,
Syne efter that far hungrier cums than. 630
And thus gait ay the puir folk ar at under:
This world to sink for sin quhat is it wonder?
Thairfoir now, be this exampil we may se,
That ane new servant is lyke ane hungrie fle.
Than, quod the King, quhat say ye to our fule? 635
Suppois that he had bene ane clark at scule?
To God now, quod the King, I make ane vow,
Ye are not sik ane fule as ye set yow.

 Thus wonderit al, the King that sat about,
And of this fule had ferly, dreid, and dout. 640

Thocht he was fule in habit, in al feiris,
Ane wyser speik thay hard never with thair eiris.
Thus ferlyit al thair was, baith he and he,
Quhat manner of ane thing this micht be;
And lyke to ane was nocht into Rome,   645
Yit than his word was full of al wisdome,
For he as fule began guckit and gend,
And ay the wyser man neirar the end.
And thus the King and al his cumpany
Upon this fuil had wonder and ferly.   650

Of the slaying of the man.

SYNE efter this ane gentleman percace
Had slane ane man, al throw his raklesnes.
And to the court he come, and tald this thing
Unto ane man was inward with the King;
And said, sir, lo! I am in the King's grace,   655
That hes ane man slane in my fault, allace!
And will ye gar the King to that consent,
For it I sal yow pay, and content.
This courteour held on this to the King;
And tald him al this tail to the ending.   660
And than the King, for his lufe and instance,
Bad bring the man that happened that mischance.
Unto the King his taill quhen he had tald;
Ful sharplie to this man he could behald:
Ane semelie man of mak sa semit he.   665
To slay that man he thocht ane greit pitie.
And bad him passe quhair he lykit to ga;
And be gude man and efter sla na ma.
Sone efter that, within half a yeir,
Ane uther man he slew withoutin weir.   670

Of the second slayne man.

THAN to the court he cummin is agane,
Unto this man befoir his gold had tane;

And said, sir, I have slane, allace!
Ane uther man, throw misfortune and cace.
And wald ye help me, befoir as ye have done, 675
Ane sowme of silver ye sould have ful sone:
Another sowme I sall give to the King;
Me hartlie to forgive into this thing.
Help me now, for God's owin deid:
Nane uther buit at yow I get remeid. 680
This courteour him answered thus agane:
This deid to do I am uncertane.
Quhen that thow slew bot ane throw raklesnes,
Of that thow micht have gotten forgivenes:
Sa may it nocht, quhen thow hes slane thus twa; 685
Notwithstanding I wil for the ga;
The for to help I sal get sib assay;
And for the do alsmekil as I may.
Unto the King than come this courteour,
And lukit weil baith to his tyme and hour: 690
He lukit quhan the King was blyth and glad,
And nocht quhen he was heavie nor sad.
Ful lawlie set he doun upon his kne,
Lo, sir, he said, ane thing of greit pitie!
The man that ye forgave, syne half ane yeir, 695
Another man now hes he slane but weir.
Ane certaine sowme of gold thus sal ye get,
And ye wald all your crabitnes foryet.
He wepes, and he sichs now sa sair,
That he sik misse will efter do na mair: 700
In all your realme thair is na wichter man;
Greit pitie is it for to tyne him than.
Ye may him have, and of his gold and geir,
He will stand yow in steid in tyme of weir.
Suppois he hes slane twa, better it is than ye 705
Have twa men slane, then thus for to sla thrie.
Thairfoir heir I beseik yow in this cace
That ye wald tak him in your gudelie grace.

The King bad than bring him to his presence,
And him forgave all fault and offence: 710
And bad him ga, and do sik misse na mair;
Thus tuke this man his leif and hame can fair.
Syne efterward this man that we of reid
The thrid man hes he slane yit indeid.

Of the thride slayne man.

THAN to the court agane maid his repair, 715
Sik grace to get agane as he did air.
Sa come hee to the courteour to tell,
His fortoun and his cace how it befell.
This courteour to speik wald not spair,
For yow forsuith, sir, dar I speik na mair: 720
Sa oft and oft ye have done sik mischeif;
I dar not speik it to the King for greif.
Now be my saul, and sa mot I do weill,
Is na remeid, als far as I can feill,
Or quhither that ye sal live the land, allace, 725
Or put yow yit into the King's grace.
This courteour agane unto the King
Now cummin is, and tald hail this thing;
And how the man, befoir the twa had slane,
The thrid man thus hes he slane agane. 730
With that the King, quhen that he hard the taill,
In grit greif than wox he wan and pail.
And sweith he said, bring him now heir to me;
Sal neyther gold nor gude let him to die.
Get he my pitie, than God put me out of mynde; 735
And he wald gif me all the Golden Inde.
Syne gart he bring to him the samyn man,
Set doun to judge, to heid or to hang.
This man, that was sa cumbred of this cace,
On kneis fel, and askit the Kingis grace: 740

The King plainly all grace can him deny;
And tald to him the caus and ressoun quhy.
With that upon ane lytil bony stule
Sat Fictus, that was the Kings fule,
And said, now an ye gar not heid or hang 745
This man, for them that he slew, it war wrang.
The first man, weil I grant, he slew;
The uther twa in faith them slew yow.
Had thou him puneist, quhan he slew the first,
The uther twa had bene levand, I wist: 750
Thairfoir, allace, this tail, sir, is over trew,
For, in gude faith, the last twa men ye slew.
The Psalmes, sayis David war and wyse;
Blist mot thay be that keips law and justice:
Thairfoir I wald that ye sould not presume 755
Na to have count, upon the day of Dome,
For mans body thair to give ane yeild,
Quhome to ye sould be sickar speir and sheild,
Of all the realme, quhom of ye beir the croun,
Of lawit and leirit; riche, pure; up and doun; 760
The quhilk, and thay be slane with mans hand,
Ane count thairof ye sall gif, I warrand;
Lesse that it be throw sum grit negligence,
Quhairin his mercy or in his defence.
And on the day of Dome, be Sanct Paull, 765
The Bishops mon ay answer for the saull;
Gif it be lost, for fault of priest or preiching,
Of the richt treuth it haif na chesing;
In sa far as the saull is forthy
Far worthier is than the blait body; 770
Many Bishops in ilk realme wee see:
And bot ane King into ane realme to be.
Thus hes the saull mair work and cure
Than the body, that is of na valure.
By this was said, the King sayis, wa is mee! 775
For I am fule of fules [I] weill see.

I se weill I have lytil part of scule,
That thus sould be informit with ane fule :
I se weil be this taill this fule can tel
That I had greatly neid of wyse counsell. 780
To send for all my Lords I consent ;
I desyre this to be in Parliament.
And it be trew my fule hes said me heir,
I sal weil reward him withouttin weir :
And be it fals, and ful of fantasy, 785
Ane fule he is, and fule him hald sal I.
And, throw this fule, this man-slayer did get
Unto the Parliament perfyte respet.
And efter quhan thir Lords al can cum
Unto this Parliament, baith al and sum, 790
Be al the thrie Estaits it was found,
Considerand al the mater, crop and ground,
This Fictus, that was callit the fule,
Was wyse in word, thocht he was clark in scule.
The King bad al the thrie Estaits that thay 795
Sould sit doun al, and sic a ganand way,
Quhat men in hous war meit with him to dwell,
Of wisdome for to gif him counsel ;
And for to mak, be his Estaits thrie,
Into this realme concordant unitie. 800
And quhen that al this deid was dewlie done,
The King sweir, be his sceptour and his croun,
That he sould never gif mercie to nane.
That slauchter in his realme committit than,
Aganis his will, bot throw his negligence, 805
Or ellis that it be fund in his defence.
And sik ane rewll made he into his land,
That luck and grace in it was ay growand.
And than this nobill King all lichtnes left ;
All bot ane thing that was not fra him reft. 810
The quhilk for ill toungs long had bene :
Ane still strangenes betwixt him and his Queene.

He beddit nocht right oft, nor lay hir by,
Bot throw lichtnes did lig in lamenry.
    AS happenit throw cace, into the toun,   815
Into ane burges innis he maid him boun ;
Ane lytill wie before the feist of Yule,
In cumpanie bot fyvesum and his fule.
This burges had ane dochter to him deir,
Ane bonie wench she was withoutin weir :   820
The King on hir he casts his lustie eine,
And with hir faine wald in ane bed haif bene.
Hee wist full weill that nane had hee
That was sa subtill as Fictus was, and slee ;
He callit him, and privilie can say,   825
Sic fantesie hes put me in effray,
I am sa ful of lust and fantesy
With this madyn, on benk that sits me by,
For gold, for gude ; for wage or yit for wed ;
This nicht I wald have hir to my bed.   830
Than, quod the fuill, I understand yow weill ;
I tak on hand to do it everie deill.
Sit still now, Sir, wil ye let me allane ;
Be mee this eirand sall be undertane.
Sone efter, quhan thay war at sport and play,   835
The fule came to this bonie prettie may ;
And said : Madyn, wist ye of the degrie
How pleasant it is to God virginitie ?
Tak exampill S. Margaret and Katrine ;
And monie uther sants that are sine :   840
In Hevins blesse that hes sik joy and grie,
With crown on heid, for thair virginitie.
I wait, for all the gold into this toun,
Of madynheid ye wald not tyne the croun.
Bot ay the King went he had besie bene   845
Of the mater that was thir twa betwene :
And to the virgine yong thus spak the King,
Quhat my fule sayis a trow be na lesing.

Sir, quod sho, his saw was suffisand;
And as he sayis I sall do, God willand. 850
Be that the Kings Stewart cummin is
To have the King to his supper, I wis;
The King said to his fule in privatie:
Of the eirand, Fictus, how sal it be?
Now hard yow not hirself consent thairto, 855
That as I said to yow sho hecht to do?
Bot ane thing have I hecht sickerly
That nane sal cum about hir, Sir, bot I.
The virgine is bot yong, and thinkis shame;
And is full laith to cum in ane ill name. 860
And quhan the Kings supper was at end,
Fictus the fule unto the Queene can wend;
And to hir said, do my counsel, Madame,
To yow it sal be nouther sin nor shame.
A burges dochter, to her father deir, 865
This nicht the King thinks to have but weir,
And tald her all the cace, and manner how
Hir for to have he gart the King weil trow;
Bot that, be God, that with his blude us bocht,
With hir to gar him sin was never my thocht. 870
The King commands to his chief Chalmerlane,
Quhan ever I cum with hir I be in tane;
And in his bed sal prively in creip,
Quhil that the King sal cum thair and sleip;
And privelie thus, be the day agane, 875
Away with me the madyn sal be tane.
Thairfoir, madame, for God, be not agast,
Abovt your heid your cloke clenlie cast:
Quhairfoir sould ye dout or be a-drad?
Is nane bot ye sould bruik the King's bed. 880
The warst may fall, suppose it wittin war,
Methocht he hang yow wil he never skar.
And thus is my counsel, Madame, ye do.
In faith, quod sho, and I consent thairto.

All thus and thus, befoir as ye have hard. 885
The Queene is brocht unto the King's bed;
The quhilk all nicht in uthers arms lay;
Quhat man to tel of al thair sport and play?
The King thocht never nicht to him so short;
Sa lykit he that nichtis play and sport. 890
And on the morne, a lytil befoir day,
The fule came in and tuke the Queene away.
And thus and thus, efter nichts thrie,
With his awin Queene grit gaming had and glie;
And west he wend that it had bene but weir 895
That with him lay the burges dochter deir;
Quhome throw he had sik joy and sik plesance,
Quhilk maid him ay the fule for to avance.
Sa was the King sa amorat of his fule,
Besyde himself ay sat upon a stule. 900
Was never yet mair joy and plesance sene
Than the King hes in bed with his awin Queene.
And that was na grit ferly to befal,
For sho was fair, and gude, and yong withal.
And thus the fule, quhen he persaving had 905
How that the King sa joyful was and glade,
Unto the King he came in privitie,
And said, now, sir, ane thing that ye tel me;
Quhairfoir it is the cace, fane wit wald I
Quhy that ye have in yow sik fantasy 910
To ly with wemen, and of law degrie,
Aganis your Queenes wil and majestie,
Considerand weil that sho is fair and gude,
With ilkane uther bewtie to conclude?
Or quhy at hir ye have al this despyte, 915
And quhy ye find in uthers sik delyte?
Or quhat plesance ye had thir nichts thrie,
With your awin Queen in bed than mair to be?
The King answerid and said, now sickarly
I cannot tel the ressoun, caus, nor quhy, 920

Fictus, my fule, with the na mair to flyte,
Bot wantonlie I followe my appetyte.
And quhan that my delyte is upon uther,
Than mony folk wil cum, and with me fludder;
And sum wil tel il tailes of the Queene, 925
The quhilk be hir war never hard nor sene.
And that I do thay say al weil is done.
Thus fals clatterars puts me out of tone:
And thus, becaus I am licht of feirs,
And heir evil tailes, and lichtly lend my eiris. 930
And thus of hir I have na appetyte,
And of al others ay have I grit delyte.
Sir, quod the fule, wil ye not consent
Thir thrie nichts that ye war weil content?
Ye, that I grant, be God that is of micht, 935
Had never nane mair plesance on the nicht.
God, quod the King, send my fortoun had bene
Sen sho I had thir nichts thrie war Queene!
Quhat wil ye gif me, than speiks the fule,
Suppose I be na cunning clark in scule, 940
Within thrie dayes to mak it weil sene,
With Goddis law for to mak hir your Queene?
And thair to do sal na man say agane;
And do I not my heid sal be the pane.
Than, quod the King, thairto I hald my hand, 945
Thow sal have gude gold, lordships, and land.
Or cast fra the thy cote, and be thow wyse,
Ane bishoprik sal be thy benefyse.
Than, quod the fule, without feinyeing or fabil,
Hald up your hand to hald this firme and stabil. 950
The King thairto sware oft and oft,
And thair he has his hand haldin on loft.
And now, quod the fule, it fallis to na King
To brek his vow, or yit his oblissing:
And it that I have hecht thus sone sal be; 955
Scho is your Queene ye had thir nichts thrie.

That, quod the King, be him that deid on rude,
Sir fule, I trow ye may not mak that gude.
Sir, I pray yow be not evil payit nor wraith,
Efter sa strait ane oblessing and aith. 960
And gif that she plesit yow thir nichts thrie;
Fra hyneforth now quhairfoir may not sa be?
Richt now ye wald have had hir to your wyfe;
And thairin now with me ye mak ane stryfe.
Quhat, quod the King, be him that was borne in Yule, 965
Thou art ane auld scollar at the scule.
I farly quhair sik sophine thou hes fund,
That with my awin band thou hes me bund.
Notwithstanding I am hartly content,
To my awin Queene I wil hartly consent: 970
And mair attour, I sweir the be the hevin,
I sal hir never displeis for od nor evin.
With thy that she may prief that it was sho,
Thir nichts thrie with quhom I had ado.
And with that word foroutin mair carping, 975
Unto the Queenes chalmer come the King,
And simply to hir presence can persew,
And tempit hir with tokens gude and trew;
And sickarly he fand that it was sho,
With quhome thay nichts thrie he had ado, 980
Than joyful was he in his hartis splene,
Of the plesance he had with his awin Queene.
Than on his kneis he askit forgivenes
For his licht laytes and his wantones:
And sho forgave him meiklie this ful tyte 985
That he had done throw lichtnes of delyte;
For weil sho saw that al was fantesy
That he usit, and richt greit foly.
And thus the King and Queene into this cace
Thankit thair God for thair weilfair and grace. 990

And syne this fule thay thankit of al,
That caused sik concord amang them fal.
And off his coate thay tirlit be the croun,
And on him kest ane syde clarkly goun;
And quhen this syde goun on him micht be,   996
Ane cunning clark and wyse than semit he.
Syne efter sone ane Bishop thair was deid,
Ful sone was he maid Bishop in his steid.
And to the King and Queene he was ful leif;
And [of] thair inwart counsell ay maist cheif.   1000
And God send sik examples ay wer sene
To ilkane King that luifit nocht his Queene!
God gif us grace and space on eird to spend!
Thus of my tail now cummin is the end.
And than spak all the fallowship thus syne,   1005
God quyte yow, sir, your tail and sant Martyne.
Sir Williame than sayis now fallis me
To tel ane tail; thoch I be of yow thrie
The febillest, and leist of literature;
Yit than, with all my diligence and cure,   1010
To tell ane taill now sik ane as I have:
Of me methink you sould na uther crave.

The thrid taill, tald be Maister Williame.

A KING thair is, and ever mair will be,
Thairfoir the KING of kings him call we.
Thus he had a man, as hes mony   1015
Into this land, als riche as uther ony.
This man, that we of speik, had freinds thrie;
And lufit them nocht in ane degrie.
The first freind, quhil he was laid in delf,
He lufit ay far better than himself: 1020
The nixt freind that alsweil luifit he,
And he himself luifit in al degrie:

The thrid freind he luifit this and swa
In na degrie like to the tother twa;
Suppois he was ane freind to him in name, 1025
To him as freind yit wald he never clame.
The tother twa his freindis war indeid
As he thocht quhen that he had onie neid.
Sa fell it on ane day sone efter than
This [King] he did send about this rich man; 1030
And sent him to his officer but weir,
Thus but delay befoir him to compeir.
And with him count and give reckning of all
He had of him al tyme baith grit and smal.
With that this officer past on gude speid, 1035
And summond this riche man we of reid;
And al the cace to him he can record,
That he in haist sould cum to his awin Lord.
This rich man be he had hard this tail
Ful sad in mynd he wox baith wan and pail. 1040
And to himself he said, sickand ful sair,
Allace how now! this is ane haisty fair!
And I cum thair, my tail it wil be taggit;
For I am red that my count be ovir raggit.
Quhat sal I do, now may I say allace: 1045
A cumbred man I am into this cace.
I have na uther help, nor yit supplie,
Bot I wil pas to my freinds thrie:
Twa of them I luifit ay sa weil,
But ony fault thair freindship wil I feil. 1050
The thrid freind I leit lichtly of ay;
Quhat may he do to me bot say me nay?
Now wil I pas to them, and preif them now,
And tel them al the caus, and maner how.

To the first friend.

THVS came he to his freind that he 1055
Lufit better than himself in al degrie.

And said: lo! friend, my hart thow ever had;
And now, allace, I am ful straitly stad.
To me the King his officer hes send;
For he wil that my count to him be kend: 1060
And I am laith, allane, to him to ga,
Without [with] me ane freind thair be or twa.
Thairfoir I pray yow that ye tel me now
In this mater quhat is the best ado?
And thus answered this freind agane, that he 1065
Over al this world lufit as *A per C*,
The devill of hell, he said, now mot me hing,
And I compeir befoir that crabit King!
He is sa ful of justice, richt, and ressoun,
I lufe him not in ocht that will be chessoun. 1070
He lufis not na riches, be the Rude,
Nor hilenes in hart, nor evil won gude.
Than evil won gude to gar men gif agane
Thair may be na war use now in ane.
Agane him can I get na gude defence; 1075
Sa just he is, and stark in his conscience.
And al things in this warld that I call richt,
It is nocht worth an eg into his sicht:
And it that is my lyking and my eis
To him alway will neither play nor pleis: 1080
And that to me is baith joy and gloir,
As fantasys judgit him befoir.
And thus he is aganis me ay and ever;
And weill I wait thairfoir he lufit me never.
He hes na lyking, lufe, nor lust of me, 1085
Na I to him, quhill the day I die.
Quhairto thairof sould [I] mak ony mair?
I cum nocht to the King, I the declair.
Fra tyme that thow art under now areist,
Of the, in faith, I have but lytle feist. 1090
Be me, I trow, thow art but lytill meind;
Pas on thy way and seik another freind.

Now is this man sair murnand in his mynde,
Sayand, allace, my freind is over unkynde!
Quhome I wend was support and supplie,   1095
And now, allace, the contrair now I sie!
Away he wend, sayand in wordis wylde,
I grant be God that I am all begylde.

The secound friend.

VNTO this tother friend cummin is this man,
That as himselfe befoir he lufit than.   1100
And said, lo! freind, the King hes send for me
His officer: and biddis that I be
At him in haist; and cum sone to his call:
And to him mak my count of grit and small,
That I of him in all my dayis had.   1105
And I sie richt I am straitlie stad!
Now, as my freind I hidder come to the
Quhome as myselfe I lufe in al degre.
For quhen I am in stryfe, or yit in sturt,
Into my hart methink thow sould be hurt.   1110
Thairfoir I pray that thow wald underta
With me unto yon king that thow wald ga.
This freind answered, and said to him agane,
I am displeisit, and ill payit of thy pane;
Bot I am nocht redie in onie thing,   1115
With thé for to compeir befoir that King.
Thoch he hes send for the his officer,
I may not ga with thé: quhat wil thou mair?
Sa with the I bid nocht for to lane;
I am ful red that I cum never agane.   1120
Quha sal me mend, and of my bail me beit,
To tak the sower and for to leif the sweit?
Quhat I have heir daylie in faith I feill;
And that quhat I sall have I weit not weill.
Thairfoir this tail is trew into al tyde,   1125
Quhair ane feiris [the bet] the langer sould he byde.

Thairfoir, methink that I sould be to sweir
Befoir yon King with yow for to appeir.
Bot a thing is to say in termes short,
With yow my friend I wil ga to the port: 1130
Trust weil of me na mair of myne ye get,
Fra ye be anis in at the kingis yet.
And thus shortly, with yow for to conclude,
Mair nor is said of me ye get na gude.
With that the man that thus charged his freind, 1135
He said, allace! I may na longer leind!
Sen I my twa best freinds couth assay:
I can nocht get a freind yit to my pay,
That dar now tak in hand, for onie thing,
With me for to compeir befoir yon king. 1140
Quhasaever vennome or poisoun taist,
That be the hand in quhom thair traist is maist.
Me to begyle quha hes mair craft and gin,
Than thay in quhome my traist ay maist is in?
Quhat ferly now with nane thoch I be meind, 1145
Sen thus falsly now failys me my freind?
Now weil I se, and that I underta,
Than feinyeit freind better is open fa.
Als suith it is as ships saillis over watters,
And weil I wait al is not gold that glitters. 1150
Now is over lait to preif my freind indeid,
Quhan that I have sik mister and sik neid:
Better had bene be tyme I had overtane,
To preif my freind, quhen mister had I nane.
Allace, quhat sal I say? quhat sal I do? 1155
I have na ma freinds for to cum to,
Bot ane the quhilk is callit my thrid freind;
With him I trow I will be lytil meind.
To ga to him I wait bot wind in waist,
For in him I have lytil trouth or traist. 1160
Becaus to him I was sa oft unkinde:
And as my freind he was not in my mynde;

Bot helelie and lichtlie of him leit,
And now to him thus mon I ga and greit,
How sould I mourne, or mak my mane him to? 1165
Befoir with him I had sa lytil ado.
Suppois to me he was ane freind in name,
Yit than as a freind to him wald I never clame,
Of him I had ful lytil joy or feist;
Of al my freinds in faith I lufit him leist. 1170
Quhat ferly is I be not with him meind;
I held him nocht bot for a quarter freind.

To the thrid freind.

NOW cummin is the man that we of reid
Unto this thrid freind, quhen he had neid,
And tald him the maner and the cace, 1175
How on him laid an officer his mace,
And summond him, and bad he sould compeir
Befoir the King, and gif ane count perqueir;
And to him mak ane sharp count of al
He had into his lyfe, baith grit and smal. 1180
And thus answered his freind to him agane:
Of thé in faith, gude freind, I am ful fane.
Of me altyme thow gave but lytil tail;
Na of me wald have dant nor dail.
And thow had to me done one thing, 1185
Nocht was with hart, bot vane gloir and hething.
With uther freinds thou was sa weill ay wount,
To me thow had ful lytil clame or count.
To thé thow thocht I was not wort ane prene,
And that I am ful rade on the will besene. 1190
And yit the lytil kyndnes that thow
To me hes had weil sal I quyte it now.
For with thé sal I ga unto the King,
And for the speik, and plie intil al thing.
Quhairever thow ga, with me thow sall be meind, 1195
And ever halden for my tender freind.

The King he lufis me weil, I wait,
Bot ever, allace, to me thow cum ouer lait;
And thow my counsal wrocht had in al thing,
Ful welcum had thou bene ay to that King. 1200
Betwixt us twa wit he of unkyndnes,
Sone wil thow feil he wil the lufe the les:
Wit he betwixt us twa be onie lufe,
He wil be richt weil payit and the apprufe:
And he to me wit thow maid ony falt, 1205
To thé that wil be ful sowre and salt.
And than weil sal thou find, as thou lufit me,
In al maner of way sa sal he thé.
Quhat is thair mair of this mater to meine?
With thé befoir the King I sal be sene. 1210
Quhairever thou ga, withoutin ony blame,
As tender freind to the I sal ay clame;
Without offence to be thy defendar,
And ay trewly to be thy protectour.
Befoir quhat judge thou appeir up or doun, 1215
Thé to defend I sal be reddie boun.
And quhither I cum agane heir ever or never
Fra thé thus sal I never mair dissever.
Thoch he the bind and cast the in a cart,
To heid or hang, fra the I sal nocht part. 1220
Quhat wil thou mair that I may say the til?
I am reddie; cum on quhanever thou wil.
Allace! allace! than sayis this riche man,
Over few I find are in this warld that can
Cheis ay the best of thir friends thrie, 1225
Quhill that the tyme be gane that they sould be.
Thow leifs nocht sin quhill sin hes left the;
And than quhan that thou seis that thow man de:
Than is ouer lait, allace! havand sik let,
Quhan deithis cart will stand befoir thé yet. 1230
Allace, send ilkane man wald be sa kynde
To have this latter freind into his mynde!

And nocht traist in this uther freinds twa,
With him befoir the King that wil nocht ga!

Quha be thir thrie freinds.

GVDE folk, I wald into this warld that ye 1235
Sould understand quhilk ar thir freinds thre;
Quha is the King; quha is this officer;
And quha this riche man is. I will declair.
The King is God, that is of michts maist,
The Father, Sone, and eik the haly Gaist, 1240
In ane Godheid, and yit in persones thre,
Thairfoir the King of kings him call we.
This officer but dout is callit Deid;
Is nane his power agane may repleid:
Is nane sa wicht, na wyse, na of sic wit, 1245
Agane his summond suithly that may sit.
Suppose thay be als wicht as ony wall,
Thow man ga with him to his Lords hall.
Is na wisdome, riches, na yet science,
Aganis his officer may mak defence: 1250
Is neyther castell, torret, not yet tour,
May scar him anis the moment of ane hour.
His straik it is sa sharpe it will not stint,
Is nane in eird that may indure his dint;
He is sa trew in his office, and lele, 1255
Is na praktik agane him to appele.
Gold, nor gude, corn, cattell, nor yit ky,
This officer with bud may nocht overby.
This riche man is baith thow and he,
And al that in the warld is that mon die. 1260
And als sone as the deid till us will cum,
Then speik we to our freinds all and sum.

Quhat is menit be the first freind.

THE first friend is bot gude penny and pelfe,
That mony man lufis better than himselfe.

And quhan to me or the cumis our deid,   1265
Our riches than will stand us in na steid:
To pairt fra it suppose we graine and greit,
It sayis fairweil! agane we will never meit!
Thus have we ever sa mekill gold and gude,
With us nane may we turs, suppose we wod.   1270
The mair golde and gude that ever we have,
The mair count thairof this King will crave.
And thus the day of deid, quhan we mon die,
Fra us away full fast all riches will flie.
Thus hald I man unwyse, I underta,   1275
That halds ane for his friend, and is his fa.
Thir thre ar ay haldin for fais evill,
Our awne flesche, the warld, and the devill.
And thus thy freind, sa mekil of the mais,
Is countit ane of thy maist felloun fais;   1280
And now with thé he will nocht ane fute
Befoir this King, for the to count or mute,
This may thow sie this warlds wit forthy
Befoir this King is bot great fantasy.

Quha is menit be the secound freind.

THIS secund freind, lat se, quhome will we call   1285
Bot wyfe and barne, and uther freindis all?
That thus answeres, and sayis in termes schort,
We will nocht ga with thé bot to the port:
That is to say unto the Kingis yet;
With the farder to ga is nocht our det.   1290
Quhilk is the yet, that we call now the port?
Nocht but our graif to pas in, as a mort.
And than with us unto that yet will cum
Baith wyfe and bairnes, and freinds al and sum:
And thair on me and thé lang will thay greit,   1295
Into this world agane or ever we meit.

In at the yet with thé now quha will ga,
That I have tald heir of thy freinds twa?
Riches nor gude; wyfe, barne, nor freind,
Of thir foirsaid with the will never leind. 1300
And quhan that thow art laid into thy hole,
Thy heid will be na hyer than thy sole.
And than quhair is thy cod, courche or cap,
Baith goun and hude had wont thé for to hap?
Nocht bot ane sheit is on thy body bair; 1305
And as thow hes done heir, sa finds thow thair.

Quhat is menit be the thrid freind.

THIS thrid freind quhome wil we cal, let sie;
Nocht ellis bot Almosdeid and charitie.
The quhilk freind answered with words sweit:
Of me as freind suppose thou lytle leit, 1310
Yit, for the lytle quantance that we had,
Sen that I se the in sturt sa straightly stad,
Quhairever thow ga, in eird or art,
With the, my freind, yet sall I never part.
Quhairever thow ga, suppose a thousand shore thé, 1315
Even I thy Almosdeid sall ga befoir the.
For as thow seis watter dois slokkin fyre,
Sa do I Almosdeid the Judges ire.
Thairfoir, gude folkes, be exampil we se
That there is nane thus of thy freinds thre, 1320
To ony man that may do gude, bot ane;
Almosdeid that it be seindle tane.
Into this warld of it we lat lichtly,
Throw fleshely lust fulfillit with folly;
Quhill all our tyme in fantasy be tint, 1325
And than to mend we may do nocht bot minte.
It for to do we have na tyme, nor grace,
Into this eird quhill we have tyme and space.

Than cumis deid have done! do fort thy det!
Cum on away; the cart is at the yet.   1330
Than we will say, with mony woful wis,
Allace! allace! be tyme had I wittin this!
I sould have done pennance, fast, and pray;
And delt my guds in almis deids alway.
Thairfoir my counsall is that we mend,   1335
And lippin nocht all to the latter end.
And syne, to keip us fra the sinnes sevin,
That we may win the hie blys of hevin:
And thus out of this warld that we may win
But shame, or det, or deidly sin.   1340

And than speiks the tother twa full tyte,
This gude tale, Sir, I trow God will you quyte.

Finis.

Tayis Bank.

TWYSBANK, one of the popular airs mentioned in "Colkelbie's Sow," has been conjectured[1] to be the appropriate tune of the following beautiful song, which owes its preservation to George Bannatyne, in whose "ballat-buik," preserved in the Library of the Faculty of Advocates at Edinburgh, it occurs.[2] Although an affected quaintness has somewhat disfigured it by redundance of alliteration, yet, as a descriptive poem, it is possessed of considerable merit; and as few, if any, of the Scotish songs, now extant are of equal antiquity, it is remarkable that "Tayis Bank" should have escaped the notice of Ritson and other collectors of our lyric poetry. Not many years since, however, a copy of it appeared in the "British Bibliographer,"[3] to which work it was transmitted by the late Henry Weber, whose services in publishing, with great fidelity and care, several of the early Metrical Romances in our vernacular tongue, have not been duly appreciated.

From the context of this poem, says Mr. Weber, "it appears to have been composed on a lady of the noble family of Perth, named Margaret, and it may be conjectured with almost more than probability that the subject of the poem was Margaret, eldest daughter of Sir John Drummond, lord of that ilk, and Stobhall, who is stated to have been contracted to King James IV., and had a daughter by him, afterwards married to Alexander, Earl of Huntley." Should this supposition respecting the lady

---

[1] Leyden, Complaynt of Scotland, Introd. p. 283.
[2] Fol. 229.
[3] Vol. iv. p. 186.

be deemed well founded, the reader may feel some interest in the description contained in the quotation below.[1] The poem itself may unquestionably be attributed to the reign of our gallant monarch James IV.

Tayis Bank.

QUHEN Tayis bank wes blumyt brycht,
    With blosvmes blycht and bred,
Be that riuer that ran doun rycht,
    Vndir the ryss I red;
The merle melit with all hir mycht   5
And mirth in mornyng maid,
Throw solace, sound, and semely sicht,
    Alswth a sang I said.

---

[1] "Margaret Drummond, eldest daughter of John Lord Drummond, was a lady of rare perfections and singular beautie. With her the young King James the 4th was [so] deeply enamoured, that without acquainting his nobles or Council, he was affianced to her in order to have made her his Queen. But so soon as his intentions were discovered, all possible obstructions were made both by the nobility, who designed an allyance w^t a daughter of England, as a mean to procure peace betwixt the nations, and by the clergie, who declared against the lawfulness of the marriage, because they were within the degrees of consanguinity forbidden by the Canon Law. Nevertheless, the King, under promise, gott her with child, which proved a daughter [in the year 1497], and was called Lady Margaret Stewart; but he was so much touched in conscience for the engagement he had made to the young lady, that, notwithstanding the weakness of the Royal family, he rejected all propositions of marriage so long as she lived: for he was crowned in the year 1488, at the age of sixteen, and did not marry untill the year 1502, when he was near thirty, and about a year after her death, which was effected not without suspition of poison; for the common tradition goes, that a potion was provided in a breakfast to dispatch her for liberating the King from his promise, that he might match with England; but so it happened that she called two of

Vndir that bank, quhair bliss had bene,
    I bownit me to abyde;   10
Ane holene, hevinly hewit grene,
    Rycht heyndly did me hyd;
The sone schyne our the schawis schene
    Full semely me besyd;
In bed of blumes bricht besene   15
    A sleip cowth me ourslyd

About all blumet wes my bour
    With blosummes broun and blew,
O^rfret with mony fair fresch flour,
    Helsum of hevinly hew;   20
With schakeris of the schene dew schour
    Schynnyng my courtenis schew,
Arrayit with a rich vardour
    Of natouris werkis new.

Rasing the birdis fra thair rest   25
    The reid sone raiss with rawis;
The lark sang lowd, quhill lycht mycht lest,
    A lay of luvis lawis;
The nythingall woik of hir nest
    Singing the day vpdawis;   30
The mirthfull maveiss merriest
    Schill schowttit throw the schawis.

---

her sisters, then with her, Lady Flemyng and a younger [sister] Sybilla, a maid, whereby it fell out all the three were destroyed with the force of the poyson. They ly buried in a curious vault, covered with three fair blue marble stones joined closs together, about the middle of the quyre of the Cathedrall church of Dumblane: for about this time the buriall place for the family of Drummond at Innerpaffray was not yet built. The monument which contains the ashes of these three lady's stands intire to this day, and confirms the credit of this sad story."—*History of the Family of Drummond* [by William, Viscount of Strathallan], 1681. MS. folio. 188. Drumm. Castle.

All flouris grew that firth within,
    That man cowth haif in mynd ;
And in that flud all fische with fyn,   35
    That creat wer be kynd :
Vndir the rise the ra dyd ryn,
    Our ron, our rute, our rynd,
The dvn deir danfit with a dyn,
    And herdis of hairt and hynd.   40

Wod winter with his wallowand wynd,
    But weir, away wes went :
Brasit about with wyld wodbynd
    Wer bewis on the bent :
Allone vnder the lusty lynd,   45
    I saw ane lusum lent,
That farely war so fare to fynd,
    Vndir the firmament.

Scho wes the lustiest on lyve,
    Allone lent on a land,   50
And farest figour, be sct. Syve,
    That evir in firth I fand.
Hir cumly cullour to discryve
    I dar nocht tak on hand ;
Moir womanly borne of a wyfe   55
    Wes neuer, I dar warrand.

To creatur that wes in cair,
    Or cauld of crewelty,
A blicht blenk of hir vesage bair
    Of baill his bute mycht be ;   60
Hir hyd, hir hew, hir hevinly hair
    Mycht havy hairtis vphie ;
So angelik vnder the air
    Neuir wicht I saw with e'.

The blosummes that wer blycht and
    brycht
By hir wer blacht and blew;
Scho gladit all the foull of flicht
    That in the forrest flew;
Scho mycht haif comfort king or knycht
    That ever in cuntre I knew
As waill, and well of wardly wicht
    In womanly vertew.

Hir cullour cleir, hir countinance,
    Hir cumly cristall ene,
Hir portratour of most plesance
    All pictour did prevene.
Off every vertew to avance
    Quhen ladeis prasit bene,
Rychtest in my remembrance
    That rose is rutit grene.

This myld meik mensuet Mergrite,
    This perle polist most quhyt,
Dame Natouris deir dochter discreit,
    The dyamant of delyt:
Never formit wes to found on feit
    Ane figour more perfyte,
Nor non on mold that did hir meit,
    Mycht mend hir wirth a myte.

This myrthfull maid to meit I ment,
    And merkit furth on mold;
Bot sone within a wane scho went,
    Most hevinly to behold;
The bricht sone with his bemys blent
    Vpoun the bertis bold,
Farest vnder the firmament
    That formit wes on fold.

As paradyce that place but peir
    Wes plesant to my sicht;
Of forrest, and of fresch reveir,
    Of firth, and fowll of flicht,   100
Of birdis, bath on bonk and breir,
    With blumes breckand bricht,
As hevin in to this erd doun heir,
    Hertis to hald on hicht.

So went this womanly away   105
    Amang thir woddis wyd,
And I to heir thir birdis gay
    Did in a bonk abyd;
Quhair ron and ryss raiss in aray
    Endlang the reuer syd: 110
This hapnit me in a tyme in May
    In till a morning tyd.

The reuer throw the ryse cowth rowt
    And roseris raiss on raw;
The schene birdis full schill cowth schowt 115
    Into that semly schaw:
Joy wes within and joy without
    Vnder that vnlenkest waw,
Quhair Tay ran down with stremis stout
    Full strecht vnder Stobschaw.   120

Finis.

The Epistill of the Hermeit of Alareit to the Gray Freirs.

THIS satirical poem has been preserved by Knox in the "History of the Reformation," where, in reference to the contempt into which the Grey Friars had fallen in consequence of their depraved conduct, he says, "Not only did the learnit espye and detect their abominable hypocrisy, bot also men in quhom nane sick graces nor giftis were thocht to have been, began plainlie to point the same furth to the people, as this ryme, made by Alexander, Earl of Glencairne, yet alive, can witness."

Alexander Cunningham, Earl of Glencairn, early distinguished himself in promoting a reformation from the errors of Popery, and he continued a firm and zealous supporter of the Protestant faith.

Alareit, or Laureit, is evidently the chapel built in honour of "our Lady of Loretto" in the village of Musselburgh, where troops of young men and women went to pilgrimage; but, there is reason to suspect, for other purposes than those of penance or religion.

Ane Epistill directed fra the halie Hermeit of Alareit, to his brethren the Gray Freirs.

 THOMAS, hermeit in Lareit,
   Sanct Francis brother do hartilie greit;
   Beseikand you with gud intent
   To be wakryif and diligent.
Thir Lutheranis, rissen of new,   5
Our Ordour daylie dois persew:

They snaikis dois set thair haill intent
To reid the Inglische New Testament;
And sayis we have thame clein decevit,
Thairfore in haist they mon be stoppit. 10
Our Stait hypocrisie they prysse,
And us blasphemis on this wyse:
Sayand, That we are heretyckis,
And false loud lying mastis tykis;
Cumerars and quellars of Christis kirk, 15
Sweir swyngeours that will not wirk,
But idillie our leving wynnis,
Devoiring woilfis into scheipis skynnis;
Huirkland with huidis into our neck,
With Judas mynd to jouk and beck; 20
Seikand Christis pepill to devoir,
The doun-thringers of Christis gloir;
Professours of hypocrisie,
And Doctouris in idolatrie:
Stout fischeiris with the Feindis net, 25
The upclosers of Hevins yet;
Cankcart corruptors of the creid,
Humlock sawers among gud seid;
To trow in trators, that men do tyist,
The hie way kennand them fra Christ; 30
Monsters with the Beistis mark,
Dogges that nevir stintis to bark;
Kirkmen that ar to Christ unkend,
A sect that Satanis self hes send;
Lourkand in hoils, lyik trator toddis, 35
Manteiners of idollis and fals goddis;
Fantastik fuillis, and fenzeit fleicheors,
To turn fra treuth the verray teichers:
For to declair thair haill sentence,
Wald mekill cumber their conscience. 40
To say your fayth it is sa stark,
Your cord and lousie cote and sark;

Your[1] lippin may bring you to salvatioun,
And quyte excludis Chrystis passioun,—
I dreid this doctrine, and it last,
Sall outher gar us wirk or fast:
Thairfoir with speid we mene provyde,
And not our profite overslyde.
I schaip myself, within schort quhill,
To curs our Ladie in Argylle,
And thair on craftie wayis to wirk,
Till that we biggit have ane kirk;
Syne miracles mak be your advyce.
The ketterells, thocht thai had bot lyce,
The twa parte to us they will bring.
Bot ordourlie to dress this thing,
A Gaist I purpois to gar gang,
Be counsaill of frier Walter Lang;
Quhilk sall mak certane demonstratiounis
To help us in our procuratiounis,
Your halie ordour to decoir:
That practick he provit anis befoir,
Betwix Kirkaldie and Kinghorne;
Bot lymmaris maid therat sick scorne,
And to his fame maid sic degressioun,
Sensyne he hard not the Kingis confessioun.
Thoicht at that time he come no speid,
I pray yow tak gude will as deid;
And him amongest your self ressave,
As ane worth many of the lave.
Quhat I obtein may, throw his airt,
Ressone wald ye had your parte;
Your Ordour handillis no money,
Bot for uther casualitie,
As beif, meill, butter, and cheiss,
Or quhat we have, that ye pleis,

---
[1] Old copy, *ye.*

Send your brethren, *et habete*.
As now nocht ellis, bot *valete*,
   Be THOMAS your brother at comand,
   A Culrun kythit throw mony a land.   60

The Tale of Colkelbie Sow.

THE following Tale, which is of considerable antiquity, is printed from Bannatyne's Manuscript. It is contained in the *Fifth* part or division of this valuable Collection, commencing—"Heir follouis the fyift pairt of this buik contenying the ffabellis of Esop with diuerss vthir fabillis and poeticall workis maid and compyld be divers lernit men 1568."
On the back of this title is the following Address:

TO THE REDAR.

My freindis thir storeis subsequent
Albeid bot fabillis thay present
ʒit devyne doctowris of jugement
  Sayis thair ar hid but dowt
Grave materis wyiss and sapient
Vnder the workis of poyetis gent
Thairfoir be war that thow consent
  To blame thir heir set owt.

From the internal evidence, the date of "Cowkelbie Sow" or "Colkelbie," a strange and whimsical rhapsody, the moral of which is expressed in no obscure terms, and of which certain passages bespeak as the author a person who had travelled much abroad, evidently appears, from the Prohemium, to have been written during the era of Minstrelsy, although from internal evidence posterior to Chaucer.[1]

---

[1] The first wes the samyn Chanticleer to luke,
Of quhome Chaucer treitis into his buke.
      (Vide stanza 788.)

With little hesitation, therefore, it may be assigned to some time previous to the middle of the fifteenth century, since it seems at least to have been very popular considerably anterior to the age of Douglas and Dunbar, both of whom flourished in the reign of James IV.

Gawin Douglas thus enumerates Colkelbie, among other heroes of romance, represented in the Mirror of Venus:

> I saw Raf Coilʒier with his thrawin brow,
> Crabbit Johne the Reif, and *Auld Cowkellpis Sow.*[1]

In "Ane interlude of the laying of a Gaist," in the present collection, it is also noticed:

> To reid quha will this gentill geist
> ʒe herd it no^t at *Cokilby's feist.*[2]

Another allusion occurs in a poem by Dunbar, who says:

> And thocht this nobill cunning sort,
> Quhom of befoir, I did report
> Rewardit be, it war bot ressoun;
> Thairat suld no man mak enchesoun:—
> Bot quhen thir vthir fulis nyce
> That feistit at Colkelbie's gryce,
> Ar all rewardit, and nocht I,
> Than on this fals warld, I cry fy!

And the same writer, in his "General Satire," quotes the poem in the following passage:

> Sic knavis and crakkaris to play at carts and dyce
> Sic halland-scheckaris whilk at *Cowkelbyis gryce*
> Are halden of pryce when lymaris do convene.[3]

The humour of this very singular composition, which is professedly satirical, is certainly coarse, and the versification exceedingly irregular. But the poem, although referring in its allusions (as Dr. Leyden has observed) to local and temporary circumstances, which are not obvious at this distance of time, throws much light on the manners and

---

[1] Part iii. St. 48.   [2] Vol. i. p. clxiv.   [3] Bann. MS.

rustic festivities of the Scotish peasantry, during a very early period. From the minuteness of its description, it is also highly illustrative of the music, dances, and musical instruments in common use in Scotland in the fifteenth century. And what adds, in no small degree, to its interest is the consideration that the names of the greater proportion of the airs, dances, and songs, enumerated in "Colkelbie's Sow" are otherwise unknown.

No other copy of the poem than that from which the present transcript was made is known to exist. In the Auchinleck manuscript there appears to have been a copy; but most unfortunately it has shared the same fate with " Ralf Coilʒear" and some others of the curious tales and romances which it once contained.

Of the author there is no trace whatever in the manuscript; and neither Dr. Leyden, who, in his learned introduction to the "Complaynt of Scotland," has given various extracts from it, nor any other writer who notices its existence, seems to have known his name. The arms at the end of the Prohemium, of which an accurate facsimile has been made, seem to be those of George Bannatyne the transcriber, as they very closely correspond with the arms of the family of Bannatyne.

The orthography of the manuscript has been strictly followed; and no liberties have been taken, with the exception of a few of the contracted words, the preservation of which could have answered no good purpose, and would no doubt have been embarrassing to those unaccustomed to the perusal of ancient manuscripts.

R. P.

EDINBURGH, *Nov.* 1821.

For completing the transcript of "Colkelbie," and carefully collating it with the Manuscript, the Editor may take this opportunity of acknowledging that he is indebted to his friend Robert Pitcairn, Esq., whose zeal and knowledge in antiquarian pursuits has lately been shown in his curious publication of "Queen Mary's Funerals."

Heir begynnis Colkelbie Sow.

Prohemium.

UHEN riallest most redowttit and hé
Magnificat crownit kingis in maiesté
Princis duces and marquis curious
Erlis barronis and kny^{t}tis chevelrous
And gentillmen of hé genolegye
As scutiferais and squieris full courtlye
Ar assemblit and sett in a ryell sé
W^t namit folkis of hé nobilité
Thair talk þat tyme in table honorable
Befoir lordingis and ladeis amiable
Is oft singing and sawis of solace
Quhair melody is þe mirthfull maistrace
Ermy deidis in auld dayis done afoir
Croniculis gestis storeis and mich moir
Manestralis amang mvsicianis merely
To haif hartis in hevinly armony
So semis it weill þat suthly so war ay
Quhat is þe warld w^{t}out plesance or play
Bot passionale   Than lat ws mak sum sport
And recreatioun the cumpany to confort
Wold my lordis do sé quho wold begin it
Quho fall surthschaw or quho sall first fall in it
Quho sall w^t discreit correctioun of ʒow
Bot I quho hath begune this mat^r now
For begynnyng w^{t}out end quhat availis
Bot lyk a tré flureist quhair the fruct falis
To quhich all men of quhat estait he be
W^t recent mynd suld evir haif his E
No^t to begin flureist and syne decress
The langir lyfe the gud losp than to cess
Quhat sal be said bot at his ending hé
Frome on faire ymp fell down a widderit tré

The lyfe is gone the loss lesting is lost
The begynning thay say wes bot a wost
Quhairfoir ȝe men most honorable at all 35
Quhich eternall wald haif memoriall
Gyd ȝow so þat first ȝour God plesit be
And obtene name and wirchep quhen ȝe dé
And quho will noᵗ eftir his gudly powére
Considering his estait go profess him a m'tere 40
Or sustene lak so may he lyknit be
A fair flureiss fadit in a falty tré
All be my self is this symylitude
Suld I begin to sport and noᵗ conclude
Than wold ȝe all belyve say lo him ȝondir 45
That set to bourd and left it in a blondir
Quhairfoir I will say of my fantesy
Sum solasing to glaid this cumpany
Bot for Godis luve and his appostill Petir
Pardoun the fulich face of this mad metir 50
San þe sentence to feill is fantastike
Lat the lettir and langage be such like
Sen all the world changis so mony facis
I trest I will cast caisse vpoun caissis
And so lat sé quhat cais ȝe think most nyce 55
Wisdome vmqˡᵉ holdis þe nycest wys
So þat it be sport in discretioun
Wᵗout odius crewale comparisoun
Perticular malice and all such thing removit
The wyss nycest the wisesst quhile is provit 60
For quhich knawing myne vnsufficience
To be comprysit perticiane wᵗ prudence
I propone noᵗ as wiss presumpteouss
Bot raþir sport myne awin spereit to reioss
And my lordis to heir þat will deden 65
Now I begin wᵗ litill est Amen.

      𝕮𝖝𝖕𝖑𝖎𝖈𝖎𝖙 𝖕𝖗𝖔𝖍𝖊𝖒𝖎𝖚𝖒 𝖊𝖙 𝖘𝖊𝖖𝖚𝖎𝖙𝖚𝖗 𝖕𝖗𝖎𝖒𝖆 𝖕𝖆𝖗𝖘.

Fitt First.

HEIR I gife ȝow caiss
Vmquhile a mery man wais
Callit Cokkelbé
He had a simple blak sow
And he sald hir bot how 5
For penneis thré as eftir ȝe may see
And verrely as I hard
Thus the money he ward
THE FIRST PENNY of the thré
For a girle gaif he 10
The secund fell in a furde
The thrid he hid in a hurde
Now quhilk penny of the thré
Wes best bestowit say ȝe
The lost penny wes vplesit 15
The girle for the time plesit
Bot the penny þat wes hid
I hold leist gude did
For in old prouerbe we sing
Cumis littill gud of gaddering
Quhair wrechit awerice birnis
Hyding hurdis in to hirnis
And knawis nevir quhome till
Latting wirschep to go will
Gret laubor is to get geir 25
And to conserue it is feir
And moir angir is to leiss
Thir thré peruerst propirteiss

---

l. 6. "As eftir ȝe may see," are added in the manuscript, perhaps by the same hand, but evidently written with different ink.

l. 10. "maid" on the margin, and the word "girle" put within brackets.

I find in skars keping
And auaritious wynnyng 30
Quhair mesur is noᵗ maistress
Bot gaddering for gredeness
The hid penny thinkis me
Wes werst bestowit of the thré
For it waiss fro the vse of man 35
Lat warldis gudis go than
Wᵗ mesur and merines
ȝit thair is moir of this cais
The penny lost in þe lak
Wes fundin and vptak 40
And he þat fand it did by
Wᵗ the samyn penny
A littell pig for his prow
Off Kolkelbeis sow
A harlot wynnit neir by 45
And scho wald mak at mangery
And had no substance at all
Bot this pur pig stall
To furniss a gret feist
Wᵗ outtin stufe, bot this beist 50
And ȝit scho callit to hir cheir
On apostita freir
A peruerst pardonier
And practand palmair
A wich and a wobstare 55
A milygant and a mychare
A fond fule a fariar
A cairtar a cariar
A libbar and a lyar
And riddill revar 60
A tuttivillus a tutlar
And a fanȝeit flatterar

---

l. 43. "Gryce" on the margin, written in the same hand.

A forfarn falconar
A malgratious millare
A berward a brawlar 65
And ane aip ledar
W^t a cursit custumar
A tratlar and tinklar
And mony vþir in that hour
Of all evill ordour 70
First w^t a fulisch flour
An ald monk a lechour
A drunkin drechour
A dowble toungit counsalour
A trimpour a trvcour 75
A hangman a hasardour
A tyrant a tormentour
A truphane a tratlour
A faynit nigre mansour
A japer a juglour 80
A lase þat lufis bot for lour
And a man merrour
An evill wyffis mirrour
In all thair semblance sour
W^t a noyefull ny^{t}bour 85
A lunatik a sismatyk
An heretyk a purspyk
A lumbard a lolard
Ane vsurar a bard
Ane ypocreit in haly kirk 90
A burn grenge in the dirk
A schipman on sé & sand
That takis lyfe & gud on hand
And knawis nowp^r courss nor tyd
Bot presumpteouss in pryd 95
Practing no^t thing expert
In cunnyng cumpass nor kert

A skeg a scornar a skald
A bald strod and a bald
An vnthrifty dapill man 100
A rebald a ruffian
A murderer of leilmen
A revischer of wemen
And two lerit men thame by
Schir Ockir and Schir Symony 105
ȝit mony in a grit rout
For lak of rowme stude about
Now wald I wit at this feste
Quho fure best of this beste
I hald þe folk best fure 110
That stud fer wᵗout þe dure
Fro this cursit cumpany
And mensles mangery
ȝit of this caiss þair is moir
The pure pig gaif a rore 115
Him to kill quhen thay pynit
So soir the silly pig quhrynit
Quhill all þe swyn þrabout
Ruschit furth in a rout
I keip noᵗ now to commoun 120
All beistes for to blassoun
Of thair diuerss naturis
Complexionis and cullouris
Quhom the law levis ete
Or quho suld be no manis meit 125
Nor of the foulis of the are
How sum wᵗ closs feit thay fare
And sum diuidit the nailis
Nor of the fische wᵗ thair scalis
All this I set asyd now 130
Haif at Cokilbeis sow
For to say þe verite
Lufand beistis swyne be

Contrair houndis nature
For brawlè doggis at þe dure 135
All settis on the sory hound
That lyis euir at the grund
And he þat cryis most & roris
Ourthrawin schent & most soiris
All the remanent him ruggis 140
Sum be leggis sum be luggis
Thay ar luving to men
Bot noᵗ to thame self than
For wo is him þat hes royne
Bot noᵗ so of the swyne 145
And on of thame be ourthrawin
That his cry may be knawin
All the remanent that heiris
Cumis in thair best maneiris
To reskew as thay may 150
So did thay this day
That sowis sonis hard I nevir
Win so grit wirschep for euir
For Stiftapill all the store
Ruschit out wᵗ a rore 155
This pig quhen thay hard him
Thay come golfand full grim
Mony long tuthit bore
And mony galt come befoir
And mony grit Gunnald 160
Gruntillot and gamald
Wrotok and Writhneb
Hogy evir in the eb
Wᵗ the halkit hoglyn
Snelly Snattis Swankyn 165
Baymell bred in the bog
Hog hoppit our hog

---

l. 134. "Luvand" on margin of the MS.

Mage of the milhill
Grom Gym of the gill
The suddill sow and the sord   170
Reid Kit that eft rord
Patypull of the Pappourtis
And Knvtknot of the Kuppourtis
The gray the gerot and the grym
Hurlhekill hoblit w^t him   175
Sigill Wrigill our sow
Gret bore Tusky the grow
Mony galt mony gilt
Come let the pig to be spilt
Rowchrumple out ran   180
Weill mo than I tell can
W^t sick a din and a dirdy
A garray and a hirdy girdy
The fulis all afferd wer
And the harlot hurt thare   185
W^t bare Tuskyis tuth
And for to say the verry suth
In that fellon affray
The littill pig gat away
And ilk bore & ilk beist   190
Defoulit the fulis of the feist
Sum mokit menȝeit & merrit
Thus wer thay fro the meit skerrit
Is no^t this a nyce caiss
Bot ȝit a fer werss it weiss   195
A new noyment and nois
W^t a rumour vprois
That of that caiss to degest
It mycht be callit a tempest
For all the suynis awnaris   200
Said seilis how the fulis fairis
And seis so curst a cumpany
Herand thair awin swyne cry

Wᵗ thir myligantis machit
Afferd the fulis had thame kachit 205
As to steill thame away
Than dyn roiss and dirray
Stok hornis blew stout
Mony on ischit out
Gilby on his gray meir 210
And Fergy on his sow fair
Hoge Hygin by þe hand hint
And Symy þat was sone brint
With his lad Loury
And his gossep Gloury 215
Fergy in frunt past
And Fynny followit him fast
Thurlgill thrang till a club
So ferss he flaw in a dub
Quhill Downy him abak drewgh 220
Than Rany of þe Reidhewch
Wᵗ Gregry the bowman
For lufe of his leman
Licht lap at a lyn
He felȝeit and he fell in 225
Hnd Hoge was sa haisty
That he sualterit him by
Quhil Thoby carioʳ him tuk
To land wᵗ a scheip cruk
Schipirdis schowit to schore 230
And Fergy Flitsy ȝeid befoir
Chiftane of that chef chak
A ter stowp on his bak
Wᵗ his lad Luddroun
And his hound Hunddroun 235
Mony schiphird with him is
Fro brokis brois and brymmis

---

l. 232, the word "ȝeid" is interlined in the original.

Off two ram crukit hornis
Thair baner on a birk born is
With Barmyberd thair banerman 240
And his cousing Cachcran
Thair menstrall Diky Doyt
Fur befoir w^t a *floyt*
Than dansit Doby Drymouth
The sone shene in the Sowth 245
And as they lukit on a lee
Thay saw an upir menʒé
Than all thay fled full afferd
And the maister schipherd
Fergy Flitsy befoir 250
Tho^t was litil on his store
His feit maid dynnyng
He lakkit breth for rynning
How q Hobby herk me
We neid no^t to fordir flé 255
ʒone folk our awin frendis ar
I knaw be thair banar
Than wer thay nevir half so fane
And glaidly turnit all againe
And knew be thair array 260
That all nolt hirdis wer thay
That ischit out to the cry
And thair banar borne by
Of Crumhorne the cowis taill
Festnitt on a lang. flaill 265
Besyd thair capitane I trow
Callit wes Colyne Cuckow
And Davy Doyle of the dale
Was thair mad menstrall
He blew on a *pype* hé 270
Maid of a borit boutré
Waytstath him by
Dansit and Dandy

The thrid fallowschip he saw
That thay wundir weill knaw 275
The swynehirdis in a rowt
And Sweirbum with his snowt
Wes captane of thame thair
And borne wes his banair
Vpoun a schule for to schaw 280
A flekkit sowis skyn faw
W*t* terletheris tyit hy
Quho bur it bot Bolgy
And Clarus the long clype
Playit on a *bag pype* 285
Haggysheid and Helly
Ballybrass and Belly
Dansit and his sone Samyn
Than all assemblit w*t* a gamyn
And all the menstralis attonis 290
Blew up and playit for the nonis
Schiphird nolt hirdis
And swynhirdis outgirdis
For to dance merily
A maistir swynhird swanky 295
And his cousing Copyn Cull
Fowll of bellis fulfull
Led the dance and began
Play us *Joly lemmane*
Sum trottit *Tras and Trenass* 300
Sum balterit *The Bass*
Sum *Perdony* sum *Trolly lolly*
Sum *Cok craw thou quhill day*
Twysbank and Terway
Sum *Lincolne* sum *Lindsay* 305
Sum *Joly lemman dawis it not day*
Sum *Be ȝon wodsyd* singis
Sum *Late laite on evinnyngis*

Sum *Joly Martene* wt *a mok*
Sum *Lulalow lute cok* 310
Sum bekkit sum bingit
Sum crakkit sum cringit,
Sum movit *most mak revell*
Sum *Symon sonis of Quhynfell*
Sum *Maistr Pier de Couӡate* 315
And vþir sum *in consate*
At leser drest to dance
Sum *Ourfute* sum *Orliance*
Sum *Rusty bully with a bek*
And Every note in vþeris nek 320
Sum vsit the dansis to deme
Of *Cipres* and *Boheme*
Sum *The faites full ӡarne*
Off *Portingall* and *Naverne*
Sum countirfutit the *gyss of Spane* 325
Sum *Italy* sum *Almane*
Sum noisit *Napillis* anone
And vþir sum of *Arragone*
Sum *The Cane of Tartary*
Sum *The Soldane of Surry* 330
All his dansis defynd
Sum *Pretir Johnie of grit Ynd*
Sum As the *Ethiopis* vsit
Sum futit and sum refusit
Sum had dansis mony ma 335
Wt all the dansis of *Asia*
Sum of *Affrickis* age
And principale of *Cartage*
Thair pressit in *Pery Pull*
Full of bellis fulfull 340
Maistr Myngeis *The mangeis*
Maistr Tyngeis *La tangeis*
Mr Totis *La toutis*
And *Rousty rottis the routis*

Maist^r Nykkis *La nakkis*   345
And Sr Jakkis *La jakk[is]*
The Hary hurlere husty
And *Calby the curst custy*
*Mony laddis mony lownis*¹
Knowf knois kynnis culrownis   350
Curris kenseis and knavis
Inthrang and dansit in thravis
W^t thame *Towis the mowis*
And *Hary w^t the reid howis*
Than all arrayit in a ring   355
Dansit *My deir derling*
And all assentit in a sop
To the vse of *Ewrop*
That for so much thay beleuit
That expert and weill preuit   360
Thay war in the Est warld
As is heir breuly ourharld
Thay conclud the vse plane
Of Ylandis in Occiane
And of the fermeland of *France*   365
And how the Emprio^r dois dance
Suesis in Suauia syne
And als the *Reuir of Ryne*
Off *Bretane the brod Ile*
Off *Yrland* and *Argvle*   370
Burgone and *Breband*
Hanyngo and *Holland*
Flanderis, Freisland, and eik
Brandebur^t and *Broinsweik*
Dittmer and *Baywer*   375
Pruce Poill and *Pomer*
Lubwick land and *Lunaburgh*
Malestrand and *Makilbur*

---

¹ l. 349. "Mony laddis mony townis" on margin of the MS.

The steidis sevin and sevinty
And all boundę thameby 380
The *Rerall*[1] and *Rusland*
Sclauia and *Gotland*
Denmark and *Norroway*
All thair dansis and play
Thay movit in thair mad muting 385
And all thay falit in futing
For m'rit wes thair menstralis
Thair instrumentis in tonis felis
And all thair plat pure pansis
Coud no^t the fete of ony dansis 390
Bot such thing as affeiris
To hirdis and their maneris
For thay hard speik of men gud
And small thairof vndirstud
Bot hurlit furth vpoun heid 395
A copyne cull coud thame lede
And so thay wend thay weill dansit
And did bot praclit, and pransit
And quhen thay had all done
It was a tratlyng out of tune 400
Than thay began for to chyd
Quhill *Quhorlorehusty* cryd
Oe ceiss this brangling and bere
Remembir quhy ӡe come here
That ilk knave and ilk cust 405
Comprysit *Horlore hust*
For a witté man commendit
And thus thair dansing thay endit
And so concluding thay past
To thair maisteris als fast 410
The silly pig to reskew
All the samyn are thay met trew

---

[1] Perhaps *Revel*.

Be than wes matchit on mold
Als mony as thay wold
Lord God so lowd as thay cryd 415
Full oft the fulis thay defyd
And on them semblit att onis
Bot thair was breking of bonis
Hold how he wes heir
Thay chace with fresch cheir 420
Fy^ll on the foirsaid sottis
And ourthrew all the ydiottis
Both of the swyne & the men
Be this ȝe may weill ken
That foly is no sapience 425
For multitud in negligence
He seldin palme of victory
Bot God & gud wit gy
And all this grit brawling
Babling and up^r thing 430
Wes for a pig as ȝe hard sayn
Ȝit he eskapit vnslane
Now juge as ȝe lift by
For this is bot a fantesy [1]
And littill a poynt of poetry 435
Bot sport to mak ws mirry
And ȝit this is a strange caiss
Bot eftirward this pig waiss
Growin to grit boir
Lo such is this warldis glore 440
Now law now he [2]
Nothing stable we sé
In this warld of variance
Ȝit fell a caiss and new chance
This pig quhen he a boir wes 445
Off micht he grew maikles

---

[1] Old copy reads *fancé sly*.   [2] Now low, now high.

As to fecht for awant
W^t Antelop or Oliphant
Tiger Pard or Pantere
Bull Wolf or Wyld bere [1]   450
W^t the awfull Vnicorne
Nor ony beist that wes borne
For he faucht wichtly w^t Wad
And w^t Melliager mad
W^t anterouss Hercules   455
He did a battell in pres
And huntit was in the plane
Befoir the goddes Dyane
Bot he eskapit harmeles
And killit houndis in the chase   460
The rich king of Sydon
And his knychtis ilk on
For thir bere afferd wer
For vmquhile he wonit thair
And gaif a battell curious   465
To Eglamoir of Artherus
The vgly worme nevir so weill preuit
Quhill this bald bore leuit
Nor ȝit as I vnderstand
The dragone in the holy land   470
Is no^t this a nyce cais
That first this pig so pure waiss
And in so many dengeris
He eskapit with weris
ȝe may consaue be this twich   475
That oft of littill cumis mich
No contempne a small fo
Quhill he haith grace to ryd or go
At liberty and fredome
I hold it no wisdome   480

---

[1] Old copy reads *bore*.

Or for loif of pennyis
To suffer honour perreis
And thus is the cais endit
Of the penny þat wes spendit
That grew to so grit priss   485
Scarss spending skathis gentriss
Thus haif I tald ȝow a caiss
To sett ȝow in solaiss
For our exceding study
May causs quhyle malancoly   490
Thairfoir to mak ws mirryar
Thus did my fantesy fair
And [of] this hirdy girdy I
And dirdy cry ȝow mercy

     Explicit Prima Pars.

     Fitt Secound.

Off thir mokking meteris and mad matere   495
ȝour hé reuerence humly eft I requyre
All ȝe hereris pardoun w^t patience
My noyous noyiss nycetie and negligence
And to satisfie my foirsaid symple dyte
In recompance of it now will I wryte   500
Of ȝE SECUND PENNY ffor the girle cost
How it did thryve ȝat onis was thrall half lost
A ȝeir eftir walking in his disport
By a rever Cokelby saw resort
Ane auld blind man w^t a pretty maid   505
No^t twelf ȝeir hold [1] I hold of age scho haid
Bot suth to say scho was no^t lyk to be
A worldly wicht so wundir fair wes sche
So weill nurtourit as scho had nurischeit bene
In closter or court dochter to kyng or quene   510

---

[1] So in MS.

Innocentlie scho salust on hir kné
This carlage man this foirsaid Colkelbé
ʒit for to tell þe werray treuth of it
He was ane man boith of substance & wit   614
And said dochter have goddis blyssing & myne
The auld man askit *le pour amour deuine*
Cherité & he said father cum to my houss
He had him home and gaif him fair almouss
And intentlie inquireit quhair he had
Gottin that fair innocent gudelie maid   620
And gif scho war his dochter or kyn to say
He said suithlie scho is nother *perfay*
Bot ane palmar ane honest man was he
Ane aliane come frome beyond þe sé
With his awin wyf a blyssit creatour   625
Lougeit[1] with me suppoiss that I be peur
And throuch þe will of God so as it was
Thay war weseit with suddane soir seikness
And deceissit thairin boith in ane hour
This little maid this tender creatour   630
Was thair dochter and beluiffit with me
That leddis me now sence myself may nocht sé
Colkelbé said I beleif it is so
Bot quhat cuntré that ewer thai folk come fro
It semis thai war of kynreid full potent   635
Be the dochteris feris this innocent
Bot guid father gif that ʒe wald aggree
To lat þe maid remane heir still with me
For hir honour and elss so wald I reid ʒow
Bot ʒe sall haif ane boy of myne to leid ʒow   640
The blynd man said thré soneis at home I have
And war I thair no moir gyding I crawe
Bot for þe maide hath bene a quhill with me
And ʒe hir haue I suld the better be

---

[1] Old copy, *longeit.*

Cokkelby said I had thré pennyis round
The first wes lost onys in a lak and found
And with it coft a pig sum callis a gryss
Quhich increscit to he wirschip and pryss
So mervellous mony men of him reidis
He wes the caus of feill ferlifull deidis
As his legend beris witness luke quho so list
The secound penny I haif heir in my fist
On lyis in hurd this is the caiss of thame
Thré silly pennyis suthly I hald the same
The said secound penny I sall gife thé
For this young maid gif þat thow will and sche
W^t my favoris in tyme to cum also
Thay agreit and thus I lat thame go
This Colkelby nvreist hir in his houss
Quich grew so fair and verry verteouss
So gentill in all hir gestis and appliable
And sobir in s'uice and amiable
That all þat hir saw thay luvit hir as thair lyfe
And specialy this Colkelbeis wyfe
A worschepfull woman in to her houss
Thay callit hir to name Bellamerouss
Betuix hir and hir husband Colkelby
Thay had a sone callit Flammislie
Galland he wes and gud in all his feir
And of all vperis odly the best archeir
In ony land ry^t wirschepfull and wyse
Big of bonis a strong man of dewyse
And as his fader and moder did oft espy
He coppeit this ʒoing wench attentely
In his consait w^t sad deʒestioun
Hir most plesand perfyt pure persoun

---

l. 550. The words "the caus" are repeated by mistake in the manuscript.

Hir fresche figour formyt of forme & face
Gevin to all gud fulfillit of Godis grace
That all bonty and bewty that myᵗ be
Worthy compryss þairof anewch had sche 680
He lovit so weill þair was non vthir
Bot wᵗ consent of freindis fadir & moder
He weddit hir to wyfe wit ʒe for ay
This amiable innocent Adria
Wes callit to name and this in France fell 685
Into the first orising of it to tell
Or it prevelit planeist and popelus
Quhair now Pareiss citie is situat thus
This Colkelby wonit þair quhair the caiss
Of þe pig fulis and all þat foirsaid was 690
Till on a tyme þat he [of] France the king
Roid to vesy the boundis thair as regne
And in the place þʳ as Cokkelby dwelt
A man of scoir with such thing he delt
For than non could haif craft cornis to win 695
That king of mycht lugit into his In
And on the morne a grit schoting thay did try
Quhair Flamslie our all wan victory
The king saw him so big a man and strong
And gudly als to tary ʒow noᵗ lang 600
For his body a squyer he him maid
And in his weiris so weill he him behaid
He was maid knycht in court to continew
And than he send for his fair lady trew
Dame Adria quhome the king did commend 605
In his chalmer vpoun the quene to attend
Best belouit and most perfyte wes sche
For hir gestis and bewtie and bontie
Our all the laif the ladeis þat thair ware
And Flammislie so weill in weiris him bare 610

---

l. 589. "ʒair" interlined in manuscript.

That the king efter maid him erle ryall
And a cornar of a cuntre seuerall
No^t that invent inhabit as it lay
Gaif him be seile heretable for ay
Quhich he plenyssit w^t peple and polesy 615
And namit it efter him and his lady
This is to say Flammislie and Adria
His hole erldome callit Flandria
Flan fra the first sillab of Flammislie
And Dria drevin fra Adria the fré 620
The quhich famouss erldome of Flanderis ay
Haldis of Frankland and Duchpeir to this day
Off the secound penny thus cum grit grace
W^t correctioun and this I call a cace
I reid no^t this in story autentyfe 625
I did it leir at ane full auld wyfe
My gritgraundame men callit hir Gurgunnald
Scho knew þe lyfe of mony faderis ald
Notable gestis of peas and weiris in storye
Fresche in hir mynd & recent of memorye 630
No$^{tw^t}$standing scho was weill sett in eild
Hir aige I hald of sevin scoir of winteris heild
And saw sumdeill bot for to say the suth
Into hir heid I trest was no^t a tuth
Thairfoir grwew most gredely eit sche 635
And laking teith famvlit hir faculté
That few folk mycht consaue hir mvmling mowth
Bot I þat was expert þ^{r}in of ӡowth
Than wald I say scho had grit grace of God
Quhy so q^d scho my son and maid a nod 640
Madame q^d I for thair be mony wyffis
Throw haboundance of spech þat nevir tryffis

---

l. 635. The word "grwew" in the manuscript seems unintelligible. Perhaps it is an error of the transcriber for "grwell."

And I wald chenge my^t it be at my reid
For a gud toung all the teith in thair heid
As ȝe ar now so suld thay no^t be namit   645
Skaldis baldis and þairthrow schent and schamit
Than angrit scho and said Sanct Johne to borrow
Thow licht boy thow menis mekle sorrow
And sall do moir gife thow in lyfe may byd
Madame q^d I that tak I on ȝour syd   650
Than wald scho preiss bett me in angry wyss
Bot weill was me scho my^t no^t ryn nor ryss
And I wald vp and wisk away full wyld
Than wald scho flattir cum in agane my chyld
And thow sall haif lo standing in the skelf   655
Quheit breid and reme conservit for my self
Than sett scho me to leir littell at the scule
Nowdir lyk to be a wys man nor a fule
And oft w^t pyne scho maid me to report
Of hir tailis and to conclud in schort   660
Scho said my sone be this said taill thou sall
Lerne fyve wittis and the first of thame all
Is to concidder of fulis the foly
Set in nummer thay ryss and multeply
Thay may nevir moir fruct in felicity   665
Thair ignorance requyris no^t it so be
Experience and testimoniall
Off þe saidis fulis my sone consaif thow sall
That a pure pig in þair possessioun
Thay had and tuk for ferme conclusioun   670
To kill þe samyn and mak of it a feist
And syne thay war ourthrawin most and leist
For sory swyne for thair golfing affraid
Till þat þe pig brak fra thame in a braid
And syne knavis ourcome þame w^t a crye   675
Thairfoir my sone fra sic fulich foly
And fallowschip keip thé for the *first* wit
The *secund* is my sone will thou lerne it

Presume nevir bot povert may prewaill
Be it ry^t wiss aganis men of grit availl 680
That ar no^t wyiss bot wranguss in þ^r deidis
In cais þai mak thé quhiles vex^t at nedis
Witnes this pig sone be experience
That was fangit in þe fulis offence
To be killit and recouerit agane 685
To so grit grace as is foirsaid certaine
Thairfoir my sone leif no^t thy gud quarrell
For apperance of dangeris and parrell
For be thow just God sall thy juge be
In all perrellis and weill deliuer thé 690
And the danger passit thow art als sure
As evir thow was and stranger in nature
To aventure agane in richtowsnace
Bot quho so will cowardly hyd his face
In defens of his just actioun 695
Quhen he trestis him for such fowll affectioun
Most in surty suppressit sone sal he be
Quhair the richtouss frome all feir sall go fré
Lychtly nevir thy gud querrell for feir
Off all perellis dowt damage or dangeir 700
Suld it so be nevir suld martirdome
Fortefie fath nor win the sege of Rome
Quho þat surest dois keip him sonest dois flyd
Bot gud quarrell and grace God be thy gyd
The *thrid* wit is my sone gif thow will ken 705
Quhair evir thow seis grit wit in virtewiss men
Tho^t thay be pure auld or ȝong specially
Contempne thame no^t sone and lo the quhy
This maid this girle this pure Adria wes
ȝoung faderles leuit and eik moderles 710
In strenge lond and ȝit the Holy Gost
Vpliftit hir for wit to wirschep most

And in lykwayiss hir lord Erle Flannyslie
Quho wold haif þame opprest for þʳ pouirte
Remembir now in such hicht as thay are
Quhat may thay do to þair party contrare
Thay may weill quyt and ouirthraw þame at all
Dispyss nevir wyiss vertewis in purall
The *ferd* wit is lat nevir thy penny be
Nor warldis gud my sone mastir of thé
For littill thing weill spendit may incres
To hé honour wirschep and gritt riches
As did thir tuo pennyis spendit weill
Vpoun þe pig and the pure damesell
I neid no moir of thame to multeply
Thow knawis befoir how they did fructefy
Thairfoir hald noᵗ pennyis our pretiouss
Bot suffer thame pass prospering commodiouss
Forsuth a tyme a penny thow may spend
That may awaill thé to thy lyvis end
Thairfoir my sone gife thow thinkis to indure
Spend wᵗ mesure for luk wit and mesure
The *fyift* wit is my sone set nevir thy harte
To mak an hurd suffering honoʳ by starte
For littill watt thow how sone þᵗ thow may slid
Frome it slely or it fra þe to glid
And at the leist in þe hurd quhill it lyis
It servis nowdir þe warld nor multeplyis
And gif thow deis it is unknawin to men
In avarice quhat cheir is wᵗ thé then
For quich this man this worthy Colkelby
That in his dayis gat nevir bot pennyis thré
Saw two thryve weill and the thrid did noᵗ
Incontinent þat penny out he brocht
And awowit to God in solempne word
That he suld nevir study to mak ane hord
Ryᵗ so my sone I chairge thé to dude
Spend wᵗ wirchep and spair nᵗ Godis gud

How littill wat thow ane vdir tyme quho may
Bruk thy wyfe & baggis eftir thy day 750
Thus Gurgunnald my grit grandame me kend
Haif I myssaid in ocht I sall amend.

Explicit Secunda Pars.

Fitt Thrid.

AND w^t pardoun now of ȝour hé lordschippis
And correctioun of ȝour reuerend maisterschippis
Heir wald I tell of THE THRID HID PENNY 755
As I haif told ȝow two did fructefy
This Cokelby concidering weill the cais
That of wrechit awarice grew nevir grace
Having in hairt the hole experience
How þat the two pennyis raiss in ascenss 760
Tho^t he wald preve the thrid penny quhyle hid
Quhilk for þe tyme no fruct nor proffeit did
To suffer it spreid in warld and fructefy
And gif sum folk wald say þat I go by
How suld a penny fruct contrair nature 765
Sen gold siluer mettell alkyn vre
Fynit be folkis vanisis and no^t incressis
Sum wold allege my lewit langage a less is
Bot or I waid moir in this wildirnes
Off such weir I will declair the cass 770
Quhill þat the vre is in the awin nature
And no^t fynit nor forgit be manis cure
So long the forss of the four elementis
And most þe erth mynisteris it nvtrimentis
To incressing as herbis stone or tré 775
Frome thair orising stok cuttit quhill thay be
And frome thair ferm first rutit grund dewydit
Thay may no^t than be natur so abscidit

Do fructifie and flureiss as afoir
Lyk as a man heidit he may no moir 780
Bot þat the saule throw grace of God only
In spirituall joyis only dois fructefy
So þe mettell abscidit be þe man
Not fructefeis of nature bot quhat than
Manly resoun and wit of Godis gift 785
Fyndis menis the money to vplift
And multeply in moir memoir & mycht
Than evir it did in erd quhill it plycht
For quhy so long as it lay on the ground
It was vnfynit as fruct nevirmoir found 790
And quhan it was vptak be manis wit
Throw out the warld alway welcome wes it
And set in cas and menissit a lyte
Vsit and handlit be men ʒit quhair a myte
Failis þairof manis wit bringis agane 795
A thowsand pundis fynit out of vris plane
The examplis þat quhoso hath a vertew
Vss it wysly eft syiss ten from it grew
And in schort my long legend quho so lestis
The euwangell the trewt þairof attestis 800
Goddis awin word quhich tuk frome on fule man
A pure penny having no moir as than
And gaif the wyss that had ten pennyis tald
Bot quhy was that for the fule man no wald
Dispone wysly his penny bot abuss it 805
Hyd it and he þat had ten weill tham usit
Thairfoir god tuk frome the vnverteouss man
A penny and gaif to the gud having ten
Ryt so he þat has strente and it abusis
Not following fast the fruct but it refusis 810
God will it geif to him þat hes far moir
I cast me nocht alday to gloiss in gloir
Or to langar legendis þat are prolixt
Thairfoir I turne vnto my first text

As to declair the thrid penny quhyle hid 815
Eftir out brocht and gydit grace it did
As followis heir quho lykis to adwert
Throw consaitis of Colkelby expert
Lyk o sede sawin in erd mortificat
Flouris money fructis vinificat 820
Lyk martiris killit off quhome the mirreitis rysis
Sanctis in hevin quhome sinfull man supprysis
And herkynniss how besyd this Colkelby
Thair duelt a man was rich of stoir and fie 824
Quhair Bodyvincant castell standis now in plane
His big nyᵗbour men callit him Bleirblowane
A wirthy wyfe had he weddit and sche
Was callit Susane on quhome a sone gat he
And Colkelby was gossep to the same
And he callit him Cokalb to his rycht name 830
Colkelby wᵗ the said thrid penny bocht
xxiiij hen heggis and wᵗ them socht
To his gud sone for godfadirly reward
Him to remembir as schawit is eftirward
Susan angrit heirtit as oft woman is 835
Quhile passionat þat all consaitis kennis
Tuk in disdaine this gift this symple thing
And said gossap beir hame ȝour pure ofiring
Mene ȝe to mok my sone & me no moir
I will heirof fure it away þhairfoir 840
He said I sall keip thame to my gud sone
And had thame home to his place quhair he wone
And chairgeit sone his henwyfe to do hir cure
And mak þame fruct than to set thame scho fure
Hir best brod hen callit lady Pekle pes 845
And ȝoung Cokrell hir lord and lemman wes
Scho maid brud on thir eggis þat in schort space
Twenty four chikkynis of þame scho hes
Twelf maill and twelf famell be croniculis cleir 849
And quhat thay war wᵗ thair names we sall heir

VOL. I.   O

The first wes the samyn Chantecleir to luke
Of quhome Chaucer treitis into his buke
And his lady Partlot sister and wyfe
Quhilk wes no lyse in detis of þat lyfe
For quhy folkis levit be naturall lawis than   855
The tuther bruþir was clipit Cokademan
He tuk to wyfe his fair trew sister Toppok
Coktrawdoun was the thrid and his wyfe Coppok
And to compt just the fourt Cok lyk ouris
And littill Henpen his pretty paramo^{r}is   860
And fyift lord was Lyricok in hall
And Kekilcrouss thay did his lady call
Brid to Kittilcok that sat on reid caill stok
And Feklefaw farest of all the flok
Was the sext and Cokrusty the sevin   865
Dame Strange his wyfe quhilk had a stout stevin
Cokky the aucht his lady clepit Erok
Coknolus the nynt spowsit his sister Vrok
Cokcoby the tent and Sprutok his speciall
Cokobenar the levint his maik thay call   870
Dame Juliane the twelf wes Cokjawbert
And lady Wagtail his joy and all his hairt
So stout a stoir come of þir breþ^r twelf
And þair sisteris I can no^t say my self
The syistre[s] p^{te} thay wer so fructeouss   875
And at schreftis evin sum wes so battalouss
That he wald win to his maist^r in feild
Fourty florans w^t bill and spuris beild
Sum of þis stoir this Cokkelby did sell
Sum auld sum ȝung sum eggis in the schell   880
And cost þ^{r}w^t vþ^r ware and so it turnit
This penny that xv ȝeir it no^t fowrnit
He mvlteplyit moir than a thowsand pound
Than his gud sone he callit to him a stound
Befoir his fader moder and freindis all   885
And said Cokkalb my sone ressaif thow sall

All thir gudis for justly thay ar thyne
Off thy chyld gift storit throw grace devyne
Fro xxiiij hen eggis quiche I thé gaif
ʒet þi moder sone wald þame no^t ressaif
Than as ʒe hard he tald all þe caiss
This Cokelb grew eftir to so grit richess
Throw this penny he grew the michtiest man
In ony realme quhat did þe penny than
First hid in hurde to vertew no^t applyit
And syne outbrocht þat so fer fructefyit
Thairfoir my sone study nevir in thy day
W^t auarice warldis gud in hurd till ley
Nor be thow no^t disparit of Godis grace
The thrid penny this was and þe last caice
As my biledame old Gurgunnald told me
I allege non vþir auctorité
In this sentence maid on revill raill
Quhich semys most to be a wyfis taill
W^t correctioun quhile now I this conclud
God þat ws bocht w^t his awin blissit blud
Both ʒow and me to consarue he deden
Throw meik mirreitis of his only sone Amen.

𝕰𝖝𝖕𝖑𝖎𝖈𝖎𝖙 𝕿𝖊𝖗𝖙𝖎𝖆 𝕻𝖆𝖗𝖘 𝖊𝖙 𝖀𝖑𝖙𝖎𝖒𝖆.

The Tale of Rauf Coilȝear.

THE excellent and worthy Prelate who was the first to draw public attention to the stores of our ancient poetical literature has justly observed, that it has ever "been a favourite subject with our English ballad-makers to represent our kings conversing, either by accident or design, with the meanest of their subjects;"[1] and at the same time he states, that his manuscript volume of old Ballad and Romance Poetry contains a mutilated copy of the ancient poem of "John the Reeve," which follows in the present collection. This Poem Bishop Percy describes as "being built on an adventure of the same kind with the ballad of 'The King and the Miller of Mansfield,' which happened between King Edward Longshanks and one of his Reeves or Bailiffs. The latter (he adds) is a piece of great antiquity, being written before the time of Edward IV., and for its genuine humour, diverting incidents, and faithful picture of rustic manners, is infinitely superior to all that have since been written in imitation." The originality of conception, thus assigned to this poem, appears rather questionable, as there are several English ballads (such as the "King and the Barker"[2]) that may vie with it in point of antiquity: and certainly it can by no means be esteemed so ancient as "Ralf Coilȝear."

"Rauf Coilȝear," in common with the greater number of the ancient tales and romances in our vernacular language, might have been referred by conjecture to some Frankish original, if it had not been the case that the writer has borrowed one of his heroes from a period when the modern French capital was hardly known or used as such. It

---

[1] Reliques of Ancient English Poetry, vol. iii. p. 179.
[2] Hazlitt's "Popular Poetry," 1864-66, i. 3-10.

purports to relate an adventure between Charlemagne or Karl and a collier in the vicinity of Paris—a city which the Emperor-king rarely visited. It is rather, then, the composition of a Scot, who, like many of his countrymen, had received his education in France, and was tempted to adopt the names without much reflection or inquiry. But it deserves notice that, whoever was the author, he followed the example of the writer of *Colkelbie Sow* in laying his scene there in the only passage where a locality is specified. The language of this tale, with the peculiar structure of the stanza and its alliterative style, refer the composition to a period not later than the fourteenth or the beginning of the fifteenth century; but we are not possessed of such evidence as might entitle us to ascribe it in particular to any one Scotish poet. That at an early period it enjoyed much popularity in Scotland is sufficiently evident. Dunbar in one of his poems addressed to James IV. mentions,

"Gentill and semple, of every clan,
   Kyne of Rauf Colȝear and Johne the Reif."

And Bishop Douglas, in the "Palice of Honour," written in the year 1503, among other characters of notoriety, says,

"I saw Rauf Colȝear with his thrawin brow."

It is also enumerated by the author of the "Complaynt of Scotland," printed at Paris about 1549, among the "tailis, fabillis, and plesand stories" recited by "the scheiperdis," whereof "sum vas in prose and sum in verse, sum vas storeis, and sum vas flet taylis."

This tale, however, was, for a length of time, considered no longer to be in existence. The short notice which occurs in Jos. Ames's "Typographical Antiquities," 1749, 4to, p. 583, is the only intimation respecting any printed edition; but so completely had every copy eluded detection, that the repeated search and inquiry of more than half a century failed in gratifying the curiosity excited by these different allusions, among our poetical antiquaries. In the index to the Auchinleck Manuscript: "Item þe buke of ralf colȝear," appears as the LXIV. article,—but this, and some other portions of the same volume, have long since been lost.

The present re-impression has been made from a printed copy discovered in 1821 in a volume of English tracts of extreme rarity in the Library of the Faculty of Advocates. In the original (of the title of which a correct *facsimile* is here given, although seemingly printed with more accuracy than is usually met with in such publications, two lines in the XIth and one line in the LVth stanza appear to have been omitted. The tract is in 4to, and contains sixteen leaves in black letter. The only liberty that has been taken, besides the change of letter, is the substitution of "th" in the few instances where the Anglo-Saxon "þ" had been introduced.

The tale of "Rauf Coilȝear" has claims to public attention altogether independent of its uncommon rarity, as it possesses no inconsiderable share of poetical merit, and the versification or rhythm is remarkable as the prototype of "Peblis to the Play," "Christ's Kirk on the Green," and other Scotish productions. Indeed, it may be worth considering whether it is not probable that this and "Peblis to the Play" were from the same pen. Although, like most poems of the same age and character, many words are altered from their usual acceptation, or introduced merely for the sake of the alliterative style, the language is by no means obscure. The narrative is simple and circumstantial; the characters are well described; and a vein of comic humour runs through the whole. The adventure with the Saracen towards the conclusion of the poem (very skilfully introduced, to prevent the author from committing the reputation, either of "Schir Rauf," his hero, or of the "gentill knycht," "Schir Rolland"—the Roland or Orlando of history), which terminates so happily in "Magog's" conversion to the Christian faith, and his marriage with the "Gentill Duchess," may, perhaps, be considered as the strongest evidence of its foreign original.

It may be stated that a very rude woodcut follows the imprint in the original, and has been omitted, as it would not have been any ornament, and, besides, has not the slightest allusion to the poem itself; that of the two heads on the title-page occurs also in the edition of Sir D. Lyndsay's Works, 4to, 1571.

❡ Heir beginnis the taill
of Rauf coilȝear how
he harbreit King
charlis

❧ Imprentit at Sanc=
tandrois be Robert Lekpreuik. Anno. 1572.

IN the cheiftyme of Charlis that chosin Chiftane
Thair fell ane ferlyfull flan within thay fellis wyde
Quhair Empreouris and Erlis and vther mony ane
Turnit fra Sanct Thomas befoir the ȝule tyde
Thay past vnto Paris thay proudest in pane   5
With mony Prelatis 't Princis that was of mekle pryde
All thay went with the King to his worthy wane
Ouir the feildis sa fair thay fure be his syde
All the worthiest went in the morning
Baith Dukis and Duchepeiris   10
Barrounis and Bacheleiris
Mony stout man steiris
                   Of town with the King.

¶ And as that Ryall raid ouir the rude mure
Him betyde ane tempest that tyme hard I tell
The wind blew out of the Eist stiflie and sture   15
The deip durandlie draif in mony deip dell,
Sa feirslie fra the Firmament sa fellounlie it fure
Thair micht na folk hald na fute on the heich fell
In point thay war to parische thay proudest men and pure
In thay wickit wedderis thair wist nane to dwell   20
Amang thay myrck Montanis sa madlie they mer
Be it was pryme of the day
Sa wonder hard fure thay
That ilk ane tuik ane seir way
                   And sperpellit full fer.

☞ Ithand wedderis of the eist draif on sa fast   25
It all to blaisterit and blew that thairin baid

Be thay disseuerit sindrie midmorne was past
Thair wist na Knicht of the Court quhat way the
    King raid
He saw thair was na better bot God on the last
His steid aganis the storme staluartlie straid   30
He Cachit fra the Court sic was his awin cast
Quhair na body was him about be fiue mylis braid
In thay Montanis I wis he wox all will
In wickit wedderis and wicht
Amang thay Montanis on hicht   35
Be that it drew to the nicht
                        The King lykit ill.

    Euill lykand was the King it nichtit him sa lait
And he na harberie had for his behufe;
Sa come thair ane cant Carll chachand the gait
With ane Capill and twa Creillis cuplit abufe   40
The King carpit to the Carll withoutin debait
Schir tell me thy richt name for the Rude lufe
He sayis men callis me Rauf Coilȝear as I weill wait
I leid my life in this land with mekle vnrufe
Baith tyde and tyme in all my trauale   45
Hine ouir seuin mylis I dwell
And leidis Coilis to sell
Sen thow speiris I the tell.   All the suith hale.

¶ Sa mot I thrife said the King I speir for nane ill
Thow semis ane nobill fallow thy answer is sa fyne
Forsuith said the Coilȝear traist quhen thow will   51
For I trow and it be nocht swa sum part salbe thyne
Mary God forbid said the King that war bot lytill
    skill
Baith my self and my hors is reddy for to tyne
I pray the bring me to sum rest the weddir is sa schill
For I defend that we fall in ony fechtine   56

I had mekill mair nait sum friendschip to find
And gif thow can better than I
For the name of Sanct July
Thow bring me to sum harbery 60
     And leif me not behind.

I wait na worthie harberie heir neir hand
For to serue sic ane man as me think the
Nane bot mine awin hous maist in this land
Fer furth in the Forest amang the fellis hie
With thy thow wald be payit of sic as thou fand 65
Forsuith thou suld be wel cum to pas hame with me
Or ony vther gude fallow that I heir fand
Walkand will of his way as me think the
For the wedderis ar fa fell that fallis on the feild
The King was blyth quhair he raid 70
Of the grant that he had maid
Sayand with hairt glaid
     Schir God ȝow forȝeild.

Na thank me not ouir airlie for dreid that we threip
For I haue seruit the ȝit of lytill thing to rufe
For nouther hes thow had of me fyre drink nor meit
Nor nane vther eismentis for trauellouris behufe 75
Bot micht we bring this harberie this nicht weill to heip
That we micht with ressoun baith thus excuse
To morne on the morning quhen thow sall on leip
Pryse at the parting how that thow dois 80
For first to lofe and syne to lak Peter it is schame
The King said, in gude fay
Schir it is suith that ȝe say
Into sic talk fell thay
     Quhill thay war neir hame.

¶ To the Coilȝearis hous baith or thay wald blin 85
The Carll had Cunning weill quhair the gait lay
Vndo the dure beliue Dame art thow in
Quhy Deuill makis thow na dule for this euill day
For my Gaist and I baith cheueris with the chin
Sa fell ane wedder feld I neuer be my gude fay 90
The gude wyfe glaid with the gle to begin
For durst scho neuer sit sūmoundis that scho hard
    him say
The Carll was wantou̅ of word and wox wonder
    wraith
All abaisit for blame
To the dure went our Dame 95
Scho said Schir ȝe ar welcome hame
              [You] and ȝour Gaist baith.

Dame I haue deir coft all this dayis hyre
In wickit wedderis and weit walkand full will
Dame kyith I am cūmin hame and kendill on ane
    fyre
I trow our Gaist be the gait hes farne als ill 100
Ane Ryall rufe he fyre war my desyre
To fair the better for his saik gif we micht win
    thair till
Knap doun Capounis of the best but in the byre
Heir is bot hamelie fair do beliue Gill
Twa cant knaifis of his awin haistelie he bad 105
The ane of ȝow my Capill ta
The vther his Coursour alswa
To the stabill swyith ȝe ga
            Thā was the King glaid.

☞ The Coilȝear gudlie in feir, tuke him by the
    hand
And put him befoir him as ressoun had bene 110

Quhen thay come to the dure the King begouth to
    stand
To put the Colȝear in befoir maid him to mene
He said thow art vncourtes that sall I warrand
He tyt the King be the nek twa part in tene
Gif thow at bidding suld be boun or obeysand   115
And gif thow of Courtasie couth thow hes forȝet
    it clene
Now is anis said the Coilȝear kynd aucht to creip
Sen ellis thow art vnknawin
To mak me Lord of my awin
Sa mot I thriue I am thrawin   120
               Begin we to threip.

  Than benwart they ȝeid quhair brandis was bricht
To ane bricht byrnand fyre as the Carll bad
He calltt on Gyliane his wyfe thair Supper to dicht
Of the best that thair is help that we had
Efter ane euill day to haue ane mirrie nicht   125
For sa troublit with stormis was I neuer stad
Of ilk airt of the Eist sa laithly it laid
ȝit was I mekle willar than
Quhē I met with this man
Of sic taillis thay began   130
               Quhill the supper was graid.

¶ Sone was the Supper dicht and the fyre bet
And thay had weschin I wis the worthiest was thair
Tak my wyfe be the hand in feir withoutin let
And gang begin the buird said the Colȝear
That war unsemand forsuith and thy self vnset   135
The King profferit him to gang and maid ane
    strange fair
Now is twyse said the Carll me think thow hes
    forȝet
He leit gyrd to the King withoutin ony mair

And hit him vnder the eir with his richt hand
Quhill he stakkerit thair with all   140
Half the breid of the hall
He faind neuer of ane fall   Quhill the eird fand.

¶ He stert vp stoutly agane vneis micht he stand
For anger of that outray that he had thair tane
He callit on Gyliane his wyfe ga tak him be the hand   145
And gang agane to the buird quhair ʒe suld air haue gane
Schir thow art vnskilfull and that sall I warrand
Thow byrd to haue nurtour aneuch and thow hes nane
Thow hes walkit I wis in mony wyld land
The mair vertew thow suld haue to keip the fra blame   150
Thow suld be courtes of kynd and ane cunnand Courteir
Thocht that I simpill be
Do as I bid the
The hous is myne pardie   And all that is heir.

☞ The King said to himself this is ane euill lyfe   155
ʒit was I neuer in my lyfe thus gait leird
And I haue oft tymes bene quhair gude hes bene ryfe
That maist couth of courtasie in this Cristin eird
Is nane sa gude as leif of and mak na mair stryfe
For I am stonischit at this straik that hes me thus steird   160
In feir fairlie he foundis with the gude wyfe
Quhair the Coilʒear bad sa braithlie he beird

Quhen he had done his bidding, as him gude thocht
Doun he sat the King neir
And maid him glaid & gude cheir 165
And said ȝe ar welcum heir
      Be him that me bocht.

¶ Quhen thay war seruit and set to the Suppar
Gyll and the gentill King Charlis of micht
Syne on the tother syde sat the Coilȝear
Thus war thay marschellit but mair 't matchit that nicht 170
Thay brocht breid to the buird and braun of ane bair
And the worthyest wyne went vpon hicht
Thay Beirnis as I wene thay had aneuch thair
Within that burelie bigging, byrnand full bricht
Syne enteris thair daynteis on deis dicht dayntelie
Within that worthie wane 175
Forsuith wantit thay nane
With blyith cheir, sayis Gyliane
      Schir dois glaidlie.

☞ The Carll carpit to the King cumlie and cleir
Schir the Forestaris forsuith of this Forest 180
Thay haue me all at Inuy for dreid of the Deir
Thay threip that I thring doun of the fattest
Thay say I sall to Paris thair to compeir
Befoir our cumlie King in dule to be drest
Sic manassing thay me mak forsuith ilk ȝeir 185
And ȝit aneuch sall I haue for me and ane Gest
Thairfoir sic as thou seis spend on and not spair
Thus said gentill Charlis the Mane
To the Coilȝear agane
The King himself hes bene fane 190
      Sum tyme of sic fair.

¶ Of Caponnis and Cūningis they had plentie
With wyne at thair will and eik Vennysoun
Byrdis bakin in breid, the best that may be
Thus full freschlie thay fure into fusioun
The Carll with ane cleir voce carpit on he   195
Said Gyll lat the cop raik for my bennysoun
And gar our Gaist begin and syne drink thow to
    me
Sen he is ane stranger me think it ressoun
Thay drank dreichlie about thay wosche and thay
    rais
The King with ane blyith cheir   200
Thankit the Coilʒear
Syne all the thre into feir   To the fyre gais

    Quhen they had maid thame eis the Coilʒear
      tald
Mony sindrie taillis efter Suppair
Ane bricht byrnand fyre was byrnand full bald 205
The King held gude countenance and company
    bair
And euer to his asking ane answer he ʒald
Quhill at the last he began to frane farther
    mair
In faith freind I wald wit tell gif ʒe wald
Quhair is thy maist wynning said the Coilʒear 210
Out of weir said the King I waynd it neuer to tell
With my Lady the Quene
In office maist haue I bene
All thir ʒeiris fyftene
            In the Court for to dwell.

¶ Quhat kin office art thow in quhen thow art at
    hame   215
Gif thow dwellis with the Quene proudest in pane

Ane Chyld of hir Chalmer Schir be Sanct
    Jame
And thocht my self it say maist inwart of ane
For my dwelling to nicht I dreid me for blame
Quhat sal I cal yᵉ said yᵉ Coilʒear quhē thow art
    hyne gane   220
Wymond of the Wardrop is my richt Name
Quhair euer thow findis me befoir the thi harberie
    is tane
And thow will cum to the Court this I vnderta
Thow sall haue for thy Fewaill
For my saik the better saill   225
And onwart to thy trauaill
                Worth ane laid or twa

¶ He said I haue na knawledge quhair the Court
    lyis
And I am wonder wa to cum quhair I am vnkend
And I sall say thee the suith on ilk syde I wis
That thow sall wit weill aneuch or I fra the wend
Baith the King and the Quene meitis in Paris   231
For to hald thair ʒule togidder for scho is efter
    send
Thair may thow sell be ressoun als deir as thow
    will prys
And ʒit I sall help the gif I ocht may amend
For I am knawin with Officiaris in cais thow cum
    thair   235
Haue gude thocht on my Name
And speir gif I be at hame
For I suppois be Sanct Jame
                Thow sall the betetr fair.

    Me think it ressoun be the Rude that I do thy
        rid
In cais I cum to the Court and knaw bot the ane   210

Is nane sa gude as drink and gang to our bed
For als far as I wait the nicht is furth gane
To ane preuie Chalmer beliue thay him led
Quhair ane burely bed was wrocht in that wane
Closit with Courtingis and cumlie cled 245
Of the worthiest wyne wantit thay nane
The Coilȝear and his wyfe baith with him thay
    ȝeid
To serue him all at thay mocht
Till he was in bed brocht
Mair the King spak nocht 250
        Bot thankit thame thair deid.

☞ Vpon the morne airlie quhen it was day
The King buskit him sone with scant of Squyary
Wachis and Wardroparis all war away
That war wont for to walkin mony worthy
Ane Pauyot preuilie brocht him his Palfray 255
The King thocht lang of this lyfe and lap on
    in hy
Than callit he on the Carll anent quhair he lay
For to tak his leif than spak he freindly
Than walkinnit they baith and hard he was thair
The Carll start vp sone 260
And prayit him to abyde [a]none
Quhill thir wickit wedderis be done
        I rid nocht ȝe fair.

    Sa mot I thriue said the King me war lath to
        byde
Is not the morne ȝule day formest of the ȝeir 264
Ane man that Office suld beir betyme at this tyde
He will be found in his fault that wantis foroutin
    weir
I se the Firmament fair vpon ather syde

I will returne to the Court quhill the wedder is
    cleir
Call furth the gude wyfe lat pay hir or we ryde
For the worthie harberie that I haue fundin heir
Lat be God forbid the Coilȝear said   271
And thow [be] of Charlis cumpany
Cheif King of Cheualry
That for ane nichtis harbery   Pay suld be laid.

¶ ȝea sen it is sa that thow will haue na pay   275
Cum the morne to the Court and do my counsall
Deliuer the and bring ane laid and mak na delay
Thow may not schame with thy Craft gif thow
    thriue sall
Gif I may help the ocht to sell forsuith I sall assay
And als my self wald haue sum of the Fewall   280
Peter he said I sall preif the morne gif I may
To bring Coillis to the Court to se gif they sell sall
Se that thow let nocht I pray the said the King
In faith said the Coilȝear
Traist weill I salbe thair   285
For thow will neuer gif the mair
                To mak ane lesing.

Bot tell me now lelely quhat is thy richt name
I will forȝet the morne and ony man ma greif
Wymond of the Wardrop I bid not to lane
Tak gude tent to my name the Court gif thow will
    preif   290
That I haue said I sall hald and that I tell the
    plane
Quhair ony Coilȝear may enchaip I trow till en-
    cheif
Quhen he had grantit him to cum than was the
    King fane
And withoutin ony mair let than he tuke his leif

Then the Coilȝear had greit thocht on the cūnand
  he had maid   295
Went to the Charcoill in hy
To mak his Chauffray reddy
Agane the morne airly
      He ordanit him ane laid.

¶ The lyft lemit vp beliue and licht was the day
The King had greit knawledge the countrie to
  ken   300
Schir Rolland and Oliuer come rydand the way
With thame ane thousand and ma of sensabill men
War wanderand all the nicht ouir 't mony ma
  than thay
On ilk airt outwart war ordanit sic ten
Gif thay micht heir of the King or happin quhair
  he lay   305
To Jesus Christ thay pray that grace thame to len
Als sone as Schir Rolland saw it was the King
He kneillit doun in the place
Thank and God ane greit space.
Thair was ane meting of grace   310
     At that gaddering.

 The gentill Knicht Schir Rolland he kneilit on
  his kne
Thankand greit God that mekill was of micht
Schir Oliuer at his hand and Bischoppis thre
Withoutin cōmounis that come and mony vther
  Knicht
Than to Paris thay pas all that Cheualrie   315
Betuix none of the day and ȝule nicht
The Gentill Bischop Turpine cummand thay se
With threttie Conuent of Preistis reuest at ane
  sicht

Preichand of Prophecie in Processioun
Efter thame baith fer and neir 320
Folkis following in feir
Thankand God with gude cheir
           Thair Lord was gane to toun.

☞ Quhen thay Princis appeirit into Paris
Ilk rew ryallie with riches thame arrayis
Thair was digne seruice done at Sanct Dyonys 325
With mony proud Prelat as the buik sayis
Syne to Supper thay went within the Palys
Befoir that mirthfull man menstrallis playis
Mony wicht wylis sone worthie and wise
Was sene at that semblay ane and twentie dayis 330
With all kin principall plentie for his plesance
They callit it the best ȝule than
And maist worthie began
Sen euer King Charlis was man
           Or euer was in France.

¶ Than vpon the morn eairlie quhen the day dew 335
The Coilȝear had greit thocht quhat he had vnder tane
He kest twa Creillis on ane Capill with Coillis new
Wandit thame with widdeis to wend on that wane
Mary it is not my counsall, but ȝone man that ȝe knew.
To do ȝow in his gentrise said Gyliane 340
Thow gaif him ane outragious blaw 't greit boist blew
In faith thow suld haue bocht it deir bot he had bene allane
For thy hald ȝow fra the Court for ocht that may be
ȝone man that thow outrayd
Is not sa simpill as he said 345
Thairun my lyfe dar I layd
           That sall thow heir and se.

☞ ȝea Dame haue nane dreid of my lyfe to day
Let me wirk as I will the weird is mine awin
I spak not out of ressoun the suth gif I sall say
To Wymond of the Wardrop war the suith knawin   350
That I haue hecht I sall hald happin as it may
Quhidder sa it gang to greif or to gawin
He caucht twa Creillis on ane capill 't catchit on his way.
Ouir the Daillis sa derf, be the day was dawin
The hie way to Paris, in all that he mocht   355
With ane quhip in his hand
Cantlie on catchand
To fulfill his cunnand   To the Court socht.

¶ Graith thocht of the grant had the gude King
And callit Schir Rolland him till and gaif cō-mandment   360
Ane man he traistit in maist atour all vther thing
That neuer wald set him on assay withoutin his assent
Tak thy hors and thy harnes in the morning
For to watche weill the wayis I wald that thow went
Gif thow meitis ony leid lent on the ling   365
Gar thame boun to this Burgh I tell the mine intent
Or gyf thow seis ony man cumming furth the way
Quhat sumeuer that he be
Bring him haistely to me
Befoir none that I him se   In this hall the day.

¶ Schir Rolland had greit ferly and in hart kest
Quhat that suld betakin that the King tald
Vpon solemni[s]t ȝule day quhen ilk man suld rest
That him behouit neidlingis to watche on the wald

Quhen his God to serue he suld haue him drest 375
And syne with ane blyith cheir buskit that bald
Out of Paris proudly he preikit full prest
In till his harnes all haill his hechtis for to hald
He vmbekest the countrie outwith the toun
Ha saw na thing on steir 380
Nouther fer nor neir
Bot the feildis in feir Daillis and doun.

¶ He huit and he houerit quhill midmorne and mair
Behaldand the hie hillis and passage sa plane
Sa saw he quhair the Coilȝear come with all his fair 385
With twa Creillis on ane Capill thairof was he fane
He followit to him haistely amang the holtis hair
For to bring him to the King at bidding full bane
Courtesly to the Knicht kneillit the Coilȝear
And Schir Rolland him self salust him agane 390
Syne bad him leif his courtasie and boun him to ga
He said withoutin letting
Thow mon to Paris to the King
Speid the fast in ane ling Sen I find na ma.

¶ I faith said the Coilȝear, ȝit was I neuer sa nyse 395
Schir Knicht it is na courtasie commounis to scorne
Thair is mony better than I cummis oft to Parys
That the King wait not of, nouther nicht nor morne
For to towsill me or tit me, thocht foull be my clais
Or I be dantit on sic wyse my lyfe salbe lorne 400
Do way said Schir Rolland, me think thow art not wise
I rid thow at bidding be, be all that we haue sworne

And call thow it na scorning but do as I the ken
Sen thow hes hard mine Intent
It is the Kingis commandement 405
At this tyme thow suld haue went
      And I had met sic ten.

¶ I am bot ane mad man that thow hes heir met
I haue na myster to matche with maisterfull men
Fairand ouir the feildis Fewell to fet
And oft fylit my feit in mony foull fen 410
Gangand with laidis my gouerning to get
Thair is mony Carll in the countrie thow may
  nocht ken,
I sall hald that I haue hecht, bot I be hard set
To Wymond of the Wardrop I wait full weill quhen
Sa thriue I said, Rolland it is mine Intent 415
That nouther to Wymond nor Will
Thou sall hald nor hecht till
Quhill I haue brocht the to fulfill
      The Kingis cōmandment.

¶ The Carll beheld to the Knicht as he stude
  than
He bair grauit in Gold and Gowlis in grene 420
Glitterand full gaylie quhen Glemis began
Ane Tyger ticht to ane tre, ane takin of tene
Trewlie that tenefull was trimland than
Semelie schapin and schroud in that Scheild schene
Mekle worschip of weir worthylie he wan 425
Befoir into fechting with mony worthie sene
His Basnet was bordourit and burneift bricht
With stanes of Beriall deir
Dyamountis and Sapheir
Riche Rubeis in feir   Reulit full richt. 430

His plaitis properlie picht attour with precious
    stanis
And his Pulanis full prest of that ilk peir
Greit Graipis of Gold his Greis for the nanis
And his Cussanis cumlie schynand full cleir
Bricht braissaris of steill about his arme banis 435
Blandit with Beriallis and Cristallis cleir
Ticht ouir with Thopas and trew lufe atanis
The teind of his tewellis to tell war full teir
His Sadill circulit and set richt sa on ilk syde
His brydill bellisand and gay 440
His steid stout on stray
He was the Ryallest of array
                On Ronsy micht ryde.

¶ Of that Ryall array that Rolland in raid
Rauf rusit in his hart of that Ryall thing
He is the gayest in geir that euer on ground glaid 445
Haue he grace to the gre in ilk Iornaying
War he ane manly man, as he is weill maid
He war full michtie with magre durst abyde his
    meting
He bad the Coilȝear in wraith swyth withoutin baid
Cast the Creillis fra the Capill, and gang to the
    King 450
In faith it war greit schame said the Coilȝear
I vndertak thay suld be brocht
This day for ocht that be mocht
Schir Knicht that word is for nocht
                That thow Carpis thair.

¶ Thou huifis on thir holtis, and haldis me heir 455
Quhill half the haill day may the hicht haue
Be Christ that was christinnit, and his Mother cleir
Thow sall catche to the Court that sall not be to
    craue

It might be preisit[1] preiudice bot gif thow suld compeir
To se quhat granting of grace the King wald the gaif 460
For na gold on this ground wald I but weir
Be fundin fals to the King, sa Christ me saue
To gar the cum and be knawin as I am command
I wait not quhat his willis be
Nor he namit na mair the 465
Nor ane vther man to me
                Bot quhome that I fand.

¶ Thow fand me fechand nathing that followit to feid
I war ane fule gif I fled, and fand nane affray
Bot as ane lauchful man my laidis to leid
That leifis with mekle lawtie and laubour in fay 470
Be the Mother and the Maydin that maid vs remeid
And thow mat me ony mair cum efter quhat sa may
Thow and I sall dyntis deill quhill ane of vs be deid
For the deidis thow hes me done vpon this deir day
Mekle merwell of that word had Schir Rolland 475
He saw na wappinis thair
That the Coilȝear bair
Bot ane auld Buklair   And ane roustie brand.

¶ This lyked[2] Schir Rolland, and lichtly he leuch
That sic ane stubill husband man wald stryke stoutly 480
Thair is mony toun man to tuggill is full teuch
Thocht thair brandis be blak and vnburely
Oft fair foullis ar fundin faynt and als freuch
I defend we fecht or fall in that foly

---

[1] ? preifit.   [2] Laing printed *It is lyke*.

Lat se how we may disseuer with sobernes
    aneuch   485
And catche crabitnes away, be Christ counsall I
Quhair winnis that Wymond thou hecht to meit
    to day
With the Quene tauld he me
And thair I vndertuke to be
Into Paris pardie   Withoutin delay. 490

    And I am knawin with the Quene said Schir
        Rolland
And with mony byrdis in hir Bowre be buikis
    and bellis
The King is into Paris that sall I warrand
And all his aduertance that in his Court dwellis
Me tharth haue nane noy of myne erand   495
For me think thow will be thair efter as thow tellis
Bot gif I fand the sorrow now to keip my cunnand
Schir Knicht said the Coilȝear thow trowis me
    neuer ellis
Bot gif sum suddand let put it of delay
For that I hecht of my will   500
And na man threit me thair till
That I am haldin to fulfill
                And sall do quhill I may.

¶ ȝea sen thow will be thair thy cunnandis to new
I neid nane airar myne erand nor none of the day
Be thow traist said the Coilȝear man as I am
    trew   505
I will not haist me ane fute faster on the way
Bot gif thow raik out of my renk, full raith sall
    thow rew
Or be the Rude I sall rais thy Ryall array
Thocht thy body be braissit in that bricht hew
Thow salbe fundin als febil of thy bone fay   510

Schir Rolland said to him self this is bot foly
To striue with him ocht mair
I se weill he will be thair
His leif at the Coilȝear   He tuke lufesumly.

¶ Be Christ said the Coilȝear, that war ane foull scorne   615
That thow suld chaip bot I the knew that is so schynand
For thow seis my weidis ar auld and all to worne
Thow trowis nathing thir taillis that I am telland
Bring na Beirnis vs by, bot as we war borne
And thir Blonkis that vs beiris thairto I mak ane band   620
That I sall meit the heir vpon this mure to morne
Gif I be haldin in heill, and thairto my hand
Sen that we haue na laiser at this time to ta
In ane thourtour way
Seir gaitis pas thay   625
Baith to Paris in fay   Thus partit they twa.

The gentill Knicht Schir Rolland come rydand full sone
And left the Coilȝear to cum, as he had vndertane
And quhen he come to Paris the hie Mes was done
The King with mony cumly out of the Kirk is gane   630
Of his harnes in hy, he hynt withoutin hone
And in ane rob him arrayit richest of ane
In that worschipfull weid he went in at none
As he was wont with the wy, that weildit the wane

On fute ferly in feir formest of all 635
Richt weill payit was the King
Of Schir Rollandis cumming
To speir of his tything   Efter him gart call.

    The King in counsall him callit, cū hidder
        Schir Knicht
Hes thow my bidding done as I the command 640
In faith said Schir Rolland I raid on full richt
To watch wyselie the wayis that I sall warrand
Thair wald na douchtie this day for Iornay be
        dicht
Fairand ouir the feildis full few thair I fand
Saif anerly ane man that semblit in my sicht 645
Thair was na leid on lyfe lent in this land
Quhat kin a fallow was that ane Schir I the
        pray
Ane man in husband weid
Buskit busteously on breid
Leidand Coillis he ȝeid   To Paris the way. 650

    Quhy hes thow not that husband brocht, as I
        the bad?
I dreid me sa he dantit the, thow durst not with
        him deill
In faith said Schir Rolland gif that he sa had
That war full hard to my hart, and I ane man in
        heill
He saw the King was engreuit and gat furth
        glaid 655
To se gif the Coilȝearis lawtie was leill
I suld haue maid him in the stour to be full hard
        stad
And I had witten that the Carll wald away steill

Bo I trowit not the day that he wald me beget
As he went outwart bayne   560
He met ane Porter swayne
Cummand raith him agayne   Fast fra the ʒet.

¶ Quhair gangis thow Gedling thir gaitis sa gane?
Be God said the Grome, ane gift heir I geif
I deuise at the ʒet thair is ane allane   565
Bot he be lattin in beliue him lykis not to leif
With ane Capill and twa Creillis cassin on the
    plane
To cum to this Palice he preissis to preif
Gif thow hes fundin that Freik in faith I am fane
Lat him in glaidly it may not engreif   570
Bot askis he eirnestly efter ony man
Than said that Gedling on ground
ʒe forsuith in this stound
Efter ane Wymound   In all that he can.

☞ Pas agane Porter, and let him swyith in   575
Amang the proudest in preis plesand in pane
Say thow art not worthy to Wymond to win
Bid him seik him his self, gif thair be sic ane
Agane gangis Schir Rolland, quhair gle suld begin
And the ʒaip ʒeman to the ʒet is gane   580
Enbraissit the bandis beliue or that he wald blin
Syne seik the wy at his will wend in the wane
Gang seik him now thy self he said vpon hicht
My self hes na lasair
Fra thir ʒetiis to fair   585
Be Christ said the Coilʒear   I set that bot licht.

¶ Gif thow will not seik him, my awin self sall
For I haue oft tymes swet in seruice ful sair
Tak keip to my Capill that na man him call
Quhill I cum fra the Court said the Coilʒear   590

My laid war I laith to lois, I leif the heir all
Se that thow leis thame not, bot ʒeme thame full
    ʒair
In that hardy in hy, he haikit to that hall
For to wit gif Wymondis wynning was thair
He arguit with the Ischar ofter than anis   595
Schir can thow ocht say
Quhair is Wymond the day
I pray the bring him gif thow may
                      Out of this wanis.

  He trowit that the wy had wittin of Wymond
    he wend
Bot to his raifand word he gaue na reward   600
Thair was na man thairin that his name kend
Thay countit not the Coilʒear almaist at regaird
He saw thair was na meiknes nor mesure micht
    mend
He sped him in spedely and nane of thame he
    spaired
Thair was na fyue of thay Freikis, that micht him
    furth fend   605
He socht in sa sadly, quhill sum of thame he
    saird
He thristit in throw thame thraly with threttis
Quhen he come amang thame all
ʒit was the King in the hall
And mony gude man with all   610
                      Vngane to the meit.

¶ Thocht he had socht sic ane sicht all this seuin
    ʒeir
Sa solempnit ane semblie had he not sene
The hall was properly apperrellit and paintit but
    peir
Dyamountis full dantely dentit betwene

It was semely set on ilk syde seir 615
Gowlis glitterand full gay glemand in grene
Flowris with Flourdelycis formest in feir
With mony flamand ferly ma than fyftene
The rufe reulit about in reuall of Reid
Rois reulit Ryally 620
Columbyn and Lely
Thair was ane hailsum harbery   Into riche steid.

¶ With Dosouris to the duris dicht quha sa wald
    deme
With all diuers danteis dicht dantely
Circulit with siluer semely to sene 625
Selcouthly in seir he was set suttelly
Blyth byrdis abufe, and bestiall full bene
Fyne foullis in Fyrth, and Fischis with fry
The flure carpit and cled and couerit full clene
Cummand fra the Cornellis closand quemely 630
Bricht Bancouris about browdin ouir all
Greit Squechonis on hicht
Anamalit and weill dicht
Reulit at all richt   Endlang the hall.

Heir is Ryaltie said Rauf, aneuch for the nanis 635
With all nobilnes anournit and that is na nay
Had I of Wymond ane word, I wald of thir wanis
Fra thir wyis I wis, to went on my way,
Bot I mon ʒit heir mair quhat worthis of him anis
And eirnestly efter him haue myne E ay. 640
He thristit in throw threttie all atanis
Quhair mony douchtie of deid war Ioynit that day
For he was vnburely on bak thay him hynt
As he gat ben throw
He gat mony greit schow 645
Bot he was stalwart I trow
                And laith for to stynt.

¶ He thristit in throw thame, and thraly can thring
Fast to the formest he foundit in feir
Sone besyde him he gat ane sicht of the Nobill
    King
ʒone is Wymond I wait it worthis na weir   650
I ken him weill thocht he be cled in vther clething.
In clais of clene gold kythand ʒone cleir
Quhen he harbreit with me be half as he is heir
In faith he is of mair stait than euer he me tald
Allace that I was hidder wylit   655
I dreid me sair I be begylit
The King preuilie smylit
                    Quhen he saw that bald.

¶ Thair was seruit in that saill Seigis semelie
Mony Senʒeorabill Syre on ilk syde seir
With ane cairfull countenance the Coilzear kest
    his E   660
To the cumely Quene courtes and cleir
Dame of thy glitterand gyde haue I na gle
Be the gracious God that bocht vs sa deir
To ken Kingis Courtasie, the Deuill come to me
And sa I hope I may say or I chaip heir   665
Micht I chaip of this chance, that changes my
    cheir
Thair suld na man be sa wyse
To gar me cum to Parise
To luke quhair the King lyis
                    In faith this seuin ʒeir.

¶ Quhen worthie had weschin, and fra the buirdis
    went   670
Thay war forwonderit I wis of thair wyse Lord
The King fell in carping, and tauld his Intent
To mony gracious Grome he maid his record

How the busteous Beirne met him on the bent
And how the Frostis war sa fell, and sa strait
    ford
Than the Coilȝear quoke as he had bene schent
Quhen he hard the suith say how he the King
    schord
Greit God gif I war now and thy self with all
Vpon the mure quhair we met
Baith all suddandly set
Or ony Knicht that thow may get
                Sa gude in thy hall.

¶ Thir Lordis leuch vpon loft, and lystinit to the
    King
How he was ludgeit and led, and set at sa licht
Than the curagious Knichtis bad haue him to hing
For he hes seruit that thay said be our sicht
God forbot he said my thank war sic thing
To him who succourit my lyfe in sa euill ane nicht
Him semis ane stalwart man and stout in stryking
That Carll for his Courtasie salbe maid Knicht
I hald the counsall full euill that Christin man
    slais
For I had myster to haue ma
And not to distroy tha
Tha war worthie to ga
                To fecht on Goddis fais.

¶ Befoir mony worthie he dubbit him Knicht
Dukis and digne Lordis in that deir hall
Schir se for thy self, thow semis to be wicht
Ta keip to this ordour, ane Knicht I the call
To mak the manly man I mak the of micht
Ilk ȝeir thre hundreth pund assigne the I sall
And als the nixt vacant be ressonabill richt
That hapnis in France, quhair sa euer it fall

Forfaltour or fre waird, that first cummis to hand
I gif the heir heritabilly
Sa that I heir quhen I haue hy
That thow be fundin reddy   705
                    With Birny ʼt brand.

¶ It war my will worthy, thy schone that thow wan
And went with thir weryouris wythest in weir
Heir ar curagious Knichtis, suppois thay the nocht ken
For thy simpill degre that thow art in heir
I beseik God of his grace to mak the ane gude man   710
And I sall gif the to begin glitterand geir
Ane Chalmer with Armour the King gart richt than
Betaucht to ane Squyar, and maid him keipeir
With clois Armouris of steill for that stout Knicht
Sextie Squyaris of fee   715
Of his retinew to be
That was ane fair cumpany
                    Schir Rauf gat that nicht.

¶ Vpon the morne airly Schir Rauf wald not rest
Bot in Ryall array he reddyit him to ryde
For to hald that I haue hecht I hope it be the best   720
To ȝone busteous Beirne that boistit me to byde
Amang the Galȝart Gromis I am bot ane Gest
I will the ganandest gait to that gay glyde
Sall neuer Lord lauch on loft quhill my lyfe may lest
That I for liddernes suld leif, and leuand besyde   725
It war ane graceles gude that I war cummin to
Gif that the King hard on hicht
That he had maid ane carll Knicht
Amang thir weryouris wicht
                    And docht nocht to do.

¶ Vpon ane rude Runsy he ruschit out of toun 730
In ane Ryall array he rydis full richt
Euin to the Montane he maid him full boun
Quhair he had trystit to meit Schir Rolland the Knicht
Derfly ouir Daillis discouerand the doun
Gif ony douchtie that day for Jornayis was dicht 735
He band his blonk to ane busk on the bent broun
Syne baid be the bair way to hald that he had hecht
Quhill it was neir time of the day that he had thair bene
He lukit ane lytill him fra
He sa cummand in thra 740
The maist man of all tha
                That euer he had sene.

¶ Ane Knicht on ane Capeill come cantly at hand
With ane curagious countenance and cruell to se
He semit badly to abyde with Birny and with brand
His blonk was vnburely, braid and ouir hie 745
Schir Rauf reddyit him sone, and came rydand
And in the rowme of ane renk in fewtir kest he
He seimit fer fellonar than first quhen he him fand
He foundis throw his forcenes gif he micht him se
He straik the steid with the spurris he sprent on the bent 750
Sa hard ane cours maid thay
That baith thair hors deid lay
Thair speiris in splenders away
                Abufe thair heid sprent.

¶ Thus war thay for thair forcynes left on fute baith
Thay sture hors at that straik strikin deid lay than 755
Thir riche restles renkis ruschit out full raith
Cleikit out twa swordis and togidder ran

Kest thame with gude will to do vther skaith
Bast on thair basnetis thay Beirnis or thay blan
Haistely hewit thay togidder, to leif thay war laith 760
To tyne the worschip of weir that thay air wan
Na for dout of vincussing thay went nocht away
Thus ather vther can assaill
WIth swordis of mettaill
Thay maid ane lang battaill 765
     Ane hour of the day.

¶ Thay hard harnest men thay hewit on in haist
Thay worthit heuy with heid and angerit with all
Quhill thay had maid thame sa mait thay failʒe
 almaist
Sa laith thay war on ather part to lat thair price fall
The rich restles men out of the renk past 770
Forwrocht with thair wapnis, and euill rent with all
Thair was na girth on the groūd, quhill ane gaif
 the gaist
ʒarne efter ʒeilding, on ilk syde thay call
Schir Rauf caucht to cule him, and tak mar of the
 licht
He kest vp his Veseir 775
With ane Cheualrous cheir
Sa saw he cummand full neir
     Ane vther kene Knicht.

¶ Now be the Rude said Schir Rauf, I repreif the
Thow hes brokin conditioun, thow hes not done richt
Thow hecht na bakheir to bring, bot anerly we 780
Thairto I tuik thy hand, as thow was trew Knicht
On loud said the Saraʒine, I heir the now lie
Befoir the same day I saw the neuer with sicht
Now sall thow think it richt sone, thow hes met
 with me
Gif Mahoun or Termagant may mantene my micht 785

Schir Rauf was blyth of that word ʒt blenkit with
    his face
Thow sayis thow art ane Saraȝine
Now thankit be Drichtine
That ane of vs sall neuer hine
                Vndeid in this place.

¶ Than said the Saraȝine to Schir Rauf succu-
    drously   790
I haue na lyking to lyfe to lat the with lufe
He gaue ane braid with his brand to the Beirne by
Till the blude of his browis brest out abufe
The kene Knicht in that steid stakkerit sturely
The lenth of ane rude braid he gart him remufe 795
Schir Rauf ruschit vp agane, and hit him in hy
Thay preis furth properly thair pithis to prufe
Ilk ane a schort knyfe braidit out sone
In stour stifly thay stand
With twa knyfis in hand   800
With that come Schir Rolland
                As thay had neir done.

The gentill Knicht Schir Rolland come rydand
    ful richt
And ruschit fra his Runsy, and ran thame betwene
He sayis thow art ane Saraȝine I se be my sicht
For to confound our Christin men that counteris
    sa kene   805
Tell me thy name tyte, thow trauelland Knicht
Fy on thy fechting fell hes thow bene
Thow art stout and strang, and stalwart in fecht
Sa is thy fallow in faith, and that is weill sene
In Christ and thow will trow thow takis nane outray
Forsuith the Saraȝine said   811
Thy self maid me neuer sa affraid
That I for souerance wald haue praid
                Na not sall to day.

¶ Breif me not with ʒour boist, but mak ʒow
    baith boun
Batteris on baldly the best I ʒow pray   815
Na said Schir Rolland that war na resoun
I trow in the mekle God, that maist of michtis may
The tane is in power to mak that presoun
For that war na wassalage sum men wald say
I rid that thow hartfully forsaik thy Mahoun   820
Fy on that foull Feind for fals is thy fay
Becum Christin Schir Knicht, and on Christ call
It is my will thow conuert
This wickit warld is bot ane start
And haue him halely in hart   825
                      That maker is of all.

¶ Schir Rolland I rek nocht of thy rauingis
Thow dois bot reuerance to thame that rekkis it
    nocht
Thow slane hes oft thy self of my Counsingis
Soudanis and sib men that the with schame focht
Now faindis to haue fauour with thy fleichingis 830
Now haue I ferlie gif I fauour the ocht
We sall spuilʒe ʒow dispittously at the next springis
Mak ʒow begginnis full bair bodword haue I brocht
Chace Charlis ʒour King fer out of France
Fra the Chane of Tartarie   835
At him this message wald I be
To tell him as I haue tauld the
                      Withoutin plesance.

¶ Tyte tell me thy name it seruis of nocht
ʒe Saraʒeins ar succuderus and self wiliit ay
Sall neuer of sa sour ane brandane bricht fyre be
    brocht   840
The Feynd is sa felloun als fers as he may

Sa thriue I said the Sarazine to threip is my thocht
Quha waitis the Christin with cair my cusingis ar thay
My name is Magog in will and I mocht
To ding thame doun dourly that euer war in my way
For thy my warysoun is full gude at hame quhair I dwel
In faith said Schir Rolland
That is full euill wyn land
To haue quhill thow ar leuand
              Sine at thine end hell.

¶ Wald thow conuert the in hy, and couer the of sin
Thow suld haue mair profite and mekle pardoun
Riche Douchereis seir to be sesit in
During quhill day dawis, that neuer will gang doun
Wed ane worthie to wyfe, and weild her with win
Ane of the riche of our Realme be that ressoun
The gentill Duches Dame Iane that clamis to be hir kin
Angeos and vther landis with mony riche toun
Thus may thow and thow will wirk the best wise
I do the out of dispair
In all France is nane sa fair
Als scho is appeirand air
              To twa Douchereis.

¶ I rek nocht of thy riches, Schir Rolland the Knicht
Said the rude Sarazine in Ryall array
Thy God nor thy Grassum set I bot licht
Bot gif thy God be sa gude as I heir the say

I will forsaik Mahoun, and tak me to his micht
Euer mair perpetuallie as he that mair may
Heir with hart and gude will my treuth I the plicht
That I sall lelely leif on thy Lord ay
And I beseik him of Grace and askis him mercy 870
And Christ his Sone full schene
For I haue Christin men sene
That in mony [d]angeris hes bene
     Full oft on him cry.

¶ I thank God said Rolland that word lykis me
And Christ his sweit Sone, that the that grace send 875
Thay swoir on thair swordis swyftlie all thre
And conseruit thame freindis to thair lyfis end
Euer in all trauell to leif and to die
Thay Knichtis caryit to the court, as Christ had thame kend
The King for thair cumming maid game and gle 880
With mony mirthfull [a] man thair mirthis to mend
Digne Bischoppis that day, that douchtie gart bring
And gaue him Sacramentis seir
And callit him Schir Gawteir
And sine the Duches cleir 885
     He weddit with ane ring.

¶ Than Schir Rauf gat rewaird to keip his Knichtheid
Sic tythingis come to the King within thay nyne nicht
That the Marschell of France was newlingis deid
Richt thair with the counsall of mony kene Knicht
He thocht him richt worthie to byde in his steid 890
For to weild that worschip worthie and wicht
His wyfe wald he nocht forȝet for dout of Goddis feid
He send efter that hende to leif thame in richt

Syne foundit ane fair place quhair he met the King
Euer mair perpetually 895
In the Name of Sanct July
That all that wantis harbery
                            Suld haue gestning.

Finis.[1]

---

[1] The colophon at the end is: "Imprentit at Sanctandrois be Robert Lekpreuik. Anno. 1572."

John the Reeve.

"JOHN THE REEVE," a Northumbrian or Durham tale of the fourteenth century (at present known to us only in an ignorant transcript of a fifteenth-century recension, when the art of cookery had been developed, and other social refinements, and the English table had grown comparatively luxurious and festive in taste), belongs to a rather large group of legendary productions emanating from England and the sister-kingdom and the Border during the Middle Ages. Nearly all of these have been printed in various collections of Ballad and Romance poetry; and the present piece forms part of that long-looked-for-come-at-last treasury, Bishop Percy's Folio MS.[1] Although the former owner was evidently aware of the corrupt nature of the text throughout, he did not quite prepare us for the ultimate rather startling revelation; but we have the whole truth before us, and we can see plainly enough what the MS. is, as well as what it is not.[2] For our present purpose it has yielded nothing beyond the story which follows, and which,

---

[1] Edited by Furnivall and Hales, 1867, 8vo, 4 vols. The text is very unsatisfactory. Some of the Northern forms of words could have been easily restored, and in certain places the language is clearly false or corrupt.

[2] The scribe who copied out from printed and perhaps occasionally MS. sources the contents of the Bishop's Folio was a worthy precursor of Percy, and between the two we have had what might have been a valuable body of popular literature almost utterly ruined. There is the excuse for the first copyist that he was an illiterate mechanic, with all his diligence and comprehensive zeal; but the Bishop knew better, and it must be deliberately affirmed that his lordship was not only injudicious, but dishonest.

with "Sir Eger," may be treated as the chief title of the relic to our consideration and gratitude. Nor should we have admitted a poem already rendered so accessible, and exhibited in the Percy MS. with manifest disregard to accuracy and fidelity on the part of the seventeenth-century copyist, had not the late David Laing evidently set such store by the possible opportunity of adding to a future edition of his book or books a legend which is mentioned by Bishop Douglas in his "Palace of Honour" (1503), in conjunction with "Colkelbie Sowe" and "Ralph the Collier," as popular among the Scots, and familiar to himself in his youth. Under the circumstances, we judge it sufficient to refer the reader to the introduction to the text of 1867,[1] where the peculiar value of this tale is pointed out, and where it is shown to differ in its political and social drift from its congeners in subject among the popular and national series. At the same time it is difficult to see how the narrative illustrates more than casually the state of vilainage, as John the Reeve—unquestionably, as generally happens in these cases, the hero of the situation—was not a member of that class, and merely discriminates between the nobility and bourgeoisie in his remarks to his unknown visitors. The King found him a bondman, *i.e.*, a man who gave sureties to the Crown for the performance of certain duties, and made him a franklin, conferred on him his "manor-place." Even persons in a good and substantial position in remote provincial districts would then, as now, be uncourtly and underbred enough, yet it strikes us as almost an offence against dramatic propriety to depict a man living in a sumptuous style, and able to dispense profuse hospitality, as little better than a clown when he comes to town to wait upon the King.

The citation in the text of the Bishop of Durham and the Earl of Gloucester as the neighbours of John does not assist us in fixing either the exact scene or home of the tale, nor its chronological rank. The modifications which it has evidently undergone may explain the topographical inconsistencies, where the North in one place, and Windsor and the "south-west country" in others, are said to have witnessed this adventure. It is, from its internal structure, most probably later than the "King and the Hermit."

---

[1] Bishop Percy's Folio MS., ii. 550 *et seqq.*

John the Reeve.

[Fit I.]

GOD ! through thy might and thy mercy,
All that loueth game and glee,
   Their soules to heauen bringe !
Best is mirth of all solace ;
Therfore I hope itt betokens grace,   5
   Of mirth who hath likinge.

As I heard tell this other yeere,
A clarke came out of Lancashire :
   A rolle he had reading,
A bourde written therein he ffound,   10
That some time ffell in England,
   In Edwards dayes our King.

By East, west, north, and Southe,
All this realme well run hee cowthe,
   Castle, tower, and towne.   15
Of that name were Kings 3 ;
But Edward with the long shankes was hee,
   A Lord of great renowne.

As the King rode a hunting vpon a day,
Three ffawcons fflew away ;   20
   He ffollowed wonderous ffast.
Thé rode vpon their horsses that tyde,
They rode forth on euery side,
   The country they out cast ;

From morning vntill eueninge late,   25
Many menn abroad they gate
   Wandring all alone ;

The night came att the last;
There was no man that wast
   What way the King was gone,   30

Saue a Bishopp & an Erle ffree [1]
That was allwayes the king ffull ne,
   And thus then gan they say:
"Itt is a ffolly, by St. Iohn,
For vs thus to ryde alone   35
   Soe many a wilsome way;

"A King and an Erle to ryde in hast,
A bishopp ffrom his coste to be cast,
   For hunting sikerlye.
The wether happneth wonderous ill,   40
All night wee may ryde vnskill,
   Nott wotting where wee bee."

Then the King began to say,
"Good Sir Bishopp, I you pray
   Some comfort, if you may."   45
As they stoode talking all about,
They were ware of a carle stout:
   "Good deene, ffellow!" can they say.

Then the Erle was well apayd:
"You be welcome, good ffellow!" hee sayd,   50
   "Of ffellowship wee pray thee!"
The carle ffull hye on horsse sate,
His leggs were short and braid [a-gate?]
   His stirropps were of tree;

---

[1] Presumably the Bishop of Durham and the Earl of Gloucester, whom the hero of the tale subsequently mentions as his neighbours. The last *Earl* of Gloucester died in 1347. That the Reeve did not recognise the two personages is not necessarily a difficulty, as they might never have been in that neighbourhood before, though possessing jurisdiction over it.

A payre of shooes were stiffe & store, 65
On his heele a rustye spurre,
   Thus fforwards rydeth hee.
The Bishopp rode after on his palfray :
"Abyde, good ffellow, I thee pray,
   And take vs home with thee!" 60

The carle answered him that tyde,
"From me thou gettest[1] noe other guide,
   I sweare by sweete St. Jame!"
Then said the Erle ware and wise,
"Thou canst litle of gentrise! 65
   Say not soe ffor shame!"

The carle answered the Erle vnto,
"With gentrise I haue nothing to doe,
   I tell thee by my ffay."
The weather was cold & euen roughe; 70
The King and the Erle sate and loughe,
   The Bishopp did him soe pray.

The King said, "soe mote I thee!
Hee is a carle, whosoeuer hee be!
   I reade wee ryde him neere." 75
Thé sayd [to him] with word[e]s hend,
"Ryd [more] saftlye, gentle ffreind,
   And bring vs to some harber."

Then to tarry the carle was lothe,
But rode forth as he was wrothe, 80
   I tell you sickerlye.
The king sayd, "by Mary bright,
I troe wee shall ryde all this night
   In wast[e] vnskillffullye;

---

[1] Percy Folio MS. reads *gett oft*.

"I ffeare we shall come to no towne ; 85
Ryde to the carle and pull him downe
   Hastilye without delay."
The Bishopp said soone on hye,
"Abyde, good ffellow, & take vs with thee !
   For my loue, I thee pray." 90

The Erle said, "by god in heauen !
Oft men meete att vnsett steuen ;
   To quite thee well wee may."
The carle sayd, "by St. Iohn
I am affraye of you eche one, 95
   I tell you by my ffay !"

The carle sayd, "by Marye bright,
I am afrayd of you this night !
   I see you rowne and reason,
I know you not, & itt were day, 100
I troe you thinke more then you say,
   I am affrayd of treason.

"The night is merke : I may not see
What kind of men that you bee.
   But & you will doe one thinge, 105
Swere to doe me not desease,
Then wold I ffaine you please,
   If I cold, with any thinge."

Then sayd the Erle with words ffree,
"I pray you, ffellow, come hither to mee, 110
   And to some towne vs bringe ;
And after, if wee may thee kenn,
Amonge Lords and gentlemen
   Wee shall requite thy dealinge."

"Of lords," sayes hee, "speake no moe : 116
With them I haue nothing to doe,
   Nor neuer thinke to haue ;
For I had rather be brought in bale,
My hood or that I wold vayle,
   On them to crouch or craue." 120

The King sayd curteouslye,
"What manner of man are yee
   Att home in your dwellinge?"
"A husbandman fforssooth I am,
And the Kings bondman ; 125
   Thereof I haue good likinge."

"Sir, when spake you with our King?"
"In ffaith, neuer, in all my liuing !
   He knoweth not my name ;
And I haue my Capull & my crofft ; 130
If I speake not with the King oft,
   I care not, by St. Iame !"

"What is thy name, ffellow, by thy leaue?"
"Marry," quoth hee, "Iohn the Reeue ;
   I care not who itt heare ; 135
For if you come into my inne,
With beeffe & bread you shall beginn
   Soone att your supper ;

"Salt Bacon of a yeere old,
Ale that is both sower & cold,— 140
   I vse neither braggat nor beere,—
I lett you witt withouten lett,
I dare eate noe other mette,
   I sell my wheate ech yeere."

"Why doe you, Iohn, sell your wheate?" 145
"For [I] dare not eate that I gett.
  Therof I am ffull wrothe;
For I loue a draught of good drinke as well
As any man that doth itt sell,
  And alsoe a good wheat loffe. 150

"For he that ffirst starueth Iohn the Reeue,
I pray to god hee may neuer well cheeue,
  Neither on water nor land,
Whether itt be Sherriffe or King
That makes such statuinge, 155
  I outcept neuer a one!

"For and the Kings penny were layd by mine,
I durst as well as hee drinke the wine
  Till all my good were gone.
But sithence that wee are mett soe meete, 160
Tell mee where is your recreate,
  You seeme good laddes eche one."

The Erle answered with words ffaire,
"In the kings house is our repayre,
  If wee bee out of the way." 165
"This night," quoth Iohn, "you shall not spill;
Such harbour I shall bring you till;
  I hett itt you to-day.

"Soe that yee take itt thankeffullye
In gods name & St. Iollye, 170
  I aske noe other pay;
And if you be sturdy & stout,
I shall garr you to stand without,
  For ought that you can say.

"For I haue 2 neighbors won by mee 175
Of the same ffreeledge that am I,
   Of old band-shipp are wee:
The Bishopp of Durham this towne oweth,
The Erle of Gloster—who-soe him knoweth [1]—
   Lord of the other is hee. 180

"Wist my neighbors that I were thratt,
I vow to god thé wold not lett
   For to come soone to mee;
If any wrong were to mee done,
Wee 3 durst ffight a whole afternoone, 185
   I tell you sikerlye."

The King sayd, "Iohn, tell vs not this tale;
Wee are not ordayned ffor battell,
   Our weeds are wett and cold;
Heere is no man that yee shall greeue. 190
But helpe vs, Iohn, by your leaue,
   With bright a ffeeare and bold."

"Ifaith," sayd Iohn, "that you shall want,
For ffuell heere is wonderous scant,
   As I heere haue yee told. 195
Thou getteth noe other of Iohn the Reeue;
For the kings statutes, whilest I liue,
   I thinke to vse and hold.

"If thou find in my house pain-main,[2]
Or in my kitchin poultry slaine, 200
   Peraduenture thou wold say

---

[1] See what is said above.
[2] See Hazlitt's Cookery Books, 1886, p. 195. Percy Folio MS. reads *payment fine*.

That Iohn the Reeue his band hath broken:
I wold not that such words weere spoken
   In the kings house another day,

"For itt might turne me to great greeffe; 205
Such proud ladds that beare in chief[1]
   Wold danger a pore man aye;
And or I wold pray thee of mercy lange,
Yett weere I better to lett thee gange
   In twentye twiine devills way." 210

Thus thé rode [un]to the towne:
Iohn the Reeue lighted downe
   Beside a comlye hall.
Four men beliue came wight;
They hasted them ffull swyth 215
   When they heard Iohn call;
Thé served him honestly and able,
And [led] his horsse to the stable,
   And lett noe term misfall.

Some went to warne their dame 220
That Iohn had brought guests hame.
   Shee came to welcome them tyte
In a side kirtle of greene,
Her head was dight all by-deene,
   The wiffe was of noe [mickle] pryde; 225

Her kerchers were all of silke,
Her hayre as white as any milke,
   Loue-some of hue and hyde;
Shee was thicke, & some deal braid,
Of comlye ffashyon was shee made, 230
   Both belly, backe, and side.[2]

---

[1] Percy Folio MS., *beare office*.
[2] A phrase which reminds us of the famous song in Gammer Gurton's Needle.

Then Iohn called his men all,
Sayes, "build me a ffire in the hall,
   And giue their Capulls meate ;
Lay before them corne and hay ;   235
For my loue rubb of the clay,
   For they beene weary and wett ;

"1 - - - - - -
Lay vnder them straw to the knee,
For courtye[r]s comonly wold be Iollye,
   And [they] haue but litle to spend."

Then hee said, "by St. Iohn,
You are welcome euery one,   245
   If you take itt thankefullye !
Curtesye I learned neu[e]r none,
But after mee, ffellowes, I read you gone."
   Till a chamber they went all 3 ;

A charcole ffire was burning bright,   250
Candles on chandlours light,
   Eche ffreake might other see.
"Where are your s[u]ords ?" quoth Iohn the
     Reeue.
The Erle said, "Sir, by your leaue,
   Wee weare none, pardye."   255

Then Iohn rowned with the Erle soe ffree :
"What long ffellow is yonder," quoth hee,
   "That is soe long of lim and lyre ?"
The Erle answered with words small,
"Yonder is Peeres pay-ffor-all,   260
   The Queenes Cheefe ffawconer."

---

[1] Half a stanza is lost.

"Ah, ah!" quoth Iohn, "ffor gods good,
Where gott hee that gay hood,
   Glittering as gold itt were?
And I were as proud as hee is like,   265
There is no man in England ryke
   Shold garr me keepe his gleads one yeere.

"I pray you, sir, ffor gods werke,
Who is yond in ondir[1] serke
   That rydeth Peeres soe nye?"   270
The Erle answered him againe,
"Yonder is a pore chaplaine,
   Long aduanced or hee bee;

"And I my selfe am a sumpter man,
Other craft keepe I nane,   275
   I say you withouten misse."
"You are ffresh ffellowes in your appay,
Iolly Ietters in your array,
   Proud ladds, & I trow penyles."

The King said, "soe mote I thee,   280
There is not a penny among[e]st vs three
   To buy vs bread and fflesh."
"Ah, ha!" quoth Iohn, "there is small charge;
For courtye[r]s comonlye are att large,
   If they goe neuer soe ffresh.   285

"I goe girt in a russett gowne,
My hood is of homemade browne,
   I weare neither burnett nor greene,
And yett I troe I haue in store
A 1000ᴸⁱ and some deale more,   290
   For all yee are proude[2] and ffine;

---

[1] Percy Folio MS., *yonder*.   [2] Percy Folio MS., *prouder*.

"Therfore I say, as mote I thee,
A bondman itt is good [to] bee,
   And come of carles kinne ;
For and I bee in tauerne sett, 295
To drinke as good wine I will not lett,
   As Edward[1] or his Queene."

The Erle sayd, "by gods might,
Iohn, thou art a comly knight,
   And sturdy in euerye ffray." 300
"A knight!" quoth Iohn, "doe away, ffor shame!
I am the King's bondman.
   Such wast words doe away!

"I know you not in your estate ;
I am misnurtured, well I wate ;[2] 305
   I will not therto say nay.
But if any such doe me wrang,
I will ffight with him alang,[3]
   When I am cladd in mine array."

The Bishopp sayd, "you seeme sturdye : 310
Trauelled you neuer beyond the sea?"
   Iohn sayd sharplye "nay!
I know none such strange guise,
But att home on my owne wise
   I dare hold the hye way ; 315

---

[1] Percy Folio MS., *London Edward ;* but the former word is not necessary to the rhythm, and is probably an interpolation.
[2] Percy Folio MS., *wott.*
[3] Percy Folio MS., *hand to hand.*

"And that hath done Iohn [the] Reeue scath,
For I haue made such as you wrath
   With choppes and chances yare."
"Iohn the Reeue," sayd our King,
"Hast thou any armouringe,   320
   Or any weapon to weare?"

"I vow, Sir, to god," sayd Iohn thoe,
"But a pikefforke with graines 2—
   My ffather vsed nane[1] other speare:—
A rusty sword that well will byte,   325
And a thyttille a handffull syde[2]
   That sharplye will stare,

"An acton & a habargyon a ffoote side;
And yett peraduenture I durst abyde
   As well as thou, Peeres, ffor all thy painted
      geere."   330
Quoth Iohn, "I reede wee goe to the hall,
Wee 3 ffellowes; & peeres pay-for-all
   The proudest before shall fare."

Thither they raked anon-right:
A charcole ffyer brenned[3] bright   335
   With manye a strang brand.
The hall was large & some deale wyde,
Thir bords were couered on euerye syde,
   Their mirth was comand.[4]

---

[1] Percy Folio MS., *neuer*.

[2] There is an erroneous transposition in the Percy Folio MS.

[3] Percy Folio MS., *burning*.

[4] Percy Folio MS., *comanded*. The sense appears obviously to be, Their mirth was beginning or coming.

Then the good wiffe sayd with a seemlye cheere,
"Your supper is readye there."   341
   "Yett watter,"[1] quoth Iohn, "letts see."
By then came Iohn's neighbors 2,
Hobkin long and hob alsoe:
   The ffirst ffitt here end[2] wee.   345

[Fit II.]

Iohn sayd, "for want of a marshall, I will take
   the wand:
Peeres ffauconer before shall gange;
   Begin the dish shall hee.
Goe to the bench, thou proud chaplaine,
My wiffe shall sitt thee againe;   350
   Thy meate-fellow shall shee bee."
He sett the Erle against the King;
They were ffaine att his bidding.
   Thus Iohn marshalled his meanye.

Then Iohn sperred where his daughters were:
"The ffairer shall sitt by the ffawconere;   355
   He is the best ffarrand man:
The other shall the Sompter man haue."
The Erle sayd, "soe god me saue;
   Of curtesye, Iohn, thou can."   360

"If my selfe," quoth Iohn, "be band,[3]
Yett my daughters beene well ffarrand,
   I tell you sickerlye.
Peeres, & thou wedded a daughter of Iohn
   the Reeue,[4]
There were no man that durst thee greeue   365
   Neither ffor gold nor ffee.

---

[1] Hot water, before they sat to table, an usual practice.
[2] Percy Folio MS., *ffind*.   [3] Percy Folio MS., *bound*.
[4] Percy Folio MS., *thou had wedded Iohn daughter Reeue*.

"Sompter man, & thou the other had,
In good ffaith then thou were made
   For euer in this cuntrye ;
Then, Peeres, thou might beare the prize.   370
Yett I wold this chaplaine had a benefize,
   As mote I thriue or thee ! [1]

"In this towne a kirke there is ;
And I were king, itt shold be his,
   He should haue itt of mee ;   375
Yett will I helpe as well as I may."
The King, the Erle, the Bishopp, can say,
   "Iohn, wee [2] shall quitte thee."

When his daughters were come to dease,
"Sitt ffarther," quoth Iohn withouten leaze,   380
   "For there shalbe no moe.
These strange ffellowes I doe not ken ;
Peraduenture they may be some gentlemen ;
   Therfore I and my neighbors tuo [3]

"Att side end bord wee will bee,   385
Out of the gentles companye :
   Thinke yee not best soe ?
For itt was neuer the Law of England
To sett gentle blood with band ;
   Therfore to supper will wee goe."   390

By then came in beane bread,
Salt Bacon rusted and redd,
   And brewice in a blacke dish,
Leane salt beefe of a yeere old,
Ale that was both sower & cold :   395
   This was the ffirst service :

---

[1] Percy Folio MS., *thariue or three.*
[2] Percy Folio MS., *& we liue we.*
[3] Percy Folio MS., *towe.*

Eche one had of that ylke a misse.
   The king sayd, "soe haue I blisse,
Such service ne erst[1] I see."
Quoth Iohn, "thou gettest noe other of mee   400
[2] - - - - - - -
   Att this time but this."

"Ye,[3] good fellow," the King gan say,
"Take this service here away,
   And better bread vs bringe;   405
And gett vs some better drinke;
We shall thee requite, as wee thinke,
   Without any letting."

Quoth Iohn, "beshrew the morsell of bread
This night that shall come in your head   410
   But thou sweare me one thinge!
Swere to me by booke and bell
That thou shalt neuer Iohn Reeue bettell
   vnto Edward our kinge."

Quoth the king, "to thee my troth I plight,   415
He shall nott witt our service [to-night]
   No more than he doth nowe,
Neuer while wee 3 liue in land."
"Therto," quoth Iohn, "hold vp thy hand,
   And then I will thee trowe."   420

"Loe," quoth the king, "my hand is heere!"
"Soe is mine!" quoth the Erle with a merry
   cheere,
   "Thereto I giue god a vowe."
"Haue heere my hand!" the Bishopp sayd.
"Marry," quoth Iohn, "thou may hold thee
   well apayd,   425
   For itt is ffor thy prowe.[4]

---

[1] Percy Folio MS., *nerest*.   [2] A line has been lost.
[3] Percy Folio MS., *Yes*.   [4] Percy Folio MS., *power*.

"Take this away, thou hobkin long,
And let vs sitt out of the throng
 Att a side bords end ;
These strange ffellowes thinke vncouthlye 430
This night att our Cookerye,
 Such as god hath vs send."

By then came in the pain-main[1] bread,
Wine that was both white and redd
 In siluer cupp[e]s cleare. 435
"A ha!" quoth Iohn, "our supper begins with
 drinke !
Taste itt, ladds ! & looke how yee thinke,
 For my loue, and make good cheere !

"Of meate & drinke you shall haue good ffare ;
And as ffor good wine, wee will not spare, 440
 I gie[2] you to vnderstand.
For euerye yeere, I tell thee tho,
I will haue a tunn or tuo
 Of the best that may be ffand.

"Yee shall see 3 Churles heere 445
Drinke the wine with a merry cheere ;
 I pray you doe you soe ;
And when our supper is all doone,
You and wee will dance soone ;
 Letts see who best can doe." 450

The Erle sayd, "by Mary bright,
Wheresoeuer the King lyeth this night,
 He drinketh no better wine
Than thou selfe does att this tyde."
"Infaith," quoth Iohn, "soe had leeuer I dyde
 Than liue ay in woe & pyne. 450

---

[1] Percy Folio MS., *them* and *payment*.
[2] Percy Folio MS., *goe*.

"If I be come of Carles kinne,
Part of the good that I may winne,
 Some therof shall be mine.
He that neuer spendeth but alway spareth, 400
Comonlye oft the worsse he ffareth ;
 Others will broake itt ffine."

By then came in red wine & ale :
The bores head into the hall,
 Then [a] shield with sauces seere ; 465
Capons both baked & roste,
Woodcockes, venison, without boste,
 And dish meate dight ffull deere.

Swannes they had piping hott,
Coneys, curleys, well I wott, 470
 The crane, the hearne in ffere,
Pigeons, partrid[g]e, with spicerye,
Elkes, fflomes, with ffroterye.
 Iohn bade them make good cheere.

The Erle sayd, "soe mote I thee, 475
Iohn, you serue vs as royallye !
 As yee had att London woned,[1]
If king Edward were here,
He might be a-payd with this supper,
 Such ffreindshipp wee haue ffound." 480

"Nay," sayd Iohn, "by gods grace,
And Edward wer in this place,
 Hee shold not touch this tonne.
Hee wold be wrath with Iohn, I hope ;[2]
Thereffore I beshrew the soupe 485
 That shall in his mouth come !"

---

[1] Percy Folio MS., *If yee had dwelled att London.*
[2] I.e., *I expect.*

Theratt the King laughed & made good cheere.
The Bishopp sayd, "wee fare well heere!"
 The Erle sayd as him thought.
They spake lattine amongst them there :   490
"Infayth," quoth Iohn, "and yee greeue mee [here],
 Full deere itt shalbe bought.

"Speake English euerye-eche ane,
Or else sitt still, in the devills name!
 Such talke loue I nought.   495
Lattine spoken amongst lewd men,
Therin noe reason do I ken :[1]
 For ffalshood itt is wrought.

"Row[n]ing I loue itt nother young nor old;
Therefore yee ought not to bee to bold,   500
 Nother att Meate nor meale.
Hee was ffalse that rowning begane;
Theerfore I say to you certaine
 I loue itt neuer a deale :

"That man can [nought] of curtesye   505
That lets att his meate rowning bee,
 I say, soe haue I seile."
The Erle sayd right againe,
"Att your bidding wee will be baine,
 Wee thinke you say right weele."   510

By this came vp ffrom the kitchin [2]
Sirrupps on plates good and ffine,
 Wrought in a ffayre array.

---

[1] Percy Folio MS., *ffind I can*. The Reeve's guests were whispering together, and more probably in French.

[2] This description of the entertainment furnished by the Reeve leads us to suspect that the story is not, at all events, prior to the fourteenth century.

"Sirrah," sayth Iohn, "sith wee are mett,
And as good ffellowes together sett,   615
    Lett vs be blythe to-day.

"Hodgkin long, & hob of the Lath,
You are counted good ffellowes bath,
    Now is no time to tine;¹
This wine is new come out of ffrance;   620
Be god! me list well to dance,
    Therfore take my hand in thine;²

"For wee will ffor our guests sake
Hop and dance, & Reuell make."
    The truth ffor to know,   625
Vp he rose, & dranke the wine:
"Wee must haue powder of ginger therein,"
    Iohn sayd, as I trow.

Iohn bad them stand vp all about,
"And yee shall see the carles stout   630
    Dance about the bowle.
Hob of the lathe & Hodgkin lang,
In ffayth you dance your mesures wrang!
    Methinkes that I shold know.³

"Yee dance neither Gallyard nor hawe,   635
Trace nor true mesure, as I trawe,
    But hopp as yee were woode."
When they began of ffoote to ffayle,
Thé tumbled top ouer tayle,
    And faster and faster⁴ they yode.   640

---

¹ Percy Folio MS., *thrine*.

² This is analogous to the incident in one of the Robin Hood ballads, where Robin makes the bishop dance after dinner.

³ This line is apparently a later substitution.

⁴ Percy Folio MS., *M.* and *M.*, which in printed text of 1867 is expanded into *Master and Master*,

Forth they stepped on stones store;
Hob of the lathe lay on the fflore,
   His brow brast out of blood.
"Ah, ha!" quoth Iohn, "thou makes good
    game!
Had thou not ffalled, wee had not laught [for
    shame];   545
   Thou gladds vs all, by the rood."

Iohn hent vp hobb by the hand [sae strange],
Sayes, "methinkes wee dance our measures
    wrange,
   By him that sitteth in throne."
Then they began to kicke & wince,   550
Iohn hitt the king ouer the shinnes
   With a payre of new clowted shoone.

Sith King Edward was mad a knight,
Had he neuer soe merry a night
   As he had with Iohn the Reeue [here].   555
To bed thé busked them anon,
Their liueryes were serued them vp sone
   With a merry cheere;

And thus they sleeped till morning att prine
In ffull good sheetes of line.   560
   A masse he garred them to haue,
And after they dight them to dine
With boyled capons good & ffine.
   The Erle[1] sayd, "soe god me saue,
If euer wee come to our abone,   565
We shall thee quitt our warrison;
   Thou shalt not need itt to craue."

---

[1] An alteration, perhaps made by the transcriber from the original text, unless we are to read *King*. The first Duke of Gloucester was not created till 1385.

[Fit III.]

The king tooke leaue att man & maye ;
Iohn sett him in the rode waye ;
  To windsor¹ can hee ryde.   570
Then all the court was ffull faine
That the king was comen againe,
  And thanked chr[i]st that tyde.

The Ierfawcons were taken againe
In the fforrest of windsor without laine   575
  The Lords did soe provyde,
They thanked god & St Iollye.
To tell the Queene of their harbor[ye]
  The lords had ffull great pryde.

The Queene sayd, "Sir, by your leaue,   580
I pray you send ffor that noble Reeue
  That I may see him with sight."
The Messenger was made to wend,
And bad Iohn Reeue goe to the King [hend]
  Hastilye with all his might.   585

Iohn waxed vnfaine in bone & blood :
Saith, "dame, to me this is nae good,
  My truth to you I plight."
"You must come in your best array."
"What to?" sayd Iohn ; "Sir, I thee pray :   590
  "Thou must be made a Knight."

"A knight," said Iohn, "by Mary myld
I know right well I am beguiled
  With the guests I harbord late.

---

[1] This is, no doubt, a change similarly made by the same hand, as the Court would have been more probably in the North.

To debate they will me bring; 695
Yett cast I mee ffor nothinge
   Noe sorrow ffor to take;

"Allice, ffeitch mee my side Acton,
My round pallett to my crowne,
   Is made of Millayne plate, 600
A pitch-fforke and a swerd."
Shee sayd shee was afferd [1]
   This deede would make debate.

Allice ffeitched downe his acton syde;
Hee tooke itt ffor no muckle [2] pryde, 605
   That hee must itt weare.
The scaberd was rent withouten doubt,
A large handfull the bleade hanged out:
   Iohn the Reeue saw [3] there,

"Gett lether & a nayle," Iohn can say, 610
"Lett me sow itt a chape to-day,
   Lest men scorne my geere.
Now," sayd Iohn, "will I see
[W]hether itt will out lightlye
   Or I meane itt to weare." 615

Iohn pulled ffast att the blade:
I wold hee had kist my arse that itt made:
   He could not gett itt out.
Allice held, & Iohn droughe,
Either att other ffast loughe, 620
   I doe yee out of doubt.

---

[1] Percy Folio MS., *sword* and *affrayd*. In the first line the Folio MS. reads *ffeitch mee downe*.

[2] Percy Folio MS., *little*, and in the next line *yett*. But the Reeve is ashamed of the condition of his armour.

[3] Percy Folio MS., *sayd;* but he has yet to speak.

Iohn pulled att the scaberd soe hard,
Againe a post he ran backward
   And gaue his head a rowte.
His wiffe did laughe when he did ffall,
And soe did his meanye all .
   That were there neere about.

Iohn sent after his neighbors bath,
Hodgkine long & hobb of the lath.
   They were be him[1] att his biddinge.
Three pottles of wine in a dishe
They supped itt all off, as I wis,
   All there att their partinge.

Iohn sayd, "& I had my bucklere,
Theres nothing that shold me dere,
   I tell you all in ffere.
Feitch me downe," quoth he, "my mittons;[2]
They came but on my hands but ons
   This 22 yeere.

"Feitch mee my Capull," sayd hee there.
His saddle was of a new manere:
   His stirropps were of a tree.
"Dame," he sayd, "ffcitch me wine;
I will drinke to thee once againe,
   I troe I shall neuer thee see.

"Hodgkin long & hob of the lathe,
Tarry & drinke with me bathe,
   For my cares are ffast comande."
They dranke 5 gallons verament:
"Farwell ffellowes all present,
   For I am readye to gange!"

---

[1] Percy Folio MS., *beene*. They were with or by him at his call. The form might, perhaps, be *be 'm*. In the second line of stanza *Hob of the lath* is to be understood as Hob of the Leet Court. He was an officer of that tribunal.

[2] Percy Folio MS., *gloues;* but comp. line 727.

Iohn was soe combred in his geere
Hee cold not gett vpon his mare
   Till hodgkinn heaue vp behind.
- - - - - - - -[1]

"Now ffarwell, Sir, by the roode!"
To neither Knight nor Barron good
   His hatt he wold not vayle
Till he came to the Kings gate :
The Porter wold not lett him in therat,
   Nor come without[2] the walle,

Till a Knight came walking out.
They sayd, "yonder standeth a carle stout
   In a rusticall arraye."
On him they all wondred right,
And said he was an vnseemelye wight,
   And thus to him gan say :

"Hayle, ffellow! where wast thou borne?
Thee beseemeth ffull well to weare a horne!
   Where haddest thou that ffaire geere?
I troe a man might seeke ffull long,
One like to thee ar that hee fong,[3]
   Tho he sought all this yeere."

Iohn bad them kisse the devills arse :
"For you my geare is much the warse!
   You will itt not amende,
By my ffaith, that can I rede![4]
Vpon the head I shall you shread
   But if you hence wende!

---

[1] Three lines are lost.   [2] Percy Folio MS., *within*.
[3] Percy Folio MS. reads *ffound*. This emendation was proposed by Dyce. It is the right word.
[4] Percy Folio MS., *lead*.

"The devill him speede vpon his crowne
That causeth me to come to this towne,
　Whether he weare Iacke or Iill!
What shold such men as I doe heere　　　696
Att the kings Manere?
　I might haue beene att home still."

As Iohn stoode fflyting ffast,
He saw one of his guests come att last;
　To him he spake ffull bold,　　　690
To him he ffast ffull rode,
He vayled neither hatt nor hode;
　Sayth, "thou hast me betold!

"Full well I wott by this light
That thou hast disdainde mee right;　　　695
　For wrat[h] I waxe neere wood!"
The Erle sayd, "by Mary bright,
Iohn, thou made vs a merry night;
　Thou shalt haue nothing but good."

The Erle took leaue att Iohn Reeue,　　　700
Sayd, "thou shalt come in without greeue;
　I pray thee tarry a while."
[1] - - - - -

The Erle into the hall went,
And told the King verament
　That Iohn Reeue was att the gate;
"To no man list hee lout;
A rusty sword gird him about,　　　710
　And a long ffawchyon, I wate."

The King said, "goe wee to meate,
And bringe him when wee are sett;
　Our dame shall haue a play."

---

[1] Three lines are lost.

"He hath 10 arrowes in a thonge, 715
Some are short & some are long,
 The sooth as I shold say;

"A rusty sallett vpon his crowne,
His hood were made [of] home browne;
 There may nothing him dare; 720
A thytill hee hath ffast in his hand
That hangeth in a peake band,
 And sharplye itt will share.

"He hath a pouch hanging ffull wyde;
A rusty Buckeler on the other syde, 725
 His mittons are of blacke clothe.
Who-soe to him sayth ought but good,
[I swear it to you by the rood,]
 Full soone hee wilbe wrothe."

Then Iohn sayd, "Porter, lett mee in! 730
Some of my goods thou shalt win;
 I loue not ffor to pray."
The Porter sayd, "stand abacke!
And thou come neere I shall thee rappe,
 Thou carle, by my ffay!" 735

Iohn tooke his fforke in his hand,
He bare his fforke on an end,
 He thought to make a ffray;
His Capull was wight, & corne ffedd;
Vpon the Porter hee him spedd, 740
 And him had welnye slaine.

He hitt the Porter vpon the crowne,
With that stroke hee ffell downe,
 Forsooth as I you tell;
And then hee rode into the hall, 745
And all the doggs both great & small
 On Iohn ffast can thé yell.

Iohn layd about as hee were wood,
And 4 hee killed as hee stood ;
   The rest will now be ware.   750
Then came fforth a squier hend,
And sayd, "Iohn, I am thy ffrend,
   I pray you light downe heere."

Another sayd, "giue me thy fforke,"   754
And Iohn sayd, "nay, by S. William of Yorke,
   First I will cracke thy crowne !"
Another sayd, "lay downe thy swerde ;
Sett vp thy horsse ; be not afferd ;
   Thy bow, good Iohn, lay downe ;

"I shall hold your stirroppe ;   760
Doe of your pallett & your hoode
   Ere thé ffall, as I troe.
Yee see not who sitteth att the meate ;
Yee are a wonderous silly ffreake,
   And alsoe passing sloe !"   765

1 - - - - - - -

"What devill," sayd Iohn, "is that ffor thee?
Itt is my owne, soe mote I thee !   770
   Therfore I will itt weare."

The Queene beheld him in hast :
"My lord," shee sayd, "ffor gods ffast,
   Who is yonder that doth ryde ?
Such a ffellow saw I neuer yere ;   775
Shee saith, "hee hath the quaintest geere,
   He is but simple of pryde."

Right soe came Iohn as hee were wood ;
He vayled neither hatt nor hood,
   He was a saly ffreake ;   780

---

[1] Three lines are lost ; their sense can be guessed.

He tooke his fforke as hee wold iust;
Vp to the dease ffast he itt thrust.
   The Queene ffor ffeare did speake,

And sayd, "lords, beware, ffor gods grace!
For hee will ffrowte some in the fface   785
   If yee take not good heede!"
Thé [all] laughed without[en] doubt,
And soe did all that were about,
   To see Iohn on his steede.

Then sayd Iohn to our Quceene,   790
"Thou mayst be proud, dame, as I weene,
   To haue such a ffawconere!
For he is a well ffarrand man,
And much good manner hee can,
   I tell you sooth in ffere.   795
¹ - - - - - - - -

"But, lord," hee sayd, "my good, its thine;
My body alsoe, ffor to pine,
   For thou art king with crowne.
But, lord, thy word is honorable,
Both stedffast, sure, and stable,   800
   And alsoe great of renowne!

"Therfore haue mind what thou me hight
When thou with me [harbord] a night,
   A warryson that I shold haue."
Iohn spoke to him with sturdye mood,   805
Hee vayled neither hatt nor hood,
   But stood with him checkmate.

The King sayd, "fellow mine,
For thy capons hott & good red wine
   Much thankes I doe giue thee."   810

---
¹ Something is lost.

The Queene sayd, "by Mary bright,
Award him as [it is] his right ;
  Well aduanced lett him bee !"

The King sayd vntill him than,
"Iohn, I make thee a gentleman ;   815
  Thy manor-place I thee giue,
And a 100ˡⁱ to thee and thine,
And euery yeere a tunn of red wine
  Soe long as thou dost liue."

By[1] then Iohn began to kneele :   820
"I thanke you, my Lord, as I haue seil,[2]
  Therof I am well payd."
The King tooke a coller bright,
"Iohn,[3] heere I make thee knight
  With worshippe," then hee sayd.   825

Then was Iohn euill apayd,
And amongst them all thus hee sayd,
  "Full oft I haue heard tell
That after a coller comes a rope ;
I shall be hanged by the throate ;   830
  Methinkes itt doth not well."

"Sith thou hast taken this estate,
That euery man may itt wate,
  Thou must begin the bord."
Then Iohn therof was nothing ffaine—   835
I tell you truth with-outen laine,—
  He spake neuer a word,

---

[1] Percy Folio MS., *But*.   [2] Percy Folio MS., *soule*.
[3] In Percy Folio MS. these two lines read :

  And sayd, "Iohn heere I make thee a knight
    With worshippe. When hee sayd."

But att the bords end he sate him downe;
For [all] hee had leeuer beene att home
   Then att all their ffrankish ffare;[1]   840
For there was wine, well I wott;
Royall meates [dainty and hott][2]
   Were sett before him there.

A gallon of wine was put in a dishe;
Iohn supped itt of, both more & lisse.   845
   "Feitch," quoth the King, "such more."
"By my Lady," quoth Iohn, "this is good wine!
Lett vs make merry, ffor now itt is time;
   Christs curse on him that doth itt spare!"

With that the Porter hend came in   850
And kneeled downe before the King,
   Was all berunnen with blood.
Then the King in hart was woe,
Sayes, "Porter, who hath dight thee soe?
   Tell on; I wax neere wood."   855

"Now infaith," sayd Iohn, "that same was I,
For to teach him some curtesye,
   For thou hast taught him noe good.
For when thou came to my pore place,
With mee thou found soe great a grace,   860
   Noe man bad thee vail thy hood;[3]

"For if any man had against thee spoken,
His head ffull soone I shold haue broken,"
   Iohn sayd, "with-outen doubt.

---

[1] Yet the Reeve provided an equally sumptuous repast for guests of whose station he was unaware.
[2] Percy Folio MS., *of the best sortes.*
[3] Percy Folio MS., *did bidd thee stand without.*

Therfore I warne thy porters [so] ffree, 865
When any man [comes] out of my Countrye,
 Lett¹ them not be soe stout.

"If both thy porters goe walling wood,
Begod I shall reaue their hood,
 Or I go on ffoote out.² 870
But thou, Lord, hast after me sent,
And I am come att thy commandement
 Hastilye withouten doubt."

The King sayd, "by St. Iame!
Iohn, my porters were to blame; 875
 Yee did nothing but right."
He tooke the case into his hand;
Then to kisse hee made them gange;
 Then laughed both King and Knight. 879
"I pray you," quoth the King, "good ffellows bee."
"Yes," quoth Iohn, soe mote I thee,
 We were not wrathe ore night."

The Bishopp said to him tho,
"Iohn, send hither thy sonnes tuo;
 To the schoole I shall them find, 885
And soe god may for them werke,
That either of them haue a kirke
 If ffortune be their ffrind.

"Also send hither thye daughters I craue;³
Two marryages the King will garr them haue, 890
 And wedd them with a ringe.
Wend fforth, Iohn, on thy way,
Looke thou be kind & curteous aye,
 Of meate & drinke be nere nithing."

---

 ¹ Percy Folio MS., *Another let.*
 ² Percy Folio MS., *Or go on ffoote boote.*
 ³ Percy Folio MS., *both.*

Then Iohn took leaue of King & Queene,   895
And after att all the court by-deene,
   And went fforth on his way.
He sent his daughters to the King,
And they were wedded with a ringe
   Vnto tuo squiers gay.   900

His sonnes both hardye & wight,
The one of them was made a Knight,
   And fresh in euery ffray;
The other a parson of a kirke,
Gods seruice ffor to worke,   905
   To serue god night & day.

Thus Iohn Reeue and his wiffe
With mirth & jollity ledden their liffe;
   To god they made laudinge.
Hodgkin long & hobb of the lathe,   910
They were made ffreemen bathe
   Through the grace of our hend King.[1]

Then thought [John] on the Bishopps word,
And euer after kept open bord
   For guests that god him send;   915
Till death ffeitcht him away
To the blisse that lasteth aye:
   And thus Iohn Reeue made an end.

Thus endeth the tale of Reeue soe wight.
God that is soe ffull of might,   920
   To heauen their soules bring
That haue heard this litle story,
That happed sometime in the north countrye[2]
   In long Edwards dayes our King!

---

[1] Percy Folio MS., *the King hend*.
[2] Percy Folio MS., *liued—south-west*, one reading wrong, the other a thoughtless change.

The Laping of Lord Fergus's Gaist.

THIS amusing Interlude, preserved by Bannatyne in his "Ballet Buik,"[1] 1568, has already been printed in the "Minstrelsy of the Scottish Border,"[2]—where it is said to be "in the same strain with the verses concerning the Gyre Carline. As the mention of Bettokis Bowr occurs in both pieces, and as the scene of both is laid in East Lothian, they are perhaps composed by the same author." At the close there is mention of "Cokleby's feist," in apparent recollection of the burlesque composition which has preceded. Sir Walter Scott, with his usual discrimination, at the same time observes, "The humour of these fragments seems to have been directed against the superstitions of Rome, but it is now become very obscure. Nevertheless the verses are worthy of preservation, for the sake of the ancient language and allusions."

Calderwood, in his highly valuable, but unpublished "History of the Church of Scotland," mentions James Wedderburn as one of those who, before the Reformation, being persecuted on account of their religious opinions, fled from Scotland;—and says, that "he had a good gift of poesie, and made diverse Comedies and Tragedies in ye Scotish tongue, q^{r}in he nipped the abuses and superstitions of the time." The historian adds, that "he counterfeited also ye conjuring of ane gaist, q^{ch} was indeed practised be Frier Lang, beside Kinghorn, q^{ch} Frier Lang had been Confessor to ye King;—But after ye conjuring the King was constrained

---

[1] MS. fol. 114. [2] Vol. i. p. clx.

for shame to remove him." Walter Lang is mentioned in *Colkelby's Sow*, suprà. A curious allusion to this story occurs in the "Epistle of Alareit," already given above:—

> —Bot ordourlie to dress this thing
> A gaist I purpois to gar gang
> By counsaill of Frier Walter Lang — —
> That practick he provit anis befoir
> Betuix Kyrkaldie and Kinghorne
> Bot Lymmaris maid thereat sik skorne
> And to his fame mad sik digressioun
> Sensyne he hard not the Kingis confessioun
> Thoicht at that time he come with speid.[1]

From the allusion by Calderwood it has been conjectured that Wedderburn was the author of the following burlesque poem.

The Laying of Lord Fergus's Gaist.

LISTIS lordis, I sall ȝow tell
   Off ane verry grit meruell,
   Off Lord Ferguß gaist,
   How mekle Sr Andro it chest,
   Vnto Beittokis bour,   6
The silly sawle to succour:
And he hes writtin vnto me,
Auld storeiß for to sé,
Gif it appinis him to meit,
How he sall coniure the spreit: 10
And I haif red mony quarß
Bath the Donet, and Dominusque parß,
Ryme maid, and als reiddin,
Bath Inglis and Latene:
And ane story haif I to reid   15
Passß Bonitatem in the creid—
To coniure the littill gaist ȝe mon haif
Off tod tailis ten thraif

---

[1] Knox's History, edit. 1732, p. 25.

And kast the grit haly watter
W{t} pater noster, patter patter   20
And ȝe man sitt in ane compaſs
And cry, Harbert tuthless,
Drag thow, and þiss draw,
And sitt thair quhill cok craw.
The compass mon hallowit be   25
With Aspergis me Domine;
The haly writt schawis als
Thair man be hung abowt ȝour hals
Pricket in ane woll poik
Off neiſs powder ane grit loik.   30
Thir thingis mon ȝe beir,
Brynt in ane doggis eir,
Ane plucke, ane paiddill, and ane palme corſs
Thre tuskis of ane awld deid horſs,
And of ane ȝallow wob the warp,   35
The boddome of ane awld herp,
The heid of ane cuttit reill,
The band of ane awld quheil,
The taill of ane ȝeild sow,
And ane bait of blew wow,   40
Ane botene, and ane brechame,
And ane quhorle maid of lame,
To luke owt at the litill boir,
And cry, Chrystis crosſs, ȝow befoir:
And quhen ȝe sé the kittill gaist,   45
Cumand to ȝow in all haist,
Cry lowd Chryste eleisone,
And speiris quhat law it leivis on?
And gif it sayis on Gode ley,
Than to the littill gaist ȝe say,   50
W{t} braid benedicitie;
Littill gaist, I coniure thé,
W{t} harie & larie,
Bay{t} fra God, & Sanct Marie,

First wt ane fisschis mowth,
And syne wt ane fowlis towth,
W{t} ten pertane tais,
And nyne knokę of windil strais,
W{t} thré heidę of curle doddy.
And bid the gaist turn in a boddy.
Then eſtir this coniuratioun,
The littill gaist will fall in soun,
And þ{r} eſtir doun ly,
Cryand mercy petously;
Than wt ȝour left heill it sane,
And it will nevir cum agane,
Als mekle as ane mige amaist. — —
He had a littill wé leg,¹
And it was cant as ony cleg,
It wes wynd in ane wyndin scheit,
Bay{t} the handę and the feit:
Suppois this gaist wes littill
ȝit it stall fra Godis quhitell;
It stall fra peteouss Abrahame,
Ane quhorle and ane quhū quhame;
It stall frae the carle of þe mone
Ane pair awld yrn schone;
It ran to Pencaitlane,
And wirreit ane awld chaplane
This littill gaist did na mair ill
Bot clok lyk a corne in myll;
And it wald play and hop,
Abowt the heid ane stra strop;
And it wald sing and it wald dance,
Ourefute and Orliance.
Quha coniurit the littill gaist sa ȝe?
Nane bot the littil Spenzie flé
That wt hir wit and ingyne,

---

¹ Apparently one or more lines are here omitted.

Gart the gaist leif agane;
And sune mareit the gaist the flé,
And cround him kyng of Kandelie;
And they gat thame betwene,
Orpheus king and Elpha quene,
To reid quha will this gentill geist
ӡe hard it no{t} at Cokilby's feist.

Explicit.

Sir John Rowll's Cursing.

DUNBAR, in his "Lament for the Death of the Makkaris," bewails the fate of two contemporary poets named Rowll, with whom he seems to have been familiar. He says:

> "Death hes tane Rowll of Abirdene
> And gentill Rowll of Corstorphyn;
> Two bettir fallowis did no man sie;
> *Timor mortis conturbat me!*" [1]

But so little is known concerning these two ecclesiastics, as to leave it uncertain which of them should be considered author of the following singular invective:—which, indeed, is the solitary memorial that remains of the talents of either one or other of two men who received from their illustrious friend this testimony to the excellence of their natural dispositions.

Sir David Lyndsay also names Rowll with other Scotish poets, of whom he says:

> "Thocht thay be deid, thair libellis bene levand,
> Quhilkis, to reherse, makith reidaris to rojose." [2]

Rowll's poem has been preserved both in George Bannatyne's and Sir Richard Maitland's collections of old Scotish poetry. Lord Hailes says, "Whether it was written by him, or only in his name, I know not. The following passage in it (he adds) determines the era at which he lived:

> ——"and now of Rome that beiris the rod,
> Undir the hevin to lowse and bind,
> Paip Alexander."

---

[1] Bann. MS., fol. 104.
[2] Lyndsay's Works, vol. i. p. 285.

The Pontiff here meant must have been the virtuous Alexander VI., who was Divine Vicegerent from 1492 to 1503."[1] And Dunbar's poem, which commemorates their death, was printed in the year 1508.

Pinkerton mentions the following poem, which appears to copy the extravagant vein of the strange compositions known as "Flytings," with great contempt, styling it a stupid and despicable production; and quoting the last lines,

" This *tragedy* is callit, but dreid
Rowlis cursing, quha will it reid,"

says the author "might have put a point of interrogation at the close."[2] The name of "Tragedy," in the language of those times, was applied to any descriptive poem, nor was it appropriated to dramatic compositions in England before the reign of Henry VIII., although no regular tragedy was produced earlier than January 1561, when "Ferrex and Porrex" was first represented.

Sir John Rowll's "Cursing" may be considered as a religious satire, being, as Lord Hailes justly observed, "an invective against those who defraud the clergy of their dues, and has no resemblance to any sort of dramatic composition."[3] Dr. Leyden[4] thought that in acrimony it was little inferior to Sterne's chapter of curses: and the author's invocation of all the devils to revenge the stealing of his geese, he considered as forming a curious contrast to Sir John of Grantam's curse for the Miller's eels that were stolen, recorded in Harsnet's "Detection of Egregious Impostures," 1604; but an anecdote current long before the Archbishop's day, as it is one of the "Hundred Merry Tales," 1526, and is quoted from that source by Scot in his "Discovery of Witchcraft," 1584,

" All you that have stolen the Miller's eelis,
Laudate Dominum de cælis:
And all that have consented thereto,
Benedicamus Domino.

---

[1] Bannatyne Poems, 1770, p. 272.
[2] Maitland Poems, 1786, p. 451.
[3] Bannatyne Poems, 1770, p. 270.
[4] Glossary to the Complaynt of Scotland, 1801, p. 329.

After the author has excommunicated

> " Baith the halderis and conceilaris,
> Ressetaris and the preve steilaris,"

and bade them "hy to the pot of hell," the lines

> " In hellis hoill quhair nevir is licht,
> Nor nevir is day, bot evir nicht,
> Quhair nevir is joy evin & morrow
> Bot endlis pane, dule & sorrow,
> Quhair nevir is petie nor concord,
> Nor amitie, bot discord,
> Malice, rancour, & invy," &c.,

are very striking, and remind us of the impressive description by a greater poet, of

> " A dungeon horrible on all sides round,
> As one great furnace flam'd; yet from those flames
> No light; but rather darkness visible
> Serv'd only to discover sights of woe,
> Regions of sorrow, doleful shades, where peace
> And rest can never dwell; hope never comes,
> That comes to all; but torture without end
> Still urges, and a fiery deluge, fed
> With ever-burning sulphur unconsumed."
> —MILTON.

Heir followis the cursing of Sᵣ Johne Rowlis upoun the steilaris of his fowlis.

DEVYNE power of michtis maist
Of Fadir Sone and Haly Ghaist
Jesu Chryst and his appostillis
Petir Paule and his discippillis
And all þe power vndir God
And now of Rome þat beiris the rod
Vndir þe hevin to lowse & bind
Paip Alexander þat we do fynd

W^t þat power that Petir gaif
Godis braid malesone nixt thay haif   10
And all þe blude about þair hairt
Blak be þair hour blak be þair pairt
For fyve fat geiss of sir Johne Rowlis
W^t caponis hēis and vþir fowlis
Baith þe halderis and conceilaris   15
Ressettaris and the preve steilaris
And he þat saulis saifis and dāmis
Beteich the devill thair guttis and gāmis
Their toung their teith thair handis their feit
   And all thair body haill compleit   20
That brak his ȝaird and stall his frutt
And raif his erbis vp be þe rute
His quheit his aitis his peiss his beir
In stowk or stakt to do him deir
In barne in houss in kill or mill   25
Except it had bene his awin will
His wow his lamb his cheis his stirk
Or ony teyndis of haly kirk
And all þat lattis vnkend or knawin
The vicar to dispone his awin   30
Kirkland hay or gerfs to awaill
Be thair support red or counsall
Now cursit and wareit be þair werd
Quhill thay be levand on this erd
Hungir sturt and tribulatioun   35
And nevir to be w^tout vexatioun
Of vengeance sorrow sturt and cair
Graceless thriftles and threid bair
All tymes in þair legasie
Fyre sword watter and woddie   40
Or ane of thir infirmeteis
Off warldly scherp aduerseteis
Pouertie pestilence or peplecy
Dum deif or edroposy

Maigram madness or missilry 45
Appostrum or þe perlocy
Fluxis hyvis or huttit ill
Hoist heidwark or fawin ill
Kald kanker feister or feveris
Brukis bylis blobbis and bleistiris 50
Emeroidese or the sair halss
The pokkis the spaving in þe halss
The panefull gravell and the gutt
The gulsoch that they nevir be but
Seattica and arrattica 55
The cruke the cramp the collica
The worme the wareit wedonȳpha
Rumbursin rippillis or bellythra
The choikis that haldis the chaftis fra chowing
Golkgaliter at the hairt growing 60
The stane wring stane and staneblind
The berne bed and mor behind
The strangelour and grit glengloir
The harchatt in þe lippis befoir
The mowlis and þʳ sleip the mair 65
The kanker and the kattair
Mott fall vpoun thair kankart corss
With all þe evil that evir had horss
Fische fowll beist or man
In erd sen first þe warld began 70
Till thay remember or thay dé
Repentand þair iniquitie
And draw þair inclinatioun
Fra stowth to contemplatioun
Fra feyndis fell subiectioun 75
To haly kirkis correctioun
Sua thay mak plane confessioun
Thair gud will and contritioun
Confessand þame to þair curatt
That in þair hairtis is evill indurat 80

Na vþir preist hes power nor freir
And thay that daly will perseveir
Nocht dreidand God in work nor word
Nor ȝit of haly kirk the suord
Bot in þair cursit and sinfull wayis 85
Levand and dryvand our thair dayis
Nor ask God mercy nor repent
Than this salbe þair sacrament
Fra God our Lady and all thair hallowis
To þe feynd þair saulis thair craig the gallowis 90
I gif and Cerberus thair banis sall knaw
For þair dispyt of þe kirkis law
Gog and Magog and grym Garog
The devill of hell the theif Harog
Sym Skȳnar and Sr Garnega 95
Julius appostata
Prince Pluto and quene Cokatrice
Devetinus þe devill þat maid þe dyce
Cokadame and Semiamis
Fyremouth and Tutivillus 100
And Browny als þat can play kow
Behind þe claith w^t mony mow
All thir about the beir salbe
Singand ane dolorus dergie
And vþiris devillis thair salbe sene 105
Als thik as mot in sonis beme
Thair sal thay kary in þair clukis
Sum libberlais and sum hell crukis
Sum w^t kāis and sum w^t kardis
Sum w^t quhippis of leddrin tardis 110
Sum w^t clubbis and mellis of leid
Sum w^t brandrathis birnand reid
Sum w^t rūpillis lyk a skait
And geiss and caponis rostit hait
That sal be laschit on þair lippis 115
Cum thay w^{t}in þe devillis grippis

W^t skulȝeoun clowttis and dressing knyvis
Platt for plat on þr gyngyvis
Sayis richt thus of Rowlis geiss
Thame chaftis þame chowit every peiss 120
For thow art he and thow art scho
That Rowlis blak robene put in bro
And thow art scho that stall þe hen
And put her in þe pot þair ben
Lo this is he þat w^t his hairt 125
Wald nevir gif the vicar his pairt
Bot ay abowt for to dissaif
The haly kirk þat it sowld haif
Than ruffy tasker w^t his flaill
Sall beit þame all fra top to taill 130
 And ruffy ragmē w^t his taggis
Sall ryfe þair sinfull saule in raggis
And quhen þe devillis hes þame tirvit
All þair saulis sal be transformit
Sum in bichis and sum in beiris 135
Sum in mvlis and sum in meiris
Aganis the statour þat thay wer īn
For vengence of þair deidly sin
To ryd and tak possessioun
Throw all hell vp and doun 140
And w^t grit din and deray
Compeir sall Sathan but delay
Sayand richt thus w^t sentēce hé
Vpoun þe day þat thow sall dé
I devill of deillis I ȝow cōdame 145
For geis for ȝowis for woll for lame
Thairfoir hy ȝow to þe pott of hell
W^t Sathan our Abirone to dwell
As feyndis spreitis perpetualy
For to remane in mesary 150
Deip Acheron ȝour saulis invaid
As blak as ruch as ony taid

Snaykis serpentis and edderis
Mott stuf ȝoͬ bellyis & ȝoͬ bledderis
In hellis hoill qͬ nevir is licht
Nor nevir is day bot evir nicht
Qͬ nevir is joy evin & morrow
Bot endlis pane dule & sorrow
Qͬ nevir is petie nor concord
Nor amitie bot discord
Malice rācour & invy
Wᵗ magry & malācoly
Than fra þe sentence be on þame said
Grit Baliall sall gif a braid
And bakwart leip vpon a beir
Sum on ane mvle sum on a meir
Sum on wolffis and sum on wichis
Sum on brodsowis sum on bichis
Than is þair noᵗ bot sadill & brydill
Thir outtit meiris hes lang gane ydill
Bot sic ane clawing wᵗ þair clukis
And sic ane reirding wᵗ þͬ rukis
Rāpand wᵗ ane hiddowis beir
Cryand all is ouris þat is heir
The memberis of the wickit mē
That staw the guse þe cok the hen
Thay salbe revin be þe throttis
For cutting of the fowlis croppis
Syne led in towis and in lang tedderis
And daly etin wᵗ taidis & edderis
That all þe court of hevin may knaw
Thay war the thevis þat Rowlis geiss staw [1]
For quhy grit God our hiest juge [2]
He gaif decreit but refuge
That all pykaris of pultre
Gais noᵗ to hevin bot thay sall fle

---

[1] 'Maye Ebin' in the MS.   [2] 'Evin,' MS.

To hell wtout redēptioun
Qr is no remissioun
The forme of thir vgly devillis
Thay hafe lang tailis on þair heilis 190
And rūpillis hingand on þair tailis
Dragoun heidis & warwolf nalis
Wt glowrane eyne as glitterad glass
Wt bowgillis & hornis maid of brass
And dyverss facis [1] repleit wt yre 195
Spowtād vēnū & sparkis of fyre
And sum wt teith and tegir tungis
Attour þair chin wt bludy dangis
Spottit and sprinklit vp & doun
Reid attry lyk a scorpioun 200
And sum ar smeith & sum are ruch
And sum ar lyk ane serpentis sluch
Wt prik mule eiris sum ar lyk
Thair eiris neifs ar lyk ane midding tyk
Wt gaippand mowth richt ȝaip to swelly 205
Ehe mair the less devill in his belly
Of þair fowle fegouris na mā can tell
Thot thay wer sevin ȝeiris in hell
To leir to paynt portour or blasoun
Thair forme & thayr feyndly fassoun 210
Thair vgsum horribiliteis
Nor ȝit na þt schaipis wt scheiris
Thot infineit he be of ȝeiris
Maist principaly to schaip þair graith
In hell for steilling heir of claith 215
Can conterfit nor mak it meit
Ane gabart for a deill cōpleit
And ȝit in hell ar mony ane
That said þai war als trew as stane
Gif þr be ony in þis houss 220

---

[1] 'Eyne,' MS.

That beiris þe nedill gorrit þe lowss
I þame beseik thay be no{t} wraith
Suppois they clyit haif parte of claith
Bot seik þe causs and leif þe deid
And blame þe scheiris þat raif þe skreid 225
And quha þat steilis & on stowth levis
Cursit mot thay be amang thir thevis
Now to þe effect ga will I
And speik of feyndis phantesy
In court no{t} wt þe quene of fary 230
But heltaris heidtailis sonkis or sadillis
But butis or spurris crukis or ladillis
W{t} full berdis blasand in þe wind
And hett speitis in þair taill behind
Than instar tasy wt his jaggis 235
And belly bassy wt his baggis
At hellis ʒettis sall mak sic reirding
On thir steillaris of geiss sall ding
That it beis hard in middil erd
The grit flappis wt sic faird 240
Thunder blastis & fyre sall blaw
That na devill may ane vþir knaw
For reik stynk & brynstane birnand
Devillis ʒelpand gaipand and girnand
Than sall Baliall gif ane brattill 245
And all the thevis in hell sall startill
Lyk to ane gaid of yrne or steill [1]
That doun war sinkand in ane weill
Sa sall thay ga to endles pane
And nevir to cum hame agane 250
    Now Jesu for thy passioun
And deit for our redemptioun

---

[1] 'Bla' in the MS. is inserted before 'Baliall,' apparently by mistake.

Of mākynd haif mercy sone
Latt never this sentēce sall þame vpone
Bot grant þame grace ay till forbeir 255
Resset or stowth of vþir mēis geir
And als agane þe geir restoir
Till Rowl as I hafe said befoir
And to repent thay may in tyme
Pray we to God thus endis [the] ryme 260
This tragedy is callit but dreid
Rowlis cursing quha will it reid.

Finis.

Ane Ballet of the Nine Nobles.

ON the margin of the ancient copy of Fordun's "Scotichronicon," that once belonged to the celebrated historian, Hector Boece, is written this translation of some barbarous Latin verses, added by Bower about the year 1440, and occurring in most copies of the same Chronicle.[1] It has, indeed, been already printed, but may, without much impropriety, be inserted in this place; particularly as it is given from the Manuscript itself,—the copy printed by the industrious antiquary, Thomas Hearne, not being remarkable for its accuracy:

> " On fut suld be all Scottis weir,
> Be hyll and mosse, thaim selff to 'steir.'[2]
> Llat wod for wallis be bow and speir,
> That innymeis do thaim na deir.
> In streit placis gar keip all stoir;
> And byrne the plane land thaim befor:
> Thane sall thai pass away in haist,
> Quhen that thai find na thing bot waist.
> With wyllis and waykene of the nycht,
> And mekill noyis maid on hycht:
> Thane sall thai turne with gret affrai,
> As thai war chassit with suerd away.
> This is the consall and intent
> Off gud King Robert'is Testament."

The following ballad, however, which is not known to be in print, may serve to shew the esteem in which the memory of Robert the Bruce was long held by the people of Scotland. It occurs at the end of the large and splendid copy of For-

---

[1] Lib. xii. cap. x.   [2] In the MS. 'weir.'

dun's Chronicle in the University Library of Edinburgh, and is written in the same hand with the rest of the Manuscript.

The Nine Worthies here enumerated often make a conspicuous figure in old English poems. Thus Gower, in his "Balade to King Henry the Fourth," says:

>" See Alexander, Hector, and Julius,
> See Machabeus, Dauid, and Josue,
> See Charlemaine, Godfray, and Arthus."

>" Fulfilled of warre, and of mortalite
> Her fame abitte, but all is vanite
> For death, which has the warres vnder fote
> Hath made an end, of which there is no bote."
> *Chaucer's Works*, Speght's edit., 1598, fol. 332.

The reader will remember the amusing Pageant of the Nine Worthies introduced by Shakspeare in "Love's Labour's Lost," where the King says—

"Here is like to be a good presence of worthies: He (Don Adriano de Armado) presents Hector of Troy; the swain, Pompey the Great; the parish curate, Alexander; Armado's page, Hercules; the pedant, Judas Machabæus.

" And if these four worthies in their first show thrive,
  These four will change habits and present the other five."

"De nouem nobilibus."

HECTOUR of Troy throu hard feichthyngis,
In half thrid ȝeris slew xix kyngis;
And ammirallis a hundred and mare,
Wyth small folk at vnrackynnit war;
He slew sa fell, at wes ferly,
Qwham Achilez tresnabli.

Alexander als nobil a kyng,
In xij ȝeris wan throw hard feichtyng,

Al landis vnder the formament!
Eqwhethir adai in till parlement,   10
He said, he had but variance,
Our litill in till his gouernance.

    Julius Cesar wan hailily
The ilis of Grece, and all Surry;
Affrick, Arab, Bretan wan he,   15
And discumfit his mawche Pompe:
Throw hard batell, stalward stour,
He war the first was emperour.

    The gentill Jewß Josue,
Anek xxx kyngis throw weir wan he;   20
And conquirit the landis also,
The flu Jordan pertit in two
Throw Goddis grace, and strang power;
Men suld hym loff on gret maner.

    Dauid slew mychthy Golias,   25
And Philisteus at felon was;
He wes so wycht, et weill feichtand,
That he wes neuer sene recriand;
Thair for men call him, loud and still.
A trew prophet of hardy will.   30

    Michty Judas Machabeus
Jn bathell slew Antiochus,
Appolonius and Nichanore,
At in his dais wald neuer shor,
No multitud be adred of men,   35
Thoff he war ane eganes ten.

    Arthur wan Dace, Spanʒe, and France,
And hand for hand slew giantis;

Lucius the publik procuratour
Of Rome, wyth milleonis in stalwar stour; 40
And in till Paris Schir Frollo,[1]
In lystis slew wyth outin mo.

    Charles of France slew Agramand,
And wan Spanʒe fra hethoun land;
He slew the sowden of Pavi, 45
And wan the Saxonis halily;
And quhar God deid for our safté,
He put haly the Cristanté.

    Godefrey Bolʒone slew Solimant,
Before Antioche, and Cormorant, 50
Quham he throu ful strak ha^e ourtane,
Throu cops and harmez his glave is gane;
Sere hethownis he slew throu hard feychtyng,
And of Ier'lm a ʒeir was Kyng.

    Robert the Brois throu hard feichtyng 55
With few venkust the mychthy Kyng
Off Ingland, Edward, twyse in fycht,
At occupit his realme but rycht
At sum tyme wes set so hard,
At hat nocht sax till hym toward. 60

      ʒe gude men that thir balletis redis,
    Deme quha dochtyast was in dedis.

---

[1] This personage, who is introduced to exemplify the prowess of Arthur, according to the Chronicles, was a Roman knight, governor of Gaul. His name and that of "Lucyus the emperour of Rome" are alluded to in the "Legend of King Arthur," printed in Percy's "Reliques," vol. iii. p. 79.

The Duik of Orlyance in Defence of the Scots.

THE following lines, transcribed from the Maitland MS., are merely an extract, with some occasional variations, from Androw of Wyntown's Chronicle. They may be allowed, however, to stand in opposition to some of the many ancient rhymes which the English are known to have scattered abroad against the Scots. The jealous and hostile spirit which, for so many ages, existed betwixt the inhabitants of the two kingdoms, has long happily ceased, and, we trust, for ever. Nevertheless, it is curious and interesting to observe the various manifestations of this long-cherished and deep-seated animosity;—whether we may read in our annals of strife and bloodshed in the field of battle; of border forays and predatory excursions; or discover it in the more harmless, but not less vehement and sarcastic effusions in which they mutually seem to have indulged.

The question put by the illustrious Duke of Orleans is sufficiently simple and dispassionate, and leads to a natural and satisfactory conclusion, when he asked how it came that the English, with all their boasting, never were able to vanquish " the puir folk of Scotland "—

> —— —— " whose gaddering into weiris
> Micht nocht exceid five hundreth speiris— "

but allowed themselves to be harassed night and day by those whom they pretended to hold in despite; nor could enforce that homage and obedience which, at times, they presumed to say, we owed to the Crown of England.

"Defence of the Scots."

ANE thowsand ʒeir thre hundreth nyntye
    and ane
Fra Jesus Chryst had manheid tane
The bischop of Sanct Androis se,
Maister Waltir Traill callit was he,—
Be counsale and be ordinance   6
Of Scottismen, he passit in France;
For, in to Scotland men hard tell,
At the duik Johne of Longcastell,
Be ane ordinat delyuerance
Off Inglismen he passit in France.—   10
And quhatsoeuir thay tretit had,
Our bischop thair tuell monethis baid.
And thair sayrlie the Inglismen
The Scottismen diffamit than:—
Thai said, thair gaddering in to weiris   15
Micht nocht exceid fyve hundreth speiris:
The king of France, thai said, forthy,
Suld lat of Scottis men bot lichtlye.
Thir wourdis war said in the presence
Of the duchtie Duik of Orlyance,   20
Quhilk had ane speciale effectioun
Till Scottismen and thair natioun;
And than in haist he maid ansueyr,
As it was said on this maneyr:—
ʒe wein to lak, bot ʒe commend   25
That natioun, as ʒe mak it kend:
Was neuer realme nor regioun
Wourth mair commendatioun,
Than ar the few folk of Scotland,
As that ʒe gar ws vnderstand.   30
ʒe say, thair gaddering in to weiris
May nocht exceid fyve hundreth speiris;

And ȝe ar ane michtie natioun,
Excelland in presumptioun,
For all landis lyand ȝow by   35
ȝe suppress with ȝour senȝory;
Owthir ȝe win thame to ȝour croun,
Or haldis thame in subjectioun;
Bot the few folk of Scotland,
Quhilk by dry marchis ar lyand   40
Neir on to ȝow, thai hald thair awin,
As it is maid vntill ws knawin;
And will cum with thair poweir,
Playn ȝe, or ȝour land, of weir,
And day and nycht will ly thairin,   45
And in ȝour sicht ȝour landis bryne
ȝour cattale and ȝour gudis thay ta;
And spairis nathing ȝour self to sla;
Thus suffer thay on na kin wyß,
ȝow of sic micht to do suppryß;   50
Bot euir thay quyt ȝow lill for lall,
Or that ȝe skaill the market all;
That natioun may ȝe nocht defame,
Bot gif ȝe smyt ȝour awin with schame!
The king of France thairfor think me, 55
Suld hald thame in to mair daintie,
That so few folk, of so lytill micht,
Aganis ȝow can manteine thair fecht,
Vpon the dry merchis lyand,
As it is gart ws vnderstand.—   60
 Quhen this was said the Inglismen
Was schamit of thair wourdis than,
And hold thame still, and spak no mair,
In till dispyt as thai did ayr.

**Finita responsio Illustrissimi Ducis Orlianensis
in honorem et Defensionem Scotorum.**

A Poem by Glassinberry.

OF Glassinberry the history is altogether unknown, and we can only conjecture that he flourished in the reign of James the Second of Scotland. The poem here printed is preserved in Gray's Manuscript,—a little diminutive volume, chiefly of historical pieces, written towards the close of the fifteenth century,[1] which is now in the Advocates' Library. Another copy (without any author's name) is contained in a MS. volume in the Archiepiscopal Library at Lambeth.[2] Two or three anonymous poems contained in Gray's MS. might, from a similarity of style and measure, be, with some propriety, assigned to the same author.

A stanza or two from one of them may be here subjoined. The subject is the transitory nature of the present life, illustrated by various examples; amongst which we have the "Nine Worthies" brought forward to show "this warld is very vanité."

> " Mony pape ar passit by,
> Patriarkis, prelatis, and preistis,
> Kingis and knichtis in company,
> Uncountit curiously up I kest;
> Women and mony wilsom wy,
> As wynd and wattir ar gane west:
> Fish, and foule, and froit of tree
> On feild is nane formit na fest;
> Riches adew! sen all is drest
> That thai may nocht this dule indrè!
> Sen nocht has leif that heir ma lest
> This world is bot a vanité!

---

[1] See Father Innes's Critical Essay, vol. ii. p. 627-632.
[2] It is contained in the volume, No. 853, of Mr. Todd's Catalogue of the Lambeth MSS.

"Quhar is Plato that clerk of price,
That of all poetis had no peir?
Or ʒit Catoun with his clergis?
Or Aristotill that clerk so clere?
Tullious that wele wauld tis?
To tell his trety wer full teyr!
Or Virgil that wes war and wis,
And wist all wardly werk but wer?
Is nane sa dowtit na sa dere,
Than but redemyng all mon dee!
Therfor I hauld, quha evir it heir,
This warld is verray vanité.

"Ane uthir exempill suth to say
In summeris day full oft is sene
Thir emotis in ane hillok ay
Rinnand oute befor thin ene;
With litill weit thai wit away,
Sa worthis of ws all I wene!
May nane indur ouer his enday,
Bot all ouer drivis, as dew bedene,
That on the bery bidis bene,
And with a blast away wilbe,
Quhile girse ar gray, quhile ar thai grene,
This warld is verray vanité!"

The following lines, written on the margin of one of the leaves of this MS. in the name of "Aristoteles Magnus," may remind the reader of some verses usually attributed to the author of "Hudibras:"—

"Gyf thou cummis to the flude,
And the wawis[1] be woude,
  Huse, and hald thé still;
Thou may cum ane uther day,
Quhen wynd and wawis ar away
  Than ma thou waid at will."

---

[1] Wawis—for "waves."

Poem by Glassinberry.

I.

THIS is Goddis awne complaint,
 Fro man to man that he has boucht,
And thus he sais to thame in taynt,
 Myne awne pepill, quhat have I wroucht
To thé, that is to me so faynt,
 And I thi lufe so deir has soucht?
In thyne ansuer no thing that paynt
 To me, becaus I knaw thi thoucht!
Have I nocht done all that I oucht?
 Have I left ony thing behynd?
Quhy wrethis thou me? I greif thé nocht;
 Quhy arttow to thi freind unkynd?

II.

I socht thi lufe, and that wes sene,
 Quhen that I maid thé like till me;
In erd my werk, baith quyk and grene,
 I pat undir thin awne pousté;
And fra Pharo, that wes sa kene,
 Of Egip I deliverit thé,
And drownit him and his men bedene;
 The Red sey twinit I thé to fle;
I bad all dry that it suld bee,
 I cessit baith wattir and wynd,
And brocht thé oure, and maid thé free;
 Quhy arttow to thi freind unkynd?

III.

And fourti yheir in wildernes,
 With angele fude syne I thé fed,
And til a land of grete richess,
 To wyn thi lufe, syne I thé led:

And yhit, to schaw thé mair kyndnes,
To tak thi kynd na thing I dreid;   30
I left my micht, and tuke mekenes,
Myne awne hert blude for thé I bled:
To by thi saule my blude I sched,
And band my self thé til unbynd;
Thus, with my wo, thi neid I sped,   35
Quhy arttow to thi freind unkynd?

IV.

[In] my wyneyhard I plauntit thé
Full of gude saver and swetnes;
And nobil seid of all degré,
Bettir in erd nevir sawin wes: 40
Quhy suld thou thus gat fra me flé,
And turne all in to bittirnes?
The croce, for my reward, to me
Thou grathit and gaif, this is no leis,
Yhit had I evir to thé grete hers,   45
Resistand thame that to thé rynd
And puttand thé of mony a pres;
Quhy arttow to thi freind unkynd?

V.

For thé I ordanit Paradise,
Fré will wes thi infeftment;   50
How mycht thou me mair disples,
Na brek my awn commaundiment?
And syne, in vij maner of wiis,
Til myn enemy thou has consent;
I put thé downe, thou mycht nocht ryse   55
Thi mycht, thi wit away wes went;
Baith pure, nakit, schamit and schent,
Of freindschip mycht thou no thing fynd,
Till that I on the Rude wes rent;
Quhy arttow to thi freind unkynd?   60

VI.

Man! I lufe thé, quhom luffis thou?
I am thi freind, quhy lest thé wayn?
I forgaif thé that thou me slew,
Quha has partit oure lufe in twane?
Turne to me, and unite think thou,   65
Thou has gane mys, yhit turne agane,
And thou salbe als welcum now,
As sum with syn that nevir did nane:
Think how did Mary Magdalane,
And quhat said I, Thomas of Ynd,   70
I graunt thé blis; quhy lest thé pane?
Quhy arttow to thi freind unkynd?

VII.

O a freind the best preif
Is lufe with dreid, and nocht disples,
Was nevir thing to me mair leif,   75
Na man that na thing may appes,
I sufferit for thi synis repreif,
And dulfull deid thi saul to es;
Hangit and drawin as a theif,
Thou did the deid, I haf dishes;   80
Nor can thow nother thank no ples,
No do gude deid, no have in mynd,
I am thi leich, to thi males;
Quhy arttow to thi freind unkind?

VIII.

Man unite, think thé quhat thou art?   85
Fra quhom thou come? quhar arttow bown;
All thocht thou be to day in quart,
To morn I can cum put thé down:
Let mynd and meiknes mele in hart,
And rew of my compasioun,   90

Apon my woundis, herd and smert,
Of skourgis, nalis, spere, and crowne ;
Let dreid and gude discretioun,
With lufe thi hert wp to me wynd,
Thou has v. wittis and resoun,
And gif thou will, thou may be kind !

IX.

Lord ! with thé we will nocht plete,
Bot as thou sais, It is and wes ;
We have deserwit hell heit
Now we ws held unto thi gres ;   10
We sal aby, and thou sal beit
And chasty ws for oure trespes ;
Let mercy so for ws entret,
That nevir the feynd our saulis ches.
And Mary mild ! fairest of faice,   10
Help ws, or we be fer behynd,
Or wepand, we mon say, Allace !
That we bene till our freind unkynd !

Explicit quod Glassinberry.

The Ring of the Roy Robert.

THIS poem, which is mentioned in the "Complaynt of Scotland" (1549), appears to have received, at an early period, more attention than easily can be accounted for any other way than from national feeling, which may have responded to the sentiments it expresses with regard to the independence and sovereignty of Scotland. The author, according to the Maitland MS., from which this poem is now printed, was Dean David Steill, a Scotish poet, who is supposed to have flourished about the close of the fifteenth century.[1]

The occasion to which the poem alludes is evidently what took place on the renewal of hostilities between the two kingdoms after the accession of Henry IV. According to our historians, that monarch in the year 1400, previously to his invading Scotland with a powerful army, sent a summons to King Robert III.[2] and all the prelates and nobility of Scotland, to meet him at Edinburgh on the 23rd of August, to do homage and swear fealty to him as Superior Lord of Scotland; which he affirmed all the former Kings of Scotland had done to his predecessors since the days of Brute

---

[1] Bishop Nicolson (Scottish Historical Library, 1703, p. 154) first pointed out that in the Maitland MS. this piece was given to Dean Steill, and Dr. George Mackenzie (Lives and Characters of Scotish Writers, i. p. 450), on that authority admitted the author into his work, and speaks of the production as containing the Life of King Robert III., "wherein several things are recorded of moment."

[2] In this copy an evident mistake occurs in calling Robert "the *first King* of the good Stewart," which probably occurred in one of the old printed copies, the answer being attributed to Robert II.

the Trojan. To such an arrogant demand he is said to have received a no less contemptuous answer from Prince David, Duke of Rothsay; upon which he marched forward; but ere long he returned to England, without having done anything worthy of his mighty preparations.[1]

But this poem cannot be regarded as a contemporary effusion. The probability is, that it may have been one of "those writings" handed about in the reign of Henry VII. which occasioned a remonstrance to be made on the part of the English monarch. A declaration on this subject, by the learned and upright judge, Sir John Fortescue, in the form of a dialogue, "Vpon certayn wrytingis sent oute of Scotteland, ayenst the Kingis title of his Roialme of England," is still preserved in MS.;[2] although the character of the author is sufficient, we should have supposed, to render any of his works deserving of publication.

The printed copies of this poem are considerably modernised and corrupted. One of these, printed as a broadside, about the year 1680, preserved in Pepys's library, has this title, "The reply and challenge of King Robert the second, the first of the Steuarts, unto Henry the fourth, King of England, unjustly challenging his homage." There is another edition, printed at Edinburgh, 1700, 8vo, p. 8, which has been elsewhere reprinted.[3] It is likewise included in Watson's "Collection of Scots Poems," Part II., 1709.

The Ring of the Roy Robert.

IN to the ring of the roy Robert,
The first King of the gud Stewart;
Hary of Ingland the ferd King
In Scotland send, and askit this thing
At King Robert, quhy he nocht maid   5
Him seruice for his landis braid?

---

[1] Henry's History, vol. v. p. 6. Rymer's Fœdera, tom. viii. p. 1182-1186. Pinkerton's History, vol. i. p. 56.

[2] MS. Bibl. Reg. 17 D. xv.

[3] Laing's Various Pieces of Fugitive Scotish Poetry, 1st Ser., 1825.

And quhy he causit to be spilt
Fell Cristiane blude throw his gilt?
He said, he aucht of heretage,
In Loundoun for to mak homage, 10
Eftir the richt of Brutus King,
Quhilk had all Ingland in gouerning!—
   Ffra that King Robert, wyse and wicht,
Had hard and sein this wryt be sicht;
Sa he grew in matelent, 15
On till his barounis, tauld his intent;
[He called a Council to Striviling town,
And there came Lords of great renown;]
And at thame all he askit it
That he micht ansueir be his awin wit. 20
Thay war rich joyfull of that thing,
Referrit thame to thair nobill King.
Than, without counsall of ony man,
To dyt and wryt our King began:
[This was the effect of his writeing, 25
All is sooth, and na liesing.]
   WE ROBERT, throw Godis micht,
King of Scotland and Ylis richt,
That inebbis in the Occeane see,
That to this day was euir free; 30
To thé Henrie of Longcastell,
Thy epistill we considder weill:
Duik of that Ilk thow suld be cald,—
It is thy richtest style of auld;
And I admit thé nocht as King, 35
For certane poyntis of degrading:
Thairfor, ane King I call nocht thé,
For hurt of Kingis Maiesté;
[For I will take nae heeding
Of thy unrighteous invading, 40
For what was right, as is well knawin,
Ye all defould within your awin:]

Wit thow that we haue understand
For to declayre anent Scotland :
Thy wryt be wourd we haue sene,   45
Fra first to last at thow can mein ;
Quhairthrow that thow sall answer haue,
Of my awin self, accept the laif.
And in the First, thow schawis ws till
Na Cristiane blude that thow wald spill,   50
On to the quhilk, we witnes beir,
Na blude for ws beis spilt in weir,
Bot gif it be in our defence,
Throw thy corruptit violence.

    And quhair thow wrytis and schawis till ws,   55
Sen borne was sonnis of auld Brutus,
That our successouris aucht to be
Servandis till youris, gré be gré ;
Thou leyd thairof ! it is weill knawin,
We war euir fré within our awin !   60
Thocht Johne Balʒoun maid ane band,
Contrair the richt of fayr Scotland ;
Thair he was mainsworne that we defend :
On till ws all, it is weill kend,
Anent the bairns of auld Brutus,   65
That kyndnes hes bene kepit till ws :
Scotland euir yit hes bene fré,
Sen Scota of Egipt tuik the see !
Bot ye ar thirlit and our harlit,
The grit refuse of all the warld,   70
For nichtbure tressoun amangis your sell
Four tymes, as the Cronicle will tell,
Ye haue halelie conqueist bene :
Ten thousand pvndis of gold so schene
To Julius Cesar payit ye   75
Off tribute, thus ye war nocht free.
Be Saxounis als ye war ouer thrawin
Be tua borne chiftanis of your awin,

And Germaneis in cumpany,
All borne Saraȝenis vtterlie,   80
At come with Horsus and Ingest,
And maid your auld blude richt waist;
And slew the gentillis of Ingland
At Salisberrie, I vnderstande;
And till ane takin the hingand stanis,   85
Ambrosius set vp for the naneis;
In till ane lestand memoriall,
At Saxounis had ourset yow all.
Vndir the hewin is no kinryk
Off sorrow hes bein to yow lyk   90
Ye war put syn in subiectioun
At we, nor yit nane vnder croun,
Was never in sic necessitie
As hapnit your aduersatie!
Then Henslot, sone of Denmark king   95
The thrid tyme rais o're yow to ring;
The quhilk of Ingland maid conquest,
And left amangis yow at the last
Ane Dane in ilk ane hous, was knawin,
Yow to defoull with in your awin;   100
That occupiit bayth gude and wyff;
Thus in bondage ye leid your lyff!

 Quhen this was done, and all bypast,
The ferd conquest approchit fast,
Off the Bastarde of Normandie,   105
Quhilk conqueist Ingland halelie;
Quhilk yit amangis yow ringis thair blude,
And meikill vther that is nocht gude:
And gif ye trow this nocht south be,
Reid the Registar, and ye may see,   110
And the croniclis of braid Bartane,
Quhairout of our authoris ar tane;
That this is suth thow may nocht lane,
France and Bartane kennis in plane

Thow art nocht rightuous for to ring, 115
For all realmis knawis this thing;
In Londoun thow swoir in Parliament,
Ingland ten yeiris [thou should absent,—
Then wast thou manifestlie mansworne
Or euir three yeiris] and ane half was worne; 120
Thou rais tressonablie for to ring,
And hes vndone Richart thy king.
Gif you knawis nocht thy meikle mis
The suth in proverb spokin is:
Flyt with thy nichtburis, and thai will tell 125
All the mischeif that thé befell.
Bot for our Realme, I dar weill say,
Was never none hyn to this day,
Brocht Scotland in subiectioun!
Bot ane was mansworne of your croun, 130
The quhilk of Langschankis, hecht Edwarde,
Tuik on him to declayr the parte,
Betuix the Brus and Johne Balioun;
That throw your fals illusioun,
Johne Balʒoun, quhair he had no richt, 135
Tuik tressonablie to hald with slicht,
Strenthis and castellis of our Cuntré,
Ye gat throw your subtilitie.
That Williame Wallace, wicht and wyse,
Wichtlie reskewit ws thrys; 140
And Robert the Bruce rakleslie
First tynt, syn wan ws wichtlie;
And with him James the gud Douglas
Quhilk preivit weill in everie place;
Erle Thomas Randell, wyse and wicht, 145
As than was neuer ane hardyar knycht;
Thir exilit all your fals barnageis,
And fred our realme of all thirlageis.
And gif thow trowis this nocht suth is,
Off sextie thousand, we thocht no miss, 150

At Bannokeburne discomfist was ;
Als your fals king away culd pas,
Throw an inborne tratour at was kend
Quhilk fré in Ingland he him send ;
Or ellis we had tane your king,					155
And Ingland had in gouerning.
    Quhen all this was cuming and gane,
Than Edward of Carnauerane
Discumfist he was at Biland
Be my Father, I tak on hand ;					160
Walter Stewart that in hy
Chaissit him all opinlie,
Ane hundreth myle on King Edward,
Quhill that he was reskewit be parte,
Till Scaribur castell, and thair him lest ;		165
Syn till his ost returnit Est ;
Be than your clergy of Ingland
Renewit agane with stalwart hand
At Myltoun, as it is weill knawin,
Thair haistellie ye war ourthrawin				170
Be the gud Douglas, the suth to say,
And Thomas the gud erle of Murray ;
Quhair twentie hundreth war dungin to deid,
Withoutin succour, or remeid
Off preistis, that beir schawin croun,			175
That hardie men war of renoun.
    Eftir this, Robert the Bruce
Tuik stait, and halelie cud reduce
Northummerland, all till him sell,—
Ye may nocht say nor this befell !—				180
Syn ye war fane, or ye wald ces,
To proffer mariage for peice,
And askit the Prince of Bruce Dauid
Till dame Jonet Touris till ally.
Ye maid that euidentis, and that band,			185
Vnder the grit seill of Ingland,

The quhilk ye call your goldin Chartour
In Ingland hes maid mony martyr!
Quhilk we haue plainlie for to schaw
The verité, quha will it knaw;   190
And falslie brokin is in yow,
All tyme befoir als weill as now;
And throw your fals suppleying
Quhen Edwarde Balʒoun rais to ring!
This is suth, I profer me   195
To preif on sextie agane sextie,
Or fourtie agane fourtie, gif ye lyk,
Or xx agane xx of our kinryk,
Gif tho be pacient and tholumdie
And wald nocht spill na Cristane blude   200
And gif thow thinkis it best sa
Let ws dereinʒe it betuix ws tua;
I proffer me to preif on thé
And we and Scotland yit art fré,—
And of the Paip nothing we hald,   205
Bot of the Kirk our fayth of auld,—
At we ar bunding of det to do,
At all Cristiane pepill aucht to do.
  ¶ This wryt to Londoun he hes send,
And quhen the Barounis had it kend,   210
And had considderit it in plane,—
Yit na said ansuer come agane.

Finis the Ring of the Roy Robert
maid be Dene Dauid Steill.

END OF VOL. I.

Printed by BALLANTYNE, HANSON & CO.
Edinburgh and London

www.ingramcontent.com/pod-product-compliance
Lightning Source LLC
Chambersburg PA
CBHW030002240426
43672CB00007B/798